Regional Trade Agreements in Eastern Europe, Central Asia and the Caucasus: Is Multilateralization of Regionalism possible?

ERLANGER SCHRIFTEN ZUM ÖFFENTLICHEN RECHT

Herausgegeben von Andreas Funke, Max-Emanuel Geis, Heinrich de Wall, Markus Krajewski , Jan-Reinard Sieckmann und Bernhard W. Wegener

Band 11

PETER LANG

Seljan Verdiyeva

Regional Trade Agreements in Eastern Europe, Central Asia and the Caucasus: Is Multilateralization of Regionalism possible?

PETER LANG

Bibliografische Information der Deutschen Nationalbibliothek
Die Deutsche Nationalbibliothek verzeichnet diese Publikation in der Deutschen Nationalbibliografie; detaillierte bibliografische Daten sind im Internet über http://dnb.d-nb.de abrufbar.

Library of Congress Cataloging-in-Publication Data
A CIP catalog record for this book has been applied for at the Library of Congress

Zugl.: Erlangen-Nürnberg, Univ., Diss., 2020

Umschlagabbildung:
Historisches Siegel der Universität Erlangen-Nürnberg.

D 29
ISSN 2192-8460
ISBN 978-3-631-84305-5 (Print)
E-ISBN 978-3-631-84659-9 (E-PDF)
E-ISBN 978-3-631-84660-5 (EPUB)
E-ISBN 978-3-631-84661-2 (MOBI)
DOI 10.3726/b18006

Peter Lang – Berlin · Bern · Bruxelles · New York · Oxford · Warszawa · Wien

This publication has been peer reviewed.

www.peterlang.com

Contents

Abbreviations

ASEAN – Association of South-East Asian Nations
CIS – Commonwealth of Independent States
CRTA – Committee on Regional Trade Agreements
DCFTA – Deep and Comprehensive Free Trade Agreement
EAEU – Eurasian Economic Union
EC – European Communities
EU – European Union
FTA – Free Trade Area
GATS – General Agreement on Trade in Services
GATT – General Agreement on Tariffs and Trade
GSP – Generalized System of Preferences
Mercosur – Southern Common Market
MFN – Most-favored nation
NAFTA – North American Free Trade Agreement
OECD – Organization for Economic Cooperation and Development
OPEC – Organization for Petroleum Exporting Countries
OSCE – Organization of Security and Cooperation in Europe
RoO – Rules of Origin
RTA – Regional Trade Agreement
SPS – sanitary and phytosanitary measures
TBT – technical barriers to trade
UNCTAD – United Nations Conference on Trade and Development
UN – United Nations
USA – United States of America
WIPO – World Intellectual Property Organization
WTO – World Trade Organization
WCO – World Customs Organization

Introduction

Statement of the Problem and Necessity for a Research

Global trade in the last decade has witnessed a rapid proliferation of *Regional Trade Agreements* (RTA from hereinafter). The WTO cites some 304 RTAs currently in force[1]. Even Mongolia, the only country not party to any RTA, recently ended its status as the only country without a RTA and signed a free trade and economic partnership agreement with Japan[2] . In fact, today the world has more RTAs than the number of existing countries[3]. Most countries choose to join more than one RTA at the same time, which leads to overlapping memberships and it subsequently drives to fragmentized and chaotic trade rules across the world.

Yet, historically speaking, RTAs are not a new phenomenon[4]. In fact, RTAs and the multilateral trading system have existed side-by-side for a long time as they both serve the same objective – liberalization of trade. In achieving this very objective, RTAs have had an immense effect on multilateral trading system by strengthening bilateral economic and political relations between countries, deepening trade, promoting foreign direct investment, encouraging competition and offering better market access opportunities. The positive effect of RTAs on the multilateral system can be particularly seen in the liberalization of non-tariff and services regulations, as liberalization policy in these sectors benefits not only RTA partners, but also all the other trading partners.

However, RTAs are also known for their certain negative impact on the global trading system. They derogate from the ground principle of WTO – Most

---

1 Regional Trade Agreements (WTO, 1 May 2018) <https://rtais.wto.org/UI/PublicMaintainRTAHome.aspx> accessed 04 July 2020.

2 RTA database (WTO) <http://rtais.wto.org/UI/PublicShowMemberRTAIDCard.aspx?rtaid=835> accessed 18 August 2016. Free Trade and Economic Partnership Agreement between Japan and Mongolia was signed on 10 February 2015. It covers both goods and services. The agreement entered into force on 7 June 2016. The agreement has extensive rules and provisions on issues outside the WTO agreements, such as e-commerce, investment, health and labor standards and etc.

3 UN currently has 193 members. See UN member states (United Nations) < http://www.un.org/en/member-states/> accessed 18 August 2016.

4 Ekaterina Mixaylenko, *Stariy i noviy reqionalizm: Teoreticeskiy diskurs* (Old and new regionalism: Theoretical discussion) (Izdatelstvo Uralskoqo universiteta, Ekaterinburg 2014), p.11.

Favored Nation rule, divert trade from natural trading partners, discriminate against small and vulnerable economies, discourage multilateral liberalization at the WTO by taking away resources and motivation for further liberalization, require different and complex rules of origin schemes, make the whole trading world more complex through application of different trade regimes between RTA partners. Yet, despite all of these issues, RTAs are proliferating at a tremendous rate throughout the world.

The changes in RTAs are being noticed not only in their growing numbers, but also in their scope, variety of members, geographical distribution and complexity of the coverage. If previously RTAs were including only provisions for improving market access, nowadays RTAs, in addition, cover areas such as services, intellectual property and non-tariff barriers to trade[5]. Most of the RTAs today also include policy areas far beyond the WTO agreements and include sectors like investment, environment, labor standards and competition. This leads to complexity of administration and implementation of RTAs, which is a challenge for governments, businesses and other stakeholders. It also complicates the effectiveness of trade and business relations. Furthermore, RTAs create a "spaghetti bowl" effect which can be clearly seen when different tariffs, rules of origin and other disciplines are applied for different trading partners in overlapping RTA membership[6].

It could easily be asserted that there is a growing competition between RTAs and multilateral trading system. The WTO has been vigilant about this process, trying to increase transparency on the existing and currently negotiated RTAs and analyzing their effect on the multilateral system. WTO former Director-General R. Azevedo has expressed many times that RTAs could not prevail over multilateral liberalization simply because there were certain issues that could be better tackled through multilateral agreements rather than RTAs, such as trade facilitation, services liberalization, fisheries and subsidies[7].

---

5 Andrey Spartak 'Metamorfozi Processa Reqionalizacii: Ot Reqionalnix Torqovix Soqlasheniy k Meqareqionalnim Proektam' (Metamorphosis of regionalization process: From regional trade agreements to mega-regional projects) (2017) 10 (4) Konturu qlobalnix transformaciy: politika, ekonomika, pravo, p 20 <https://cyberleninka.ru/article/v/metamorfozy-protsessa-regionalizatsii-ot-regionalnyh-torgovyh-soglasheniy-k-mezhregionalnym-proektam> accessed 23 December 2018.

6 Jagdish Bhagwati, *Termites in the Trading System: How Preferential Agreements Undermine Free Trade* (2008, Oxford University Press, Oxford) p.63.

7 Roberto Azevedo, 'Regional Trade Agreements "Cannot Substitute" the Multilateral Trading System' (WTO Seminar on Cross-Cutting Issues in Regional Trade

However, so far, multilateral trade liberalization has been lagging far behind the RTA liberalization. This is in some way due to the fact that the WTO has been unable to reach any major trade deal in the Doha Round for several decades, apart from a few exceptions[8]. This has caused certain frustration among the countries which opted to conclude RTAs and gain deeper market access instead of waiting for the conclusion of the Doha Round[9].

The stagnation of multilateral liberalization, which is the main cause accounted for proliferation of RTAs globally, has been due to a number of reasons. First and foremost, members of the WTO outnumber parties to RTAs. The WTO membership has considerably increased compared to original General Agreement on Tariffs and Trade (GATT) signatories (164 countries versus 23 original GATT signatories) and thus, it is much more difficult to reach an agreement that would be acceptable to all the members[10].

Secondly, there is a shift of power in the multilateral trade arena[11]. If the EU, USA, Canada and Japan were the main powers that influenced the trade negotiations during the GATT negotiating rounds and the WTO establishment process, now the political realities of the WTO are different. The developing countries at the WTO, as well as new members of the WTO, such as China and Russia, are more active in the trade negotiations and have complicated the decision-making process at the WTO[12].

Thirdly, business lobbies in developed countries push for non-traditional trade topics to be included in the negotiations, yet there are a growing number

---

Agreements, 25 September 2014) <https://www.wto.org/english/news_e/spra_e/spra33_e.htm> accessed 11 August 2016.

8 The exceptions are: WTO Trade Facilitation Agreement (7 December 2013), Bali Ministerial Decision , WT/MIN(13)/36 – WT/L/911, WTO Ministerial Decision on Export Competition (19 December 2015), Nairobi Ministerial Decision, WT/MIN(15)/45 — WT/L/980.

9 Oksana Shkutko 'Mnoqostoronneye Requlirovanie Torqovix Otnosheniy: Potensial i Vozmojnosti Transformachiyi' (Multilateral regulation of trade relations: potential and opportunities for transformation) (2018) 37 (1) Sbornik nauchnix trudov uchenix I aspirantov, p. 5.

10 Bernard Hoekman, 'Multilateral Cooperation in a World of Preferential Trade Agreements' (2015) 21 (2) The Brown Journal of World Affairs, p. 132.

11 Kseniya Efremova 'Ot reqionalisma k transreqionalizmu: Teoreticeskoe osmislenie novoy realnosti' (From regionalism to trans-regionalism: Theoretical thinking of new reality) (2017) 58 (2) Sravnitelnaya politika, p. 69.

12 Richard Baldwin 'The World Trade Organization and the Future of Multilateralism' (2016) 30 (1) The Journal of Economic Perspectives, p. 95.

of developing countries, such as India and Brazil, which are not willing to go for any further liberalization than is necessary[13]. Acceded countries after 1995, which were forced to take significantly more commitments and liberalize deeper than original WTO signatories, do not wish to liberalize any further as well.

Fourthly, WTO's slow liberalization process does not catch up with the fast growing realities of world trade[14]. There is a shift in trading realities across the globe with the creation of global value and supply chains. Baldwin, for example, states that WTO rules were designed for the goods that simply crossed the borders and that these rules have not caught up with the realities of global value chains where production, manufacturing and distribution could take place in various places[15]. In that aspect, RTAs are more apt to change and update than WTO agreements.

Despite all of this, there is a hope at the end of the tunnel. The conclusion of mega-regional trade arrangements, such as the Pacific Alliance[16] and Comprehensive and Progressive Agreement for Trans Pacific Partnership[17] bring major trading partners together, replace bilateral deals and thus, merge and harmonize the existing trading rules[18]. Together, these mega-regional deals have the potential to minimize the fragmented and chaotic RTA rules and lay the groundwork for future global liberalization[19]. This process introduces "multilateralisation of

13 Arvind Panagariya, 'Challenges to the Multilateral Trading System and Possible Responses' (2013) 7 Economics, p. 15.

14 Alexey Portanskiy, 'Posle Nairobi VTO Vinujdena Menyatsya' (After Nairobi, WTO must change) (2016) 3 Rosiyskiy vnesneoekonomicheskiy vestnik, p. 48.

15 Richard Baldwin 'The World Trade Organization and the Future of Multilateralism' (2016) 30 (1) The Journal of Economic Perspectives, p. 95.

16 Pacific Alliance is a regional integration of Chile, Colombia, Mexico and Peru established in 2011. The Framework Agreement on Pacific Alliance (6 June 2012) <https://alianzapacifico.net/download-category/acuerdo-marco-de-la-alianza-del-pacifico/> accessed 6 April 2019.

17 Trans-Pacific Partnership encompasses the following countries: Australia, Canada, Japan, Malaysia, Mexico, Peru, US, Vietnam, Chile, Brunei, Singapore, New-Zealand. It was signed in 2016, but did not enter into force and US withdrew its signature. The remaining countries negotiated Comprehensive and Progressive Agreement for Trans-Pacific Partnership which came into force in December 2018. The text can be accessed here: <https://dfat.gov.au/trade/agreements/in-force/cptpp/official-documents/Documents/tpp-11-treaty-text.pdf> accessed 06 April 2019.

18 See more: 'New Developments in RTAs' (WTO) <https://www.wto.org/english/tratop_e/region_e/region_e.htm#rules_ita> accessed 20 September 2018.

19 Regional Trade Agreements: Facts and Figures (WTO) <https://www.wto.org/english/tratop_e/region_e/regfac_e.htm> accessed 18 August 2016.

regionalism" – a concept developed to identify the elements of the RTAs that could be used for multilateral negotiations. This concept is aimed at harmonizing generally accepted elements of the RTAs, diminishing negative effect of regionalism and making RTAs less discriminatory. During the process of multileralization of regionalism similar provisions across the different RTAs are brought together and thus trade rules in certain areas are harmonized among a wider scope of countries. While each and every RTA has its own advantages and disadvantages, multilateralization of regionalism aims to build on the positive experiences of these RTAs and shows how elements of the RTAs can be utilized for the purposes of the globalization of trade liberalization. Multilateralization of regionalism is basically bringing regionalism closer to multilateralism.

Research Goal and Importance

The main aim of this research is to analyze multilateralization of regionalism and apply it to the RTAs in the Central Asia, Eastern Europe and the Caucasus region. This book looks into whether multilateralization of regionalism is possible in this region and if so, what are the best ways to achieve it. The region that is being analyzed is quite complex geopolitically. It comprises of post-Soviet countries, mainly the countries of Eastern Europe (Ukraine, Moldova, Belarus, Russia), the Caucasus (Armenia, Azerbaijan, Georgia) and Central Asia (Kazakhstan, Kyrgyzstan, Turkmenistan, Tajikistan). These countries share common historical, economic, cultural and political backgrounds, which will be discussed in greater detail in Chapter 2.

Even outside the concept of the multilateralization of regionalism, Eastern Europe, Central Asia and the Caucasus region has not been under much scrutiny in the trade literature. Moreover, several RTAs of the region are quite new, such as Association Agreements of the EU with Ukraine, Moldova and Georgia, as well as the Eurasian Economic Union. Accordingly, there has not been an intensive examination of these RTAs in the trade literature. In this sense, the book also gives good comparative analysis of these RTAs and their relationship with the WTO agreements.

Research Hypotheses

The research tests the following three general hypotheses in the Central Asia, Eastern Europe and the Caucasus region: First of all, RTAs are the most efficient[20]

20 The term "efficient" throughout this book refers to trade liberalization with the

tool for trade liberalization and multilateralization in this region. Secondly, innovative and progressive elements of these RTAs can be used in the multilateralization of regionalism. Lastly, multilateralization of regionalism should focus on RTA provisions with low cost and high gain.

For this purpose, the book firstly examines the RTAs in Eastern Europe, Central Asia and the Caucasus and their impact on trade liberalization. It elaborates on whether there are any innovative or progressive elements in these RTAs and if there are, whether they can they be taken as a basis of multilateral negotiations. Finally, the book discusses if any element of the RTAs could be used in multilateralization of regionalism and what potential costs and gains this process could entail.

Structure

The book consists of 5 chapters.

Chapter 1 analyzes the legal basis of the RTAs and WTO's outlook on the RTAs, as well as the concept of the multilateralization of regionalism. In this chapter the reader is shown how RTAs are regulated within the WTO, the main treaties where the general prerequisites of the RTAs are given, how the WTO is currently progressing towards the future with regard to the RTA policy, the correlation of multilateralism and regionalism in the global world, the definition of the concept of the multilateralization of regionalism, the scholarly views on its possibility and the main elements for multilateralization, as well as how mega-regional deals are benefitting this process.

Chapter 2 gives background on the RTAs of the region, mainly the Eurasian Economic Union, The EU Association Agreements with Moldova, Georgia and the Ukraine, as well as the Commonwealth of Independent States (CIS). The political realities and the dynamics of the region, as well as the main characteristic traits of the region are introduced in this chapter. The chapter also elaborates on what makes the countries within this region join RTAs and how the political agenda of the region defines the RTA realities. Contextual detail is provided for the analyzed RTAs of the region.

Chapter 3 goes into detail with the traditional topics of the RTAs in the region, such as rules of origin, trade facilitation and transparency, TBT, SPS and intellectual property. The reader is first introduced briefly on how these topics are

maximum productivity and minimum waste. Efficient tool is the tool that is fast, yields positive results and has minimum negative effect.

regulated within the WTO. Then the RTAs in the region are analyzed and lastly, findings based on the analysis are introduced.

While Chapter 3 focused on traditional topics of the RTAs, Chapter 4 analyzes the non-traditional topics found in the RTAs that are not covered or just superficially touched upon within the WTO agreements. Thus, Chapter 4 focuses on investment, competition and energy issues, which are found in the RTAs of the analyzed region. The chapter looks at the common traits of these topics within the RTAs and elaborates on the possibility of multilateralizaiton of these areas.

Chapter 5 applies the criteria developed by the OECD (Widespread nature, similarity, discrimination toward non-parties, implementation, transparency and enforceability, existence of political will to drive multilateralism) to assess whether multilateralization of regionalism is possible within a certain area. This chapter builds upon all the previous chapters, as it uses the information put forward from the findings of the previous chapters. It analyzes the possible effects of multilateralization of regionalism in Eastern Europe, Central Asia and the Caucasus.

The conclusion looks at the hypothesis raised in the introduction in the light of the information provided in the research and elaborates the possibility of multilateralization of regionalism and key steps in that regard.

Chapter 1 Legal Basis of Regional Trade Agreements in the World Trade Organization and the Importance of Multilateralization of Regionalism

The aim of this chapter is to introduce and give contextual background information for the research topic. For this purpose, it consists of two main sections.

The first section gives overview of the main legal instruments governing RTAs within the WTO, status of current negotiations on RTAs in the WTO Doha Round, as well as understanding within the WTO on RTA issues and the way forward as seen by the WTO members. This section is necessary for the reader to understand the relationship of regionalism and multilateralism, to explain how regionalism has proliferated and why the concept of multilateralisation of regionalism came into being.

The second section looks in more detail at the concept of multilateralization of regionalism. It explains the definition, its importance, the role of mega-regional arrangements in multilateralization of regionalism and scholarly views on how it can be achieved.

1. Regional Trade Agreements and the World Trade Organization

The current world is witnessing a tremendous shift in the RTA increase. All the countries in the world are a party to at least one RTA and many countries participate in various RTAs. The RTAs cover nowadays not only goods, but also services, labor movement, capital, investment, energy, environmental and other sectors. There are certain RTAs whose scope include not only trade and economic issues, but also political, military, cultural, social and other kinds of cooperation. They are thousands of pages long with detailed trade policy regulations. It is very difficult to ensure that RTA commitments remain compatible with the WTO commitments of the participating state. The importance of the WTO is rising in this context, because WTO is the only forum where RTAs are somewhat regulated.

Definition of RTAs and criteria for their set-up are provided in the following WTO documents[21] :

(i) Article XXIV of the General Agreement on Tariffs and Trade (GATT 1947)[22]
(ii) Understanding on the Interpretation of the Article XXIV of the GATT[23]
(iii) WTO Decision on Differential and More Favorable Treatment Reciprocity and Fuller Participation of Developing Countries dated 28 November 1979 – also known as the Enabling Clause[24]
(iv) Article V of the General Agreement on Trade in Services (GATS) and
(iv) Transparency Mechanism for RTAs[25].

This section will go one-by-one over each of these five legal instruments and clarify their importance within the research topic.

i. GATT Article XXIV (Territorial Application – Frontier Traffic – Customs Union and Free Trade Areas) and Understanding on GATT Article XXIV

Article XXIV of the GATT is, without any doubt, the fundamental and most controversial provision of the WTO on RTAs. Article XXIV came into life in the aftermath of World War II, aiming to unite Europe under one umbrella. In order to achieve this, there was a necessity to derogate from the principle of the GATT which called to extend the same trade benefits to all the trade partners[26] – Most-Favored Nation

21 It should be noted that, the research does not analyze Preferential Trade Agreements, therefore GSP, GSP+ schemes, as well as any agreement granting unilateral concessions are not examined here.

22 GATT: General Agreement on Tariffs and Trade (30 October1947) <http://docsonline.wto.org> accessed 20 August 2016.

23 Understanding on the Interpretation of the Article XXIV of the GATT (15 April 1994) <http://docsonline.wto.org> accessed 20 August 2016.

24 Enabling Clause: WTO Decision on Differential and More Favorable Treatment Reciprocity and Fuller Participation of Developing Countries (28 November 1979) <http://docsonline.wto.org> accessed 20 August 2016.

25 Transparency Mechanism for Regional Trade Agreements (14 December 2006) WT/L/671, 18 December 2016 <http://docsonline.wto.org> accessed 20 August 2016.

26 Kerry Chase also argues that the reason for inclusion of the Article XXIV in Havana negotiations was because of the secret negotiations on free trade area between USA and Canada held at the time. According to him, initially, negotiations on Havana Charter of International Trade Organization, whose provisions were later included in the GATT

principle[27] . Thus, Article XXIV was drafted aiming to provide for such derogation, yet to contain such a language as to minimize the abuse of the derogation from Article I of GATT (Most-Favored Nation principle) by others[28]. However, this article ended up being accountable for the rising power of regionalism[29].

Article XXIV is contextually broad and contains disciplines not only on the RTAs, but in addition, on frontier traffic and customs territories. However, the main bulk of its paragraphs are dedicated to the RTAs. This article was subsequently interpreted at the end of the Uruguay Round with the Understanding on the Interpretation of the Article XXIV of the GATT. Article XXIV applies only to the RTAs *on goods* between the WTO members[30]. The RTAs are defined here as voluntary agreements of closer integration between the economies[31]. The GATT mentions 3 types of such integration agreements: (i) customs unions, (ii) free trade areas and (iii) interim agreements necessary for the formation of either customs union or of a free trade area[32]. In comparison, subsequent WTO

1947, covered disciplines only on customs union. USA had a strict multilateralism policy at the time and opposed any regionalism. However, after the secret negotiations for a trade deal was proposed between the parties, USA came up with an arrangement that was more flexible than customs union – "free trade area" and in order to legalize this arrangement, its negotiators put a leeway in Havana Charter on establishment of free trade area, as well as interim agreements leading to free trade areas. Surprisingly though, this trade deal never came into life. However, the world ended up having Article XXIV of the GATT. See: Kerry Chase 'Multilateralism Compromised: the Mysterious Origins of GATT Article XXIV' (2006) 5(1) World Trade Review, p. 3.

27 Most-Favored Nation principle requires that if a WTO member accords any advantage, privilege or immunity to any product from its trading partners, it should accord the same treatment immediately and unconditionally to all the other WTO members. See: GATT Article I.

28 Alexey Portanskiy 'Mirovaya Tendenciya Reqionalizma I Inteqrasiya v SNQ' (The global tendency of regionalism and integration in the CIS) (2011) 11 Rossiyskoy vneshnoekonomicheskoy vestnik, p. 14.

29 Joanna Langille, 'Neither Constitution nor Contract: Understanding the WTO by Examining the Legal Limits on Contracting out through Regional Trade Agreements Note' (2011) 86 (5) New York University Law Review, p. 1482.

30 Unlike Enabling Clause, GATT Article XXIV does not differentiate between the development level of the members.

31 GATT: General Agreement on Tariffs and Trade, Article XXIV:4 (30 October1947) <http://docsonline.wto.org> accessed 20 August 2016.

32 Hilpold in his research points to the fact that GATT Article XXIV was formed just after the World War II and therefore could not possibly cover other economic integration levels that could not be predicted at that time. See: Peter Hilpold 'Regional Integration

agreements such as GATS cover broader range of integration levels, such as common space, economic union and so on.

Interim agreements: Interim agreements, in the meaning of GATT Article XXIV, are considered transitory arrangements for countries aiming to conclude free trade areas or customs union. These agreements usually do not answer to all of the criteria set in Article XXIV for free trade areas and customs union. In order for countries not to abuse the use of interim agreements, a specific time limit – 10 years – has been set for them[33]. In cases where longer periods are necessary for the formation of customs union or free trade areas, full explanation is to be provided to the WTO[34].

Customs unions: Paragraph 8 of the Article XXIV defines customs union as the substitution of a single customs territory for two or more customs territories[35]. For customs unions to be in accordance with Article XXIV, two conditions should be met[36]: (i) Customs union parties have to eliminate duties and other

According to Article XXIV – Between Law and Politics' (2003) 17 (87) Max Planck Yearbook of United Nations Law, p. 227.

33 Understanding on the Interpretation of the Article XXIV of the GATT: 3 (15 April 1994) <http://docsonline.wto.org> accessed 20 August 2016.

34 ibid, 4.

35 GATT: General Agreement on Tariffs and Trade, Article XXIV:8 (a) (30 October1947) <http://docsonline.wto.org> accessed 20 August 2016.

36 Turkey-Textile Case is interesting here to mention. This case was brought to dispute settlement by India. India was complaining on the quantitative import restrictions which Turkey imposed on textile and clothing products originated from India as a result of the Turkey – EC customs union. India claimed that these restrictions were inconsistent with Article XI (general elimination of quantitative restrictions) and XIII (non-discriminatory administration of quantitative restrictions) of the GATT, as well as Article 2.4 of the Agreement on Textile and Clothing. In its defence, Turkey justified its measure under Article XXIV of the GATT stating that quantitative restrictions were necessary for the formation of the customs union. Turkey lost this case in the dispute settlement. Yet, Appellate Body in its interpretation of the Article XXIV of the GATT, came into the following conclusions that are important to our research: (1) Article XXIV may justify a measure which is inconsistent with other GATT provisions; (2) In invoking Article XXIV as a defence for inconsistency with other GATT provisions, two pre-conditions should be met: (1) compatibility of the customs union with Article XXIV paragraph 8 requirements, (2) whether the inconsistent measure is necessary for the formation of the customs union. (3) Burden of proof is on the party who is invoking Article XXIV exception. See: WTO, *Turkey – Restrictions on Import of Textile and Clothing Products – Report of the Appellate Body* (22 October 1999) WT/DS34/AB/R.

restrictive regulations of commerce with respect to substantially all the trade between themselves or at least with respect to substantially all the trade in products originating with each other; (ii) Customs union parties have to apply substantially the same duties and other regulations of commerce to third parties[37].

Free trade areas: In comparison with customs unions, there is no requirement of establishment of a common external tariff with regard to free trade areas. The criterion for free trade area is only one. Free trade area parties have to eliminate duties and other restrictive regulation of commerce on substantially all the trade between themselves in products originating with each other [38].

GATT Article XXIV states that the motivation for conclusion of customs unions, free trade areas and interim agreements is the desire to increase freedom of trade[39] . Therefore, these agreements should "facilitate trade" between its parties and not lead to "raising barriers to the trade" of other members[40]. This is called "third party neutrality". Discipline on third party neutrality is further developed in the 5th paragraph of Article XXIV. In the general meaning of this paragraph, third party neutrality implies that duties and other regulations of commerce applied to the third parties shall not be higher or more restrictive than prior to the formation of such RTA[41].

There are a number of exclusions which are permitted under the GATT: Article XI (general elimination of quantitative restrictions), XII (restrictions to

37 ibid.

38 ibid, 8 (b).

39 ibid, 4.

40 ibid.

41 Yet, Article XXIV has used slightly different wording on this matter with regards to customs unions and free trade areas. With free trade areas and interim agreements leading to their formation, there is no derogation from third party neutrality. In comparison, the language on the same discipline for customs unions or interim agreements leading to the formation of customs unions is slightly weaker. Article XXIV paragraph 5(a) makes it possible for customs union to adopt duties and regulations of commerce that derogate from MFN principle, as long as these measures are "on the whole" not higher or more restrictive to outside parties. This is because formation of a customs union is a complex process and during this process, introduction of common external tariff is necessary, which might in its turn lead to cases that could be restrictive to outside parties. Therefore, different wording in the Article was thus introduced for customs unions during GATT negotiations in order to give some space for customs union members in their trade liberalization efforts. See: Zakir Hafez 'Weak Discipline: GATT Article XXIV and the Emerging WTO Jurisprudence on RTAs' (2003) 79 (4) North Dakota Law Review, p. 879.

safeguard balance of payments), XIII (non-discriminatory administration of quantitative restrictions), XIV (exceptions to the rule of non-discrimination), XV (exchange arrangements) and XX (general exceptions)[42]. In other words, duties and other restrictive regulations of commerce could be maintained when forming customs union or free trade area as long as they are justified under the aforementioned exclusions of GATT.

Both definitions of customs union and free trade area talk about "substantially all trade", yet the term is not defined[43]. In WTO, there have been three approaches to clarifying the wording of "substantially all trade". One group of members suggest using a quantifiable benchmark[44]. There have been numerous suggestions in different quantifiable benchmarks, but the WTO has not been able to reach a consensus on them[45]. Another group of members argue for a qualitative approach, where substantially all trade would mean that no sector is kept out of the liberalization[46]. There is a third approach suggesting using combination of quantifiable and qualitative approach[47]. Yet, the issue still remains open.

Understanding on the Interpretation of Article XXIV makes it clear that dispute settlement procedures could be invoked with respect to any matter arising from the application of the Article XXIV of the GATT provisions related to RTAs[48]. This has in years led to many members not being willing to notify their RTAs, as well as an impasse in Committee on Regional Trade Agreements in

42 GATT: General Agreement on Tariffs and Trade, Article XXIV:8 (30 October1947) <http://docsonline.wto.org> accessed 20 August 2016.

43 Chase argues that "substantially all trade" wording used in the Article XXIV was included by US, because US wanted to exclude a number of goods from the scope of trade deal with Canada. See: Kerry Chase, 'Multilateralism Compromised: the Mysterious Origins of GATT Article XXIV' (2006) 5 (1) World Trade Review, p. 15.

44 WTO, Negotiating Group on Rules 'Compendium of Issues related to Regional Trade Agreements' (1 August 2002) TN/RL/W/8/Rev.1, 18.

45 Petros Mavroidis points that an Australian proposal to clarify "substantially all trade" during the Uruguay Round by introducing a quantifiable benchmark (95% of all trade at the 6 digit HS level) failed as no other member approved it. See: Petros Mavroidis, 'Always Look at the Bright Side of Non-delivery: WTO and Preferential Trade Agreements, Yesterday and Today' (2011) 10(3) World Trade Review, p. 379.

46 WTO, Negotiating Group on Rules 'Compendium of Issues related to Regional Trade Agreements' (1 August 2002) TN/RL/W/8/Rev.1, 18.

47 Peter Hilpold 'Regional Integration According to Article XXIV – Between Law and Politics' (2003) 7 Max Planck Yearbook of United Nations Law, p. 235.

48 Understanding on the Interpretation of the Article XXIV of the GATT: 12 (15 April 1994) <http://docsonline.wto.org> accessed 20 August 2016.

delivering examination reports for the examined RTAs. Members were unwilling to submit information which could be used against them in dispute proceedings.

ii. The Enabling Clause

The GATT Contracting Parties adopted on November 28, 1979 a decision on Differential and More Favorable Treatment, Reciprocity and Fuller Participation of Developing Countries which later became known as the Enabling Clause. This decision allows members to derogate from the GATT Article I (Most-favored Nation) and to accord preferential and more favorable treatment to the developing countries.

The Enabling Clause applies to a number of cases, however, from the point of view of this research, only paragraph 2c is relevant. This is because most of the provisions of the Enabling Clause deals with preferential treatment such as Generalized System of Preferences, differentiated treatment towards developing countries. In other words, the Enabling Clause mostly regulates unilateral preferences allocated by more developed countries to lesser developed countries. However, paragraph 2c makes the Enabling Clause applicable to regional or global arrangements among less-developed countries for mutual reduction or elimination of tariffs and non-tariff measures on products imported from one-another[49]. Thus, the Enabling Clause is applicable to the RTAs between developing countries. The Enabling Clause does not cover services, it only covers *goods*. Thus, the developing countries have the choice of notifying their RTAs in goods either based on the Article XXIV of the GATT or the Enabling Clause.

Article 3 and 4 of the decision reiterates the third-party neutrality rule and requirements of notification. The rest of the decision is dedicated to recognition of the particular challenges and development needs of the less-developed countries and not expecting reciprocity for concessions and commitment levels from the developing countries.

There are a few differences between the Enabling Clause and GATT Article XXIV. In comparison to the GATT Article XIV, the Enabling Clause's language is not as strict. There is no reference to elimination of tariffs and other measures of commerce covering substantially all trade. Moreover, while the GATT Article XXIV requires elimination of duties and other measures of commerce, the Enabling Clause does not require total elimination. It gives a choice of either mutual

49 Enabling Clause: WTO Decision on Differential and More Favorable Treatment Reciprocity and Fuller Participation of Developing Countries: 2 (28 November 1979) <http://docsonline.wto.org> accessed 20 August 2016.

reduction or elimination of tariffs[50]. With regards to non-tariff measures, the same language is observed, but the decision also states that contracting parties may prescribe criteria and condition for the mutual reduction or elimination of non-tariff measures among less-developed countries[51].

It should be noted here that "less developed" or "developing" country term is defined nowhere in the WTO agreements. Neither the WTO nor any other international organization defines the criteria for a country to be eligible for being considered as a developing country[52]. The World Bank classifies countries based on their gross national income into the following categories: low-income economies, lower middle income economies, upper middle income economies and high-income economies[53]. Yet, this list has no standing in the WTO, especially in conferring privileges of developing countries embodied in WTO agreements to acceding countries claiming these flexibilities. So, WTO members may assert themselves "less developed" or "developing" and have access to the Enabling Clause, however other WTO members in this case should agree with such assertions.

iii. GATS Article V (Economic Integration)

Article V of the GATS regulates RTAs in *services* between both developing and developed countries. While the GATT Article XXIV has disciplines on free trade areas, customs unions and interim agreements only, the coverage of the GATS is broader. It disciplines economic integration agreements as well[54].

---

50 ibid, 2 (c).

51 ibid.

52 UN has an official list of least-developed countries (LDC), yet UN does not regulate the development levels of other countries. See: UN, Committee for Development Policy 'List of Least Developed Countries' <http://www.un.org/en/development/desa/policy/cdp/ldc/ldc_list.pdf> accessed 19 May 2016.

53 World Bank, World Development Indicators Database <http://databank.worldbank.org/data/reports.aspx?source=world-development-indicators> accessed 11 August 2016.

54 Economic integration agreements in general refer to preferential trade agreements, free trade agreements, customs unions, common markets and economic unions. These agreements allow free flow of goods and services, as well as factors of production among the parties to the agreement. See: Scott Baier, Jeffrey Bergstrand, Michael Feng, 'Economic Integration Agreements and the Margins of International Trade' (2014) 93 Journal of International Economics, p. 339.

Article V covers a variety of issues, such as criteria for the agreements to be compatible with Article V, considerations in evaluating such criteria, flexibilities for developing countries, third party neutrality, modification of schedules, notification requirements, treatment of service suppliers of other members and compensation.

RTAs are defined here as the agreements liberalizing trade in services, provided they answer to the following criteria: (i) They have a substantial sectoral coverage; (ii) They provide for the absence or they eliminate substantially all discrimination, in the services sectors through either elimination of existing discriminatory measures and/or prohibition of new or more discriminatory measures[55].

As was the case in GATT Article XXIV, "substantial coverage" is not defined in the GATS Article V. The footnote in Article V explains that "substantial coverage" encompasses a number of sectors, volume of trade affected and modes of supply and points that an agreement cannot have substantial coverage if it excludes a mode of supply from its coverage a priori[56]. Yet, whether an agreement which includes all modes of supply, but covers only a few sectors and some volume of trade could be considered having a "substantial coverage" is a grey area[57].

The GATS does not define the term "substantially all discrimination" either. However, it states that in evaluating whether substantially all discrimination is eliminated between the parties, relationship with wider processes of economic integration and trade liberalization could be taken into account[58].

The agreement lists measures that could be justified under the GATS Article XI (payments and transfers), XII (restrictions to safeguard balance of payments), XIV (general exceptions) and XIV bis (security exceptions) as an exception[59].

---

55 GATS: General Agreement on Trade in Services, Article V:1 (15 April, 1994), Marrakesh Agreement Establishing the World Trade Organization, Annex 1B, <http://docsonline.wto.org> accessed 20 August 2016.

56 ibid, Article V:1 (a) footnote.

57 There have been some members in the WTO who questioned whether the RTAs that required only liberalization of Mode 3 (commercial presence) for provision of some services are compatible with Article V citing that this was incompatible with Article V footnote 1. WTO, Negotiating Group on Rules 'Compendium of Issues related to Regional Trade Agreements' (1 August 2002) TN/RL/W/8/Rev.1, 17.

58 GATS: General Agreement on Trade in Services, Article V:2 (15 April, 1994), Marrakesh Agreement Establishing the World Trade Organization, Annex 1B, <http://docsonline.wto.org> accessed 20 August 2016.

59 ibid, Article V:1(b).

The GATS Article V paragraph 3 provides certain flexibilities for developing countries. This means that if the parties to an RTA in services are developing countries, overall and in individual sectors, they do not have to meet all the criteria set out in Article 5 paragraph 1, especially the requirement for elimination of substantially all the discrimination between them[60].

As in all other WTO provisions on RTAs, the GATS also has discipline on the third party neutrality rule. It explains that agreements referred to in the GATS Article V should facilitate trade between the parties and should not lead to raising the overall level of barriers in services with third parties[61]. Article V also allows for service suppliers of third parties to enjoy the benefits of the RTA when they have juridical persons in the parties to the RTA, as well as when they have substantial business operation in the territory of RTA parties[62]. What is considered as "substantial business operation" is undefined throughout WTO Agreements.

iv. Current and Future WTO Negotiations on RTAs

From the very beginning, the WTO has been vigilant to the process of conclusion of the RTAs. Prior to the formation of the WTO, RTAs were mostly being examined in ad-hoc working parties[63]. However, after the start of the proliferation of RTAs, the WTO General Council adopted a decision to establish Committee on Regional Trade Agreements (CRTA hereinafter) on 6 February 1996. Thus, the examination process of RTAs was centralized throughout the WTO. According to the terms and references of the CRTA, its functions were to examine individual RTAs and report its findings to the Council for Trade in Goods, Council for Trade in Services or Committee on Trade and Development, to adopt recommendations regarding reporting of RTAs, to develop procedures to facilitate and improve the examination of RTAs, to consider and make recommendations on systemic implications of RTAs on multilateral trading system and their relationship and to carry out additional functions entrusted by the General Council[64].

---

60 ibid, Article V:3.

61 ibid, Article V:4.

62 ibid, Article V:6.

63 Work of the Committee on Regional Trade Agreements (WTO) <https://www.wto.org/english/tratop_e/region_e/regcom_e.htm> accessed 12 August 2016.

64 WTO, General Council Decision 'WTO Committee on Regional Trade Agreements' (6 February 1996) WT/L/127, 7 February 1996 < https://www.wto.org/english/tratop_e/region_e/127.pdf> accessed 12 August 2016.

Initially, the examination of RTAs on services was not mandatory[65]. Only the RTAs notified under Article XXIV of the GATT were obligatory for examination. The notifications under Article XXIV of the GATT were made to the Council of Goods which then directed the issue to the CRTA. In the case of RTAs covering services and notified under Article V of the GATS, the notifications were made to the Council on Trade in Services which could or could not pass the RTA for examination to the CRTA. The notifications under the Enabling Clause were made to the Committee on Trade and Development which discussed the RTA itself and rarely asked the CRTA for examination. However, this process was challenging, as the Secretariat was not able to finalize any examination reports because there was frequently a lack of consensus among the members. The members could not agree on a number of issues open to interpretation[66].

When the Doha Round of negotiations was launched in 2001, disciplines on RTAs were included in the area of "WTO Rules" for further negotiations. At this time, RTAs were proliferating on a tremendous scale. To answer to this challenge, Doha Declaration stressed and emphasized the unique role of the WTO as a platform for the global trade rule-making while also recognizing some positive impacts of RTAs such as trade liberalization and development. The mandate in Doha Declaration was "to clarify and improve disciplines and procedures under the existing WTO provisions applying to regional trade agreements"[67]. From 2002 to 2011, a number of documents were submitted by members in the Doha Development Round in this respect, but there was no progress and in 2011 the work was stalled.

Yet, the most important document during the Doha Round was the adoption of provisional Transparency Mechanism on RTAs by WTO General Council on 14 December 2006. The Mechanism regulates early announcement, notification, reporting and transparency procedures related to RTAs. Based on the document, all RTAs should be notified to the WTO as soon as possible but before they are entered into force[68]. Members consider these RTAs based on the factual presentations prepared by the WTO Secretariat[69]. According to the Mechanism, all the

---

65 Up until the period when the Transparency Mechanism on RTAs was adopted.

66 WTO, Negotiating Group on Rules 'Compendium of Issues related to Regional Trade Agreements' (1 August 2002) TN/RL/W/8/Rev.1, paras 19–20.

67 WTO Doha Ministerial Declaration (adopted 14 November 2011) WT/MIN(01)/DEC/1, para 29 <https://www.wto.org/english/thewto_e/minist_e/min01_e/mindecl_e.htm> accessed 11 August 2016.

68 Transparency Mechanism for Regional Trade Agreements: 3 (14 December 2006) WT/L/671, 18 December 2016 <http://docsonline.wto.org> accessed 20 August 2016.

69 ibid, 7 (b).

RTAs notified under GATT Article XXIV and GATS Article V are considered on CRTA, while RTAs notified under the Enabling Clause 2(c) are considered under Committee on Trade and Development in its dedicated sessions[70].

The halted negotiations on RTAs in the Doha Round were re-started in 2015. The only progress so far has been the language on RTAs incorporated in the Declaration of the Nairobi Ministerial Meeting. The Nairobi Declaration itself does not clarify or improve the disciplines on RTAs as was mandated in the Doha Declaration. However, the Nairobi declaration stresses the need to ensure that RTAs should be complementary to the multilateral trading system and should not substitute it[71]. In this regard, it instructs CRTA to consider and discuss systemic issues associated with RTAs and their relationship with WTO rules, as well as to work towards transforming provisional Transparency Mechanism into a permanent mechanism without prejudice to the notification requirements[72].

Overall, based on the discussion presented in this section, it is evident that even though, the GATT and later the WTO laid the foundations of regionalism in the world, regionalism as a phenomenon has gone beyond the expectations of the legal drafters of the WTO instruments. In fact, it has become a platform of competition with multilateralism. The WTO is pursuing a policy to somehow regulate regionalism by increasing transparency and the advertising complementarity of both platforms, however this policy has yielded only limited results so far. In this context, different processes could be used to ensure that regionalism does not undermine globalization of trade and among this multilateralisation of regionalism stands out. The next section will therefore touch upon multilateralisation of regionalism in a more detailed way.

2. Multilateralization of Regionalism

With the proliferation of the RTAs, the trade literature focused intensely on discussions around the advantages and disadvantages of the RTAs and their impact on the multilateral trading system[73]. There have been opponents and

70 ibid, 18.

71 Alexey Portanskiy, 'Posle Nairobi VTO Vinujdena Menyatsya' (After Nairobi, WTO must change) (2016) 3 Rosiyskiy vnesneoekonomicheskiy vestnik, p. 51.

72 WTO Nairobi Ministerial Declaration (adopted 19 December 2015) WT/MIN(15)/DEC, para 28 <https://www.wto.org/english/thewto_e/minist_e/mc10_e/mindecision_e.htm> accessed 12 August 2016.

73 To read more about advantages and disadvantages of RTAs, see: Colin Picker 'Regional Trade Agreements v. WTO: A Proposal for Reform of Article XXIV to Counter this

proponents of both regionalization and multilateralization. Even though, there are advantages and disadvantages of both, a common ground could not be found. In this line, the WTO prompted a process called multilateralization of regionalism, to discuss how RTAs could potentially be facilitating the multilateral trade agreements and how they could grow into larger trade agreements[74].

This sub-section of the chapter aims to introduce the concept of the multilateralization of regionalism and discuss how it could possibly function.

i. Definition and Background

The concept of multilateralization of regionalism was first put forward in 2007 in the framework of the international conference organized by the WTO. In this international conference, the Director – General of the WTO at that time – Pascal Lamy – pointed that it was about time, instead of focusing on advantages and disadvantages of regionalism, to discuss how RTAs can be multilateralized. Here Pascal Lamy defined multilateralization as "expanding RTAs — or in other words, collapsing them into larger entities that bring us much closer to a multilateral system of trade arrangements"[75].

The multilateralization of regionalism is also defined as making RTAs less preferential[76]. In other words, it is aimed to join more countries in the RTAs or to make the disciplines in the RTAs apply to more countries.

Initially, when the idea of multilateralization of regionalism was first put forward, it focused mostly on tariffs and rules of origin, and creating a tariff-free global system[77]. This was because, the initial waves of RTAs focused more on

---

Institutional Threat' (2005) 26 (2) University of Pennsylvania Journal of International Economic Law 270; Sarah Barnekow, Kishore Kulkami 'Why Regionalism? A Look at the Costs and Benefits of Regional Trade Agreements in Africa' (2017) 18(1) Global Business Review , p. 103.

74 *WTO, Multilateralising Regionalism: Challenges for the Global Trading System* edited by Richard Balwin, Patrick Low(Cambridge University Press, Cambridge, 2009), p. xii

75 Pascal Lamy – Opening Speech at the conference on Multilateralising Regionalism, 10 September 2007, Geneva <https://www.wto.org/english/news_e/sppl_e/sppl67_e.htm> accessed 25 July 2018.

76 Richard Baldwin 'Multilateralising 21st Century Regionalism' (2014) OECD Global Forum on Trade Reconciling Regionalism and Multilateralism in Post-Bali World, p. 5 <https://repository.graduateinstitute.ch/record/286980/files/Baldwin_OECD_2013.pdf> accessed 23 July 2018.

77 Richard Baldwin 'Multilateralising Regionalism: Spaghetti Bowls as Building Blocks on the Path to Global Free Trade' (2006) NBER Working Paper 12545, p. 3 <https://www.nber.org/papers/w12545.pdf> accessed 7 April 2019.

tariff preferences and gaining more favorable market access to goods and services. Nonetheless, the modern wave of RTAs go beyond tariff preferences and capture market access to capital, movement of people, intellectual property and know-how[78]. This has happened because a series of WTO tariff cuts, conclusion of bilateral investment treaties and policies of unilateral tariff cuts in developing countries have made tariffs generally low across the world. As such, the focus of modern RTAs are not on tariffs, but rather on non-tariff barriers. This has also resulted in the change of impact of the RTAs. While previously RTAs were always perceived as a mechanism which would certainly have a negative affect over the non-RTA parties, the analysis of modern RTAs show that they have more and more positive spillover affect and generate trade both to members and non-members[79]. It is observed that even when RTAs discriminate between the partners, there are certain trade creation implications between non-members as well. For instance, if country A and B conclude a RTA where both countries adopt deep trade facilitation provisions, these measures will be applicable to all trading partners, so country C will benefit from this as well and it will generate trade for country C as well.

In this line, nowadays multilateralization of regionalism has also gained a completely different context. It focuses more on making non-tariff issues multilateral. Multilateralization of non-tariff issues are somewhat easier to achieve as some non-tariff issues are impossible to discriminate towards non-parties of the RTAs. While rules on market access to goods could easily differentiate among the trading partners, non-tariff barriers, if countries wish, can be instantly multilateralized. For instance, when a country adopts a competition system prescribed in the RTA, it will be applicable to all trade partners. As such, liberalization of non-trade barriers would have a positive affect for all the trade partners.

It should be noted that the multilateralization of regionalism is also impacted by the growing global supply and production chains. Current RTAs are aimed at making the trading environment for companies participating in such supply chains attractive[80]. That is to say, states aim to conclude RTAs that will

---

78 Alexey Portanskiy, 'Posle Nairobi VTO Vinujdena Menyatsya' (After Nairobi, WTO must change) (2016) 3 Rosiyskiy vnesneoekonomicheskiy vestnik, p. 51.

79 Rohini Acharya et al. "Landscape" in Preferential Trade Agreement Policies for Development: A Handbook (2011, World Bank, Washington), p. 39.

80 Richard Baldwin 'Trade and Industrialization After Globalisations' 2nd Unbundling: How Building and Joining Supply Chain are Different and Why it Matters' (2011) NBER Working Paper 17716, p. 32 <https://www.nber.org/papers/w17716.pdf> accessed 07 April 2019.

give favorable market access to their companies along the supply chain. In particular, RTAs nowadays deal with concepts such as offshoring, creation of joint ventures, combination of high-technologies from developed countries along with low wages of developing countries[81]. For instance, most companies participating in global supply and production chains seek lower wage companies in the third-nation countries for their production. When they locate their production in such countries, they also need assurance of capital movement, protection of their intellectual property and other disciplines. Furthermore, they require a cut in transaction costs associated with complying with different trade rules and regulations.

ii. How Multilateralization of Regionalism Could Function?

There are certain theoretical possibilities to take into consideration when it comes to multilateralization of regionalism. First of all, multilateralization within the WTO mostly prescribes a "one size fits all" concept, that is to say countries are applying the same set of rules with a few exceptions[82]. However, this approach might not be relevant in the case of multilateralization of regionalism. There are certain disciplines in trade where the interests of developing and developed countries collide, which is one of the reasons why such areas are not currently covered by the WTO. For instance, agriculture is one of these areas. While some developing countries allocate large subsidies to agriculture to increase the competitiveness of their exporting industry, there are certain developed countries, especially members of the WTO Cairns group, who are pursuing policies of no subsidies to agriculture[83] . In such scenarios, it is very difficult to reconcile the interests of the different countries to achieve the multilateralization process. The key is thus not having "one size fits all" concept, but rather developing a framework which could be applied based on the various countries' specificities.

Against such a background, multi-tier multilateralization might be a solution to soften considerable differences between the interests of countries[84].

81 ibid

82 Trade Facilitation Agreement is an exception. Here, parties can choose their commitment level. Also, pluryilateral agreements of the WTO are voluntary to join.

83 Cairns group members are: Argentina, Australia, Brazil, Canada, Chile, Colombia, Costa Rica, Guatemala, Indonesia, Malaysia, New Zealand, Pakistan, Paraguay, Peru, the Philippines, South Africa, Thailand, Uruguay, Vietnam

84 Richard Baldwin and Philip Thornton, "Multilateralising Regionalism" (2008) CEPR Policy Report <https://cepr.org/active/publications/books_reports/viewreport.php?cvno=P185> accessed 25 July 2018.

Here, a multilateral model framework could cover minimum standards at one tier and countries could choose implementation level of this framework on the second tier. Best practices to achieve the multilateral framework could be shared. While standards and principles would need to be complied with, the best practices would only be voluntary, but it would lead to more countries adapting this system than the current regionalism, as it would create space for countries to adapt to their specific circumstances.

Multilateralization of regionalism can be implemented globally and mega-regionally. Globally would mean that certain discipline would be harmonized in the global level. This can be done within the multilateral processes of the WTO. Mega-regionally implies harmonization of the RTA disciplines within larger regions. This can be achieved through mega-regional deals such as Comprehensive and Progressive Agreement for Trans-Pacific Partnership which joins together economies such as Japan, Canada, Australia, New Zealand, Mexico, Singapore.

It should be noted that, multilateralization is easier to achieve between hub and spoke countries[85] . Market access to hub countries is a great incentive for the spoke countries to join the RTAs. This is especially true for small countries wishing to develop their export capacities. These countries feel pressured to join RTAs with the regional hubs in order to export to a bigger market on more favorable terms[86]. An example could be the case of the EU, where Association Agreement parties need to align their legislation with that of the EU. This in turn leads to the hub country having similar or the same disciplines in its RTAs with trading partners. For instance, EU Pan-European Rules of Origin scheme is applied to a set of countries. Thus, a series of EU partners apply the same rules of origin. Of course, the situation gets complicated when the spoke country has RTAs with two different hubs or there is a rivalry between the hubs in the region[87]. For instance, Mexico needs to comply with NAFTA rules, as well as EU rules.

85 If country A has RTA with Country B and C, but the Country B and C do not have RTAs with each-other, then Country A is the hub country and Country B and C are spoke countries.

86 Richard Baldwin 'The Causes of Regionalism' (1997) 20 (7) World Economy, p. 878 <https://onlinelibrary.wiley.com/doi/abs/10.1111/1467-9701.00107> accessed 21 December 2018.

87 Christopher Dent, *New Free Trade Agreements in the Asia-Pacific* (Palgrave Macmillan, New York, 2006), p. 231.

As mentioned earlier, nowadays, multilateralization of tariff preferences might not be the primary goal of the multilateralization of regionalism. Tariffs preferences are not as important an aspect as they used to be when concluding RTAs, because tariffs worldwide are generally low nowadays[88]. The last two decades have witnessed tariff reductions worldwide which has resulted in very low or almost zero average tariffs globally. For instance, Mauritius has decreased its tariffs from 28% to 0.8% in the last 20 years[89]. For the trading partners of countries like Mauritius, achieving further tariff cuts in the RTAs are not important. Furthermore, multilateralization of tariff preferences (extending the tariff preferences to the non-RTA members) might not even be desirable, as even in the WTO, members have different applied tariffs.

Multilateralization of rules of origin surfaces as an important goal of multilateralization of regionalism. One of the greatest challenges for the multilateral system is the existence of different rules of origin. In this context, simplification of rules of origin can be a big stepping stone for the multilateralization of regionalism. Conclusion of WTO Agreement on Preferential Rules of Origin would put forward a set of rules and principles for preferential rules of origin. However, considering that these negotiations are at a stalemate currently, the likelihood of this happening soon is quite low.

Harmonizing standards and technical regulations can be another way of multilateralizing regionalism. There is a tendency for spoke countries in the world to harmonize their standards and technical regulations with those of the hub countries (for instance EU, USA, Japan). Though the standards and technical regulations of the hub countries differ, most of the hubs have mutual recognition system for standards and technical questions. It seems thus TBT is a sector where multilateralization of regionalism is naturally developing.

Disciplines with higher degree of similarity across the RTAs are valuable in the multilateralization process. These include WTO *beyond* (going beyond what is covered by the WTO agreements) and WTO *deep* (going deeper in the coverage of the disciplines already tackled in the WTO agreements) disciplines, as

---

88 Average applied tariff worldwide is around 9%. In fact, there are WTO members such as Singapore, Honkong and Macao which apply no tariffs for the majority of merchandise trade. Tariffs higher than 25% have been eliminated, while tariffs in the range of 15–25% have been decreased See: "Trade and Tariffs" (2015) WTO publication <https://www.wto.org/english/thewto_e/20y_e/wto_20_brochure_e.pdf> accessed 21 August 2018.

89 ibid

they are quite similar across the RTAs[90]. In fact many such provisions in the RTAs generally stem from the discussions held within the WTO committees, which did not lead to WTO agreements. OECD findings show that investment, services and transparency are the top three most widespread WTO *deep* and WTO *beyond* sectors[91]. Some scholars point that these sectors are easier to multilateralize because rules of origin do not matter or are weak in these sectors[92].

Institutionalizing multilateralization process and having an efficient oversight institution could help in clarifying how these provisions would be implemented and what would happen if one party fails to do so. An effective supervision mechanism would thus guarantee that parties adhere to their commitments. For instance, an OECD study shows that WTO plus provisions in the RTAs have lesser degree of implementation because there is no supervisory body such as WTO to oversee the implementation[93]. This supervision mechanism for multilateralization of regionalism could be established as an independent body or functioning within the WTO.

In conclusion, multilateralization of regionalism is different from the multilateralization process within the WTO, so different approaches should be used here than by the WTO. There are challenges to this process, however multilateralization of regionalism is quite possible and feasible. During the process, special attention could be allocated to multilateralization of disciplines with higher degree of similarity, institutionalizing the process, by not prescribing a "one size fits all" concept.

iii. The Role of Mega-regional Arrangements

The mega-regional arrangements are the new phase of regionalism[94]. Ricardo Melendez Ortiz defines them as "deep integration partnership between countries

---

90 Iza Lejárraga 'Multilateralising Regionalism: Strengthening Transparency Disciplines in Trade' (2012), 152 OECD Trade Policy Papers (OECD Publishing, Paris), p. 20.

91 Iza Lejárraga 'Deep Provisions in Regional Trade Agreements: How Multilateral-friendly?: An Overview of OECD Findings' (2014) OECD Trade Policy Papers 168 (OECD Publishing, Paris), p. 15.

92 *WTO, Multilateralising Regionalism: Challenges for the Global Trading System* edited by Richard Balwin, Patrick Low(Cambridge University Press, Cambridge, 2009).

93 Iza Lejárraga 'Deep Provisions in Regional Trade Agreements: How Multilateral-friendly?: An Overview of OECD Findings' OECD Trade Policy Papers, No. 168 (2014, OECD Publishing, Paris), p. 6.

94 Mega-regional arrangements are agreements, covering substantial world trade and aiming deep integration.

or regions with a major share of world trade and foreign direct investment, in which two or more states are in paramount driver position or serve as a hub in global value chains"[95]. Thus their major differences from the traditional RTAs lie in their larger size, their coverage, deeper integration, and most importantly their regulatory convergence. Mega-regional trade agreements aim to phase out differences in business and investment climates of the participating countries. The largest current mega-regional trade agreements are Comprehensive and Progressive Agreement for Trans-Pacific Partnership which came into force in late 2018, EU – Japan Free Trade Agreement which came into force in 2019, as well as projects such as the Transatlantic Trade and Investment Partnership and Regional Comprehensive Economic Partnership[96] . Because of their regulatory convergence, deepness, coverage and share of world trade Eurasian Economic Union and in some respect, the CIS can also be considered as mega-regional trade deals.

There are two major driving forces behind the mega-regional arrangements. First of all, development of global supply and value chains require reduction of transaction costs associated with the trade in different countries or even regions and this is not easily achieved within the WTO, hence this process leads to mega-regional arrangements to achieve it[97]. Secondly, different political considerations

95 Ricardo Melendez Ortiz 'Mega-Regionals: What is going on?' In "Mega-Regional Trade Agreements: Game Changers or Costly Distractions for World Trading System?" (2014) World Economic Forum publication <http://www3.weforum.org/docs/GAC/2014/WEF_GAC_TradeFDI_MegaRegionalTradeAgreements_Report_2014.pdf> accessed 8 April 2019.

96 Comprehensive and Progressive Agreement for Trans-Pacific Partnership came into force in December 2018. The text can be accessed here: <https://dfat.gov.au/trade/agreements/in-force/cptpp/official-documents/Documents/tpp-11-treaty-text.pdf> accessed 06 April 2019.
Economic Partnership Agreement between European Union and Japan entered into force on February 1, 2019. See: COM(2018) 192 FINAL <https://eur-lex.europa.eu/legal-content/EN/TXT/?uri=CELEX:52018PC0192#document2> accessed 8 April 2019.
Transatlantic Trade and Investment is a draft RTA between the EU and the USA, the negotiations for this agreement was halted in 2017, however the parties are negotiating new mandate for reopening the trade negotiations.
Regional Comprehensive Economic Partnership is a draft RTA between Brunei, Cambodia, Indonesia, Laos, Malaysia, Myanmar, Philippines, Singapore, Thailand, Vietnam, Australia, China, India, Japan, South Korea, New Zealand.

97 Vladislav Zaqashvili 'VTO I Meqaregionalnie Torqovie Soqlashenie' (WTO and mega-regional trade agreements) (2017) 5 Rosiyskiy vneshnoekonomiceskoy vestnik, p. 30.

and shifts of power in the world result in such mega-regional deals[98]. For instance, Regional Comprehensive Economic Partnership is China's project to assert its power in the region[99] .

For multilateralization of regionalism, mega-regionals are important from a number of aspects. First of all, these arrangements cover a broader range of countries than traditional RTAs. As discussed in the previous section, having a broader range of countries as members, makes it easier to multilateralize the disciplines[100]. Secondly, mega-regionals already have harmonized the scattered rules and disciplines existent in different RTAs and they mitigate the effects of "spaghetti bowls"[101]. They can cumulate diverse rules of origin among the different countries[102]. Thirdly, mega-regionals are directed towards elimination of non-tariff barriers[103]. They are not expected to generate substantial tariff cuts,

98 Dumulen Ippolit 'Mnoqostoronnost I Regionalism v Ramkax VTO I Sovremennoy Mejdunarodnoy Torqovle' (Multilateralislm and regionalism in the framework of the WTO and contemporary international trade) (2016) 10 Mejdunarodnaya ekonomika, p. 7.

99 Iza Lejárraga 'Deep Provisions in Regional Trade Agreements: How Multilateral-friendly?: An Overview of OECD Findings' (2014) OECD Trade Policy Papers, No. 168 (OECD Publishing, Paris).

100 Maria Tabarovskaya, Vladimir Sherov-Iqnatyev, 'VTO Posle Nayrobi: Vizovi So Storoni Meqareqionalnix Soqlasheniy I Koalichionnaya Aktivnost Rossiyi' (WTO after Nayrobi: Challenges from the mega-regional agreements and coalition activity of Russia) (2017) 1 (9) Torqovaya politika, p. 27.

101 Andrey Spartak 'Metamorfozi Processa Reqionalizacii: Ot Reqionalnix Torqovix Soqlasheniy k Meqareqionalnim Proektam' (Metamorphosis of regionalization process: From regional trade agreements to mega-regional projects) (2017) 10 (4) Konturu qlobalnix transformaciy: politika, ekonomika, pravo, p. 27 <https://cyberleninka.ru/article/v/metamorfozy-protsessa-regionalizatsii-ot-regionalnyh-torgovyh-soglasheniy-k-mezhregionalnym-proektam> accessed 23 December 2018.

102 Jeremy Harris "Building Inclusive Rules of Origin in the XXI Century" (2017) International Center for Trade and Sustainable Development and Inter-American Development Bank Publication, p. 9 <http://e15initiative.org/wp-content/uploads/2015/09/RTA-Exchange-Rules-of-Origin-Jeremy-Harris-Final.pdf> accessed 30 July 2018.

103 Vera Malceva, Darya Chupina 'Reqionalnie i Meqareqionalnie Torqovie Soqlasheniye: Torqovlya Selskoxozyaystvennoy Produkciey v Transtixookeanskim Partnerstve' (Regional and mega-regional trade agreements: Trade in agricultural products in Transpacific Partnership) (2017) Vestnik mejdunarodnix orqanizaciy: obrazovanie, nauka, 1 novaya ekonomika, p. 51 <https://cyberleninka.ru/article/v/regionalnye-i-megaregionalnye-torgovye-soglasheniya-torgovlya-selskohozyaystvennoy-produktsiey-v-transtihookeanskom-partnerstve> accessed 22 December 2018.

however it is expected that they will harmonize many non-tariff issues across the regions and will make some previously non-enforceable issues within the existing RTAs more enforceable[104]. Fourthly, getting access to the markets of mega-regional trade blocks becomes an incentive for outsiders to join the mega-regional deals[105]. In this way, mega-regional arrangements are one step closer to multilateralism than bilateral trade deals.

However, the disadvantages of RTAs apply to mega-regional arrangements as well. Firstly, as mega-regionals are also political projects, different political realities of the countries participating in these arrangements impact the process. For instance, a change of government in the USA halted the ratification of the Trans-Pacific Partnership and halted negotiations of the Transatlantic Trade and Investment Partnership[106]. Secondly, mega-regionals benefit mostly the developed countries, and not so much developing countries[107]. This is because mega-regional arrangements are not as effective as the WTO for developing countries to promote their interests. In the WTO, developing countries can group and voice their views and concerns as one block. This is not the same in the RTA platform where they are compromising their interests in order to reap the benefits of the RTA formation[108].

Despite its drawbacks, mega-regional arrangements are the ideal place to start for multilateralization of regionalism. In the context of Eastern Europe, Central Asia and the Caucasus, the Eurasian Economic Union can be considered as a mega-regional trade arrangement, as it is deep integration level and is covering substantial trade in the Eurasia region. Unlike the Eurasian Economic Union,

---

104 Chad P. Brown 'The Mega-Regional Trade Arrangements and the Future of the WTO' (2016) Council on Foreign Relations Discussion Paper, p. 108 <https://onlinelibrary.wiley.com/doi/full/10.1111/1758-5899.12391> accessed 15 August 2018.

105 Vladimir Obolenskiy 'Pereqovori o Sozdanii Torqovix Superblokov I Interesi Rossii' (Negotiation on formation of trade super-blocks and interests of Russia) (2013) 11 Rossiyskiy Vneshnoekonomiceskiy Vestnik, p. 11 <https://cyberleninka.ru/article/v/peregovory-o-sozdanii-torgovyh-superblokov-i-interesy-rossii> accessed 22 December 2018.

106 Vladislav Zaqashvili 'VTO I Meqaregionalnie Torqovie Soqlashenie' (WTO and mega-regional trade agreements) (2017) 5 Rosiyskiy vneshnoekonomiceskoy vestnik, p. 30.

107 Stefanos Katsoulis 'Multilateralising Regionalism and the Case of the EU' in "The EU at a Crossroads" edited by Despina Anagnostopoulou, Ioannis Papadopoulos and Lina Papadopoulou, p. 166 (Cambridge Scholars Publishing, Newcastle 2016).

108 Alexey Portanskiy 'O Perspektivax Meqaregionalnix Torqovix Soqlasheniy' (About the perspectives of mega-regional trade agreements) (2017) 3 Mir novel ekonomiki, p. 53.

Association Agreements of the EU with Moldova, Georgia and Ukraine or the Commonwealth of Independent States (CIS) are not mega-regional arrangement, however they also play an important role in the region in harmonizing scattered trade rules. For instance, after the collapse of the Soviet Union, it was under the leadership of the CIS that Eastern Europe, Central Asia and the Caucasus countries adopted and harmonized their SPS and TBT, rules of origin, trade remedies legislation.

3. Summary of the Chapter

This chapter examined the RTA law within the WTO. The specific provisions of the various WTO agreements covering the RTAs were elaborated. Moreover, the chapter provided information on the current processes within the WTO and how existing WTO rules affected the RTA formation across the globe.

The chapter also analyzed the concept of multilateralization of regionalism, its definition, ways of functioning, as well as the role of mega-regional arrangements in the multilateralization of regionalism. It was concluded that a "one size fits all" concept is not relevant in the multilateralization process and a multi-tier multilateralization process could be more effective. The chapter also noted that the way forward for multilateralization would be through the expansion of membership of the RTAs. It was further concluded that the goal was not to multilateralize tariff cuts, but rather to focus on the non-tariff issues. The chapter elaborated that multilateralization can be done globally or mega-regionally, while mega-regional deals were an ideal place to start for multilateralization. It was also noted that the multilateralization process is easier to achieve between RTAs of hub and spoke countries. In this context, rules of origin, investment and TBT were explored as possible sectors for multilateralization. It was also noted that institutionalization could be a useful tool in this process.

Chapter 2 The Geopolitical Situation and the Specifics of the Regional Trade Agreements in Eastern Europe, Central Asia and the Caucasus

This chapter aims to introduce the reader to the region of Eastern Europe, Central Asia and the Caucasus. In doing so, the book consists of three sub-sections. The first section provides general characteristics of the RTAs in the region. The second sub-section provides information about the main elements of geopolitical and foreign policy of the major international players in the region. The third sub-section provides background information about the Eurasian Economic Union, Association Agreements of the EU with Ukraine, Georgia and Moldova, as well as the Commonwealth of the Economic States.

1 The General Characteristics of RTAs in Eastern Europe, Central Asia and the Caucasus Region

The RTAs in the region of Eastern Europe, Central Asia and the Caucasus has been under-analyzed in the trade literature. However, the rapid growing number of the RTAs here make Eastern Europe, Central Asia and the Caucasus attractive for analysis. There are several specificities of this region. First of all, all the countries in the region transitioned from socialism to capitalism, as they all were united in Soviet Union of Socialistic Republics for around 70 years. Their transition to market economy was coupled with harsh economic difficulties, severe currency depreciations, political challenges, instabilities, conflicts and escalations. Trade policies of these countries were shaped on a large scale by this transition, but also by the specificities of their freshly-gained independence. Some of these countries like Georgia, Moldova and the Ukraine chose to align themselves with western allies which led to their alienation from Russia. On the contrary, some of them, such as the Kyrgyz Republic, Tajikistan and Kazakhstan chose to build warm and friendly relations with Russia, which is partly due to their land-locked geography.

Secondly, this is a region with diverse WTO engagement. Most of the countries in the region are WTO members and some constitute recently acceded members such as Tajikistan, Russia and Kazakhstan[109]. As recently acceded members, they have taken much more accession commitments compared to the original WTO members. The region also contains a number of countries in the accession process such as Belarus, Uzbekistan and Azerbaijan[110]. Among these countries only Belarus is in the advanced position. Uzbekistan and Azerbaijan have not been showing a political will to complete the accession process yet. Turkmenistan has not been engaging with the WTO, due to its policy of neutrality[111] .

Thirdly, most of the countries in the region are abundant with natural resources[112]. Economies of Azerbaijan, Russia, Kazakhstan and Turkmenistan are characterized by the presence of a large oil and gas sector[113]. Among them, Russia is the world's leading producer of oil and natural gas[114]. Russia is also among top exporters of ferrous metals. Apart from hydrocarbon resources, Kazakhstan has

---

109 The WTO accession date of the countries in the Eastern Europe, Central Asia and Caucasus are as following: Kyrgyz Republic – 20 December 1998, Georgia – 14 June 2000, Moldova – 26 July 2001, Armenia – 5 February 2003, Ukraine – 16 May 2008, Russian Federation – 22 August 2012, Tajikistan – 2 March 2013, Kazakhstan – 30 November 2015. See: Understanding the WTO: The organization. Members and Observers (WTO) <https://www.wto.org/english/thewto_e/whatis_e/tif_e/org6_e.htm> accessed 25 August 2016.

110 The relevant dates of establishment of WTO Working Parties for the accession negotiations of the countries in this region are as following: Belarus – 27 October 1993, Uzbekistan – 21 December 1994, Azerbaijan – 16 July 1997. See: Understanding the WTO: The organization. Members and Observers (WTO) <https://www.wto.org/english/thewto_e/whatis_e/tif_e/org6_e.htm> accessed 25 August 2016.

111 Actually, Turkmenistan had applied for observer status during the Uruguay Round in early days of its independence. Its observer status was granted, yet the country did not follow its request after the establishment of the WTO, so formally Turkmenistan is not considered as an observer.

112 'The Economic Aspects of the Energy Sectors in the CIS' (2008) Center for Social and Economic Research, 327 Economic papers, p. 3 <http://ec.europa.eu/economy_finance/publications/pages/publication12678_en.pdf> accessed 22 October 2018.

113 Serqey Zhiltsov 'Truboprovodi v Centralnoy Azii I v Kaspiyskom reqione: noviy etap borbi' (Pipelines in the Central Asia and the Caucasus region: new stage of fight) (2014) 17 (3) Centralnaya Aziya I Kavkaz, p. 141.

114 Andrey Dryakin 'Enerqeticeskaya Diplomatiya Rossii v Aziatsko-Tixookeanskom Reqione: Osnovnie Aspekti i Napravleniya' (Energy diplomacy of Russia in Asian-Paific region: main aspects and directions) (2014) 4 (32) Izvestie Vuzov: Povoljskiy reqion. Qumanitarnie nauki, p. 106 <https://cyberleninka.ru/article/v/energeticheskaya-diplomatiya-rossii-v-aziatsko-tihookeanskom-regione-osnovnye-aspekty-i-napravleniya> accessed 35 December 2018.

vast resources of uranium, zinc and copper. Uzbekistan and Turkmenistan together produce most of the cotton in the world. Existence of abundant natural resources, coupled with the big consumer market makes these countries an attractive destination for RTA formation. However, it also makes economies of these countries dependent on natural resources[115].

Fourthly, the region is geopolitically active in terms of conflicts. All the countries in the region have some sort of territorial, ethnic or economic disputes with each other which are reflected in their bilateral trade relations. Frozen conflicts and ethnic escalations are surfaced in Moldova as Transnistria conflict, in Armenia and Azerbaijan as Nagorno Karabakh conflict, in Ukraine as annexation of Crimea to Russia, in Georgia as South Ossetia and Abkhazia conflict, in Kyrgyz Republic as ethnic clashes with Uzbek population. Existence of these challenges hinders effectiveness of the RTAs, undermines regional integration as well as trade handling in general[116].

Fifthly, the analyzed region is rich with RTAs. According to Neufeld, Ukraine and Russia are among the top ten countries having the most RTAs in the world[117]. However, the administration of the RTAs are not effective in the region. This stems from the fact that the countries in the region are lagging behind in terms of good governance and rule of law[118]. Poor records of rule of law and good governance affect proper administration of the RTAs. For instance, provisions of the Eurasian Economic Community between Russia, Belarus, Kazakhstan,

115 Aleksey Portanskiy 'Ot Bretton-Vudsa do Buenos Ayresa' (From Bretton-Woods to Buenos-Aires) (2017) 3 (11) Torqovaya politika, p. 38 <https://cyberleninka.ru/article/v/ot-bretton-vudsa-do-buenos-ayresa> accessed 22 December 2018.

116 Ekaterina Mixaylenko 'Slojnosti Postroenie Rosiyskoqo Reqionalizma na Post-Sovetskom Prostranstve' (Challenges of establishment of Russian regionalism in post-Soviet space) (2015) 400 Vestnik Tomskoqo Qosudarstennoqo Universiteta, p. 83 <https://cyberleninka.ru/article/v/slozhnosti-postroeniya-rossiyskogo-regionalizma-na-postsovetskom-prostranstve> accessed 26 December 2018.

117 Nora Neufeld 'Trade Facilitation Provisions in Regional Trade Agreements: Traits and Trends' (2014) 5 (1) Journal of International Commerce, Economics & Policy, p. 14.

118 Vladimir Petrovsky 'Growth, Governance and Human Development: Post-Soviet Transition in North and Central Asia' (2002) Asia Pacific Center for Security Studies, p. 160 <https://apcss.org/Publications/Edited%20Volumes/GrowthGovernance_files/Pub_Growth%20Governance/Pub_GrowthGovernancech12.pdf> accessed October 23, 2018.

Tajikistan and Kyrgyz Republic were applied in the region only occasionally, when it served the interests of the members[119].

In general, dynamics of the RTAs are governed by the economic and foreign relations of the major players, such as Russia[120]. Countries such as Ukraine, Moldova, Belarus, Azerbaijan, Armenia, Georgia, Turkmenistan, Tajikistan, Kyrgyz Republic and Kazakhstan have little or no influence when negotiating over the provisions on the RTAs.

The RTAs of the region are concluded mostly with the neighbors and traditional trading partners. The non-traditional trading partner so far has only been Vietnam, with which Eurasian Economic Union signed a free trade area. The rationale behind that move was to increase ties with ASEAN countries in light of the mega-regional trade negotiations happening in the Asian region[121].

It can be observed that, the RTAs in the region are concluded not only based on the economic reasons, but also based on political and security considerations. A clear example for this could be Armenia's membership to the Eurasian Economic Union. Apart from economic reasons, Armenia is in the Eurasian Economic Union to ensure its security in the Caucasus region[122]. Another such example is Syria, with which Eurasian Economic Union has ongoing RTA negotiations[123].

Despite the fact that the region contains economies rich in hydrocarbon resources, energy provisions of the RTAs have a narrow scope. The main energy producing countries in the region are Azerbaijan, Kazakhstan, Russia and Turkmenistan. None of the RTAs of Azerbaijan or Turkmenistan regulates energy issues, while the Eurasian Economic Union treaty (to which Russia and

119 David Tarr 'The Eurasian Economic Union Among Russia, Belarus, Kazakhstan, Armenia and Kyrgyz Republic: Can It Succeed Where Its Predecessor Failed?'(29 September 2015) World Bank Publications, p. 3 <http://as.vanderbilt.edu/gped/documents/DavidTarrEurasianCustomsUnion--prospectsSept282015.pdf> accessed 1 April 2018.

120 ibid, p. 21.

121 Aleksey Portanskiy 'Ot Bretton-Vudsa do Buenos Ayresa' (From Bretton-Woods to Buenos-Aires) (2017) 3 (11) Torqovaya politika, p. 43 <https://cyberleninka.ru/article/v/ot-bretton-vudsa-do-buenos-ayresa> accessed 22 December 2018.

122 Golam Mostafa, Monowar Mahmood 'Eurasian Economic Union: evolution, challenges and possible future directions' (2018) 9 (2) Journal of Eurasian Studies, p. 165.

123 Andrey Yeliseyev, 'EAES I Perspektivniiye Zoni Svobodnoy Torqovli (EAEU and Prospective Free Trade Areas)' Belarus Institute for Strategic Studies (2015) 6 Evraziyskoye obozrenie, p. 10.

Kazakhstan is a member) has limited scope of provisions which stipulate creation of common energy market. This market is supposed to be created with 10 year transition period that will end by 2025[124]. The rationale is simple. The energy producing countries of the region are dependent on their energy exports and they sell their energy products with high prices in the world products. They simply do not need to be in the WTO or have RTAs to gain revenues from their energy exports. In fact, it is energy importing countries that are interested in having energy issues in the RTAs[125]. Hence, there is a reluctancy from many energy players of the region to have energy provisions in the RTAs.

Most of the RTAs in the region are free trade areas. There are some advanced economic integration levels such as the Eurasian Economic Union. The EAEU is modeled after European Union and aims for integrating not only goods, services, capital and labor, but also aims to create common energy and monetary market in the following years. The region also contains Association Agreements of EU with Georgia, Ukraine and Moldova. These Association Agreements include Deep and Comprehensive Free Trade Agreements of recipient countries with the EU. Commonwealth of Independent States (CIS) is institutionalized, has its own secretariat and an extensive list of the treaties related to its implementation. The chapter will give more attention to the EAEU and CIS treaties, as well as Association Agreements, since these agreements cover extensive trade topics and cover the main countries in the region.

2. Historical Context, Geopolitical Perspective and Foreign Policy

Political and security considerations play an important role in conclusion of RTAs in the region of Eastern Europe, Central Asia and the Caucasus. Therefore, geopolitical perspective and foreign policy of these countries needs to be analyzed to have a clear understanding on the motivations of the particular member-states in joining a given RTA.

This region is located in the crossroads of both Asia and Europe where powers of major dominant states converge. Eastern Europe, Central Asia and the Caucasus region already contains some geopolitically dominant countries like Iran,

124 Treaty on the Establishment of the Eurasian Economic Union: Article 81, 83 and 84 (29 May 2014) <docs.eaeunion.org> , accessed 2 November 2017.

125 Golam Mostafa, Monowar Mahmood 'Eurasian Economic Union: evolution, challenges and possible future directions' (2018) 9 (2) Journal of Eurasian Studies, p. 165.

Turkey and Russia. In addition, the EU, China, as well as the USA are competing in exerting their influence over this region. This sub-section analyzes the political and economic developments of post-Soviet countries, Russia, the EU, Turkey, Iran, China and the USA.

i. Post-Soviet Republics

Historically, the countries in Eastern Europe, Central Asia and the Caucasus were ruled for many years by Russian Tsar Empire and later were united in Soviet Union[126]. The Union existed between 1922 and 1991 and was a totalitarian and communist regime where member states had a very limited autonomy[127]. The economies of the republics were highly centralized, based on socialism and planned economy, and key decisions were taken through Russia[128]. Soviet republics had no control over their own foreign policy, foreign trade, distribution of their natural resources and many other aspects of economic and political policy.

When the Soviet Union came to an end and the republics gained their independence in early 1990s, they were faced to deal with an array of problems inherent to formerly centralized economies[129]. Production and distribution networks in these countries were broken, as the segments of production of the same goods were located in different countries of the Soviet Union. The economies suffered deeply, there was severe currency depreciation and there was an urgent need for massive reforms which would facilitate foreign investment and privatization[130]. This was also accompanied by political instability, conflicts and unrest.

---

126 For a more comprehensive historical outlook, please see: Georg van Rauch, *History of Soviet Russia* (Praeger Publishers, New York, 1972), p. 137.

127 In paper, all the republics in the Soviet Union had a number of rights, such as entering into relations with other states and organization, leaving the Soviet Union when they wish so and so on. However, these rights were hardly enforceable in practice. See: Constitution of the Union of Soviet Socialist Republics (7 October 1977) <www.constitution.org/cons/ussr77.txt> accessed 1 November 2016.

128 Mark Harrison 'The Soviet Economy: I917–1991. Its Life and After-life'(2017) 1137 Warwick Economic Research Papers, p. 5.

129 The declaration of independence by former Soviet Union countries are as following: Georgia 9 April 1991, Ukraine 24 August 1991, Belarus 25 August 1991, Moldova 27 August 1991, Kyrgyz Republic 31 August 1991, Tajikistan 9 September 1991, Armenia 21 September 1991, Azerbaijan 18 October 1991, Turkmenistan 27 October 1991, Russian Federation 12 December 1991 and Kazakhstan on 16 December 1991.

130 Tamaz Zubiashvili 'Aspects of Post-Soviet Economy Against the Backdrop of Association Agreement with European Union' (2017) 6 (1) Ecoforum, p. 3.

So, 1990s were mainly a transition era for post-Soviet countries that tried to revive their economies and to adapt to market economy.

In this period, former Soviet Union republics started building from scratch their relations bilaterally and multilaterally. They joined key global and regional international organizations, concluded bilateral free trade and economic partnership agreements, and implemented reforms to liberalize their trading regime and economic policy[131].

This period also coincided with the Uruguay Round and most of the former Soviet Union republics applied for an observer status in the GATT. While some of former Soviet Union republics did not follow on their observer status after the establishment of the WTO[132] , working parties for accession of countries like Russia, Belarus, Ukraine and Moldova were established in the pre-WTO era[133]. Yet, it was Kyrgyz Republic among the post-Soviet countries which first became a WTO member among them, which was followed by the other post-Soviet countries[134].

The RTAs signed within the early years of independence were mainly with the post-Soviet countries themselves. There were several attempts to join in a customs union, which were unsuccessful because these attempts did not yield equal economic benefits For instance, Eurasian Economic Community comprised of Russia, Kazakhstan, Belarus, Kyrgyz Republic, Tajikistan and for a short while Uzbekistan provided favorable access to Russia, but not to the Central Asian countries[135]. Only starting from 2010, the policies of regionalization intensified.

---

131 Andrey Spartak 'Metamorfozi Processa Reqionalizacii: Ot Reqionalnix Torqovix Soqlasheniy k Meqareqionalnim Proektam' (Metamorphosis of regionalization process: From regional trade agreements to mega-regional projects) (2017) 10 (4) Konturu qlobalnix transformaciy: politika, ekonomika, pravo, p. 19 <https://cyberleninka.ru/article/v/metamorfozy-protsessa-regionalizatsii-ot-regionalnyh-torgovyh-soglasheniy-k-mezhregionalnym-proektam> accessed 23 December 2018.

132 Azerbaijan and Turkmenistan both have been observer in the GATT period. Yet, after the WTO was established, they did not follow the request. Turkmenistan is still not an observer country. However, Azerbaijan re-submitted its request for observer status, as well as for accession in 1997.

133 Svetlana Kozlova 'Vstuplenie Rossii v VTO: Opit stran SNQ' (Russia's accession to the WTO: Experience of CIS countries' (2011) 5 Biznes v Zakone, p. 268 <https://cyberleninka.ru/article/v/vstuplenie-rossii-v-vto-opyt-stran-sng> accessed 31 October 2018.

134 This accession is also cited as the shortest accession in the WTO history so far. Kyrgyz Republic applied for membership in 1996 and became a WTO member in 1998. The accession took two and a half years.

135 David Tarr 'The Eurasian Economic Union Among Russia, Belarus, Kazakhstan, Armenia and Kyrgyz Republic: Can It Succeed Where Its Predecessor Failed?'(29

In 2014, the Eurasian Economic Union was established and the same year Association Agreements of the EU with Georgia, Moldova and the Ukraine were signed. With these RTAs, regionalization within Eastern Europe, Central Asia and the Caucasus took a completely different look. While previously it was mainly about liberalization of market access for goods, now the RTAs cover services, capital, investment, labor, mobilization and many other aspects of the economy. While previously RTAs were concluded without full commitment from the parties, now parties are more committed to the successful implementation of these RTAs.

ii. Russia

The general contours of the trade and economic relations within Eastern Europe, Central Asia and the Caucasus region is predominantly shaped by the foreign policy of Russian Federation[136]. Russia has traditionally been the main power which influenced the politics in the region because of the historical, cultural, economic and social ties. The latest Foreign Policy Concept of Russian Federation states that the member-states of Commonwealth of Independent States (CIS) share not only common historical heritage with Russian Federation, but also have vast potential of integration with Russia in different spheres, thus making this region a priority for foreign policy of Russian Federation[137].

Mentioned foreign policy goals of Russia also shapes the dynamics of RTAs in the region. The Russian scholar Alexey Portanskiy points that, in conclusion of modern RTAs for Russia the primary goal is foreign policy objectives[138]. In his opinion this foreign policy objective is twofold: first, creation of a strong economic and political entity as a way of showing its power to the world; second,

September 2015) World Bank Publications, p. 3 <http://as.vanderbilt.edu/gped/documents/DavidTarrEurasianCustomsUnion--prospectsSept282015.pdf> accessed 1 April 2018.

136 Aleksey Portanskiy 'Mirovaya Tendenciya Reqionalizma I Inteqrasiya v SNQ' (The global tendency of regionalism and integration within the CIS) (2011) 11 Rossiyskiy vneshnoekonomicheskiy vestnik, p. 12 <https://cyberleninka.ru/article/v/mirovaya-tendentsiya-regionalizma-i-integratsiya-v-sng> accessed 21 December 2018.

137 Foreign Policy Concept of Russian Federation, adopted by the Decree of President of Russia on 12 February 2013, paragraph 42.

138 Aleksey Portanskiy 'Mirovaya Tendenciya Reqionalizma I Inteqrasiya v SNQ' (The global tendency of regionalism and integration within the CIS) (2011) 11 Rossiyskiy vneshnoekonomicheskiy vestnik, p. 12 <https://cyberleninka.ru/article/v/mirovaya-tendentsiya-regionalizma-i-integratsiya-v-sng> accessed 21 December 2018.

keeping the post-Soviet countries in its of influence, which also means prevention of revolutionary events (especially in the case of Central Asian countries) or drifting towards western allies as a change of the government (in the case of Belarus), influence in their domestic policies (such as assistance in Kyrgyz Republic for keeping socio-economic conditions of the country under control or promoting Belarusian government to implement market reforms)[139]. He points that getting better market access as a result of RTA formation is more attractive to Belarus or Kazakhstan, rather than for Russia for whom trade turnover with these countries is not significant[140].

According to the mentioned Foreign Policy Concept, Russia also aims to neutralize any threats to security of this region, as well as any attempts for destabilization in the South Caucasus and Central Asia[141]. This mainly builds foundation of the relations of Russia with the EU, USA and other big powers, which is sectorial cooperation in one hand, but also geo-political power play from the other hand. In other words, any political and economic cooperation of the countries within the axis of influence of Russia, including post-Soviet countries with other key players, such as EU and USA are received with caution by Russia[142]. This was clearly seen in the case of the Ukraine and Armenia, which will be discussed in the next sub-section.

iii. The EU

The EU's policy towards post-Soviet countries is differentialized. Veronika Movchan and Volodymyr Shportyuk classify Eastern Europe, Central Asia and Caucasus countries based on their relations with EU into the following categories[143]: (1) Latvia, Lithuania and Estonia – already within the EU; (2) Armenia,

---

139 ibid

140 ibid. Portanskiy mentions that trade with Belarus and Kazakhstan is less than 8% in Russian trade turnover, hence getting better market access is not a priority for Russia.

141 Foreign Policy Concept of Russian Federation, adopted by the Decree of President of Russia on 12 February 2013, paragraph 46.

142 Abdolreza Faradjirad, Assad Xezerzadeh 'Vneshnaya politika Rossii v Yuzhnem Kafkaze pri Vladimire Putina' (Russia' foreign policy in South Caucasus in Vladimir Putin's time) (2010) 13 Centralnaya Aziya I Kafkaz 4 <https://cyberleninka.ru/article/v/vneshnyaya-politika-rossii-na-kavkaze-pri-vladimire-putine> accessed 31 October 2018.

143 Veronika Movchan & Volodymyr Shportyuk 'EU – Ukraine DCFTA: The Model for Eastern Partnership Regional Trade Cooperation' (2012) 445 CASE network Studies and Analyses, p. 5.

Azerbaijan, Belarus, Georgia, Moldova, Ukraine – neighbors, as well as Eastern Partnership countries; (3) Russia – special neighbor; (4) Kazakhstan, Kyrgyz Republic, Tajikistan, Uzbekistan and Turkmenistan – far neighbors, relations with which is lesser priority for the EU[144].

The EU's delivers its policy in post-Soviet space through various soft power instruments targeting democratization, stabilization, good governance, rule of law, respect for human rights, security[145]. In the EU Global Strategy adopted in 2016, it is once more noted that investing in resilience of the states and societies to the east stretching into the Central Asia is a priority for the EU[146]. The EU delivers these policy goals through instruments such as European Neighborhood Policy[147] , Eastern Partnership initiative, Association Agreements. Among these instruments Eastern Partnership initiative takes a special place. This initiative, the inauguration process of which was held in 2009, encompasses 6 countries: Armenia, Azerbaijan, Georgia, Moldova, Belarus and Ukraine and covers areas such as strengthening institutions, building good governance and stability, dialogue on sustainable economic development, visa facilitation, energy security[148]. Association Agreements cover only 3 countries: Georgia, Moldova and the Ukraine and envisage wide-range of cooperation, including deep and comprehensive free trade agreement between the parties.

Energy dialogue is also of great importance in the region. To decrease this dependence from Russian hydrocarbon resources, which is one of the main supplies of energy within the EU, it is supporting alternative routes and supplies of energy products, including through the territories of other post-Soviet countries. The existing Baku -Tbilisi -Jeyhan oil pipeline, Baku -Tbilisi -Erzurum gas pipeline which deliver Caspian oil and gas to the European markets, as well as currently constructed Southern Gas Corridor all bypass Russia and deliver Caspian

144 ibid

145 Teodor Moga, Denis Alexeev 'Post-Soviet States Between Russia and the EU: Reviving Geopolitical Competition? A Dual Perspective' (2013) 13 (1) Connections, p. 41.

146 "Shared vision, common action: a stronger Europe" Global Strategy for European Union's Foreign and Security Policy, June 2016 <www.eeas.europa.eu/top_stories/pdf/eugs_review_web.pdf> accessed 16 December 2016.

147 European Neighborhood Policy regulates the relationship of EU with 16 countries: Algeria, Egypt, Israel, Lebanon, Libya, Jordan, Palestine, Morocco, Syria, Tunisia, Armenia, Azerbaijan Georgia, Belarus, Ukraine and Moldova.

148 European Commission, High Representative of the Union for Foreign Affairs and Security Policy "Joint Staff Working Document: Eastern Partnership – focusing on key priorities and deliverables", Brussels, 15 December 2016.

energy resources to Europe[149]. They serve to the diversification of energy supply and transit routes in Europe, as well as counter-balancing dependence of Europe on Russian energy sources.

When examining the relationship of the EU and post-Soviet countries, one has to consider specificities of relationship between the EU and Russia which shapes the contours of cooperation in the whole region. It should be noted that the EU – Russia relations is confrontational on a geo-political level with co-existence of sectorial cooperation[150]. It is no doubt that the two parties have long-standing trade and economic relations. The EU has been the main trading partner of the Russian Federation, while Russia constitutes fourth largest trading partner of the EU[151]. Energy dialogue is the main element of this relationship, with the EU exporting Russian energy resources and Russia relying on the EU as its key energy exports market[152].

However, in the political level the relationship between the EU and Russia is confrontational. The EU's presence in the region, especially through Eastern Partnership platform is perceived as a threat for Russia due to its dominance in the region[153]. For the EU, Russia's activities in the Eastern European countries

149 Southern Gas Corridor includes three pipelines which would deliver natural gas of Caspian Sea to Europe: (1) Trans Adriatic Pipeline delivering gas to Greece, Albania and Italy (2) Trans Anatolian Pipeline delivering gas to Turkey and (3) South Caucasus Pipeline delivering gas to Azerbaijan and Georgia. See: <www.tap-ag.com> accessed 16 December 2016.

150 Tania Marocchi 'EU-Russia Relations: Towards an Increasingly Geopolitical Paradigm' (2017) Henrich Boll Stiftung publications, p. 7 <https://eu.boell.org/sites/default/files/uploads/2017/07/eu-russia-relations_towards-an-increasingly-geopolitical-paradigm.pdf> accessed 12 April 2019.

151 The source of the statistics is EU Directorate General for Trade <trade.ec.europa.eu/doclib/docs/2006/September/tradoc_122530.pdf> accessed 09 December 2016.

152 Russia is the only gas supplier for 6 EU members. Around 39% of natural gas imports and 27% of gas consumption was from Russia in 2013. EU imports around 100 billion euro oil and oil products from Russia. See: European Energy Security Strategy, Communication from the Commission to the European Parliament and the Council, Brussels, 28 May 2014, COM (2014) 330 final.

153 Alexander Serqunin, Vladimir Tixonov '"Vostochnoe Partnerstvo" I Rossiyskie Interesi na Kafkaze' ("Eastern Partnership" and Russia's interests in the Caucasus) (2010) 4 Izvestiya Vuzov: Severo Kafkazskiy region. Seriya: Obshestvennie nauki, p. 36 <https://cyberleninka.ru/article/v/vostochnoe-partnerstvo-i-rossiyskie-interesy-na-kavkaze> accessed 31 October 2018.

are perceived as security challenge[154]. This has led to the "cold war" between Russia and the EU which has echoed in the foreign policy of the countries in the region.

The increasing geopolitical confrontation between the EU and Russia was clearly seen in the case of Armenia. In 2013, Armenia was just on the footsteps of signing Association Agreement with the EU when the government shifted the policy and stopped the process. At the same time, Armenia declared the country's intention to join the Customs Union lead by Russia[155]. It should be noted that Armenia has no borders with the Customs Union member countries (Russia – Belarus – Kazakhstan) and its trade with these countries is done through the territory of Georgia. Armenia already was enjoying tariff free treatment with these countries and joining the Customs Union and subsequently the Eurasian Economic Union was perceived as an attempt of this country to maintain its security which is tremendously dependent from Russia[156]. Trying to mitigate and balance its relations with the EU, Armenia signed Comprehensive and Enhanced Partnership Agreement with the EU, however this agreement excluded free trade provisions which could contradict its obligations within the EAEU[157].

However, it was events in the Ukraine that resulted in a point of on return in EU – Russia relationship[158]. Under the Russian influence, the Ukrainian president Yanukovich backed down from the signature of an agreement with the EU and instead signed a loan agreement with Russia[159]. However, this led to massive

154 Stephanie Pezard, Andrew Radin, Thomas Szayna, Stephen Larrabee, *European Relations with Russia: Threat Perceptions, Responses and Strategies in the Wake of the Ukrainian Crisis* (2017, Rand Corporation, California), p. 3.

155 . See more: Ian Bond 'Contested Space: Eastern Europe between Russia and the EU' (2017) Center for European Reform publication, p. 7 <https://www.cer.eu/sites/default/files/pb_eastern_part_IB_9march17.pdf> accessed 12 April 2019.

156 ibid

157 Comprehensive and Enhanced Partnership Agreement with the European Union and the European Atomic Energy Community and their Member States on the One Part and Republic of Armenia on the Other Part (25 September 2017) 2017/0238 <https://eeas.europa.eu/sites/eeas/files/eu-armenia_comprehensive_and_enhanced_partnership_agreement_cepa.pdf> accessed 13 April 2019.

158 Tania Marocchi 'EU-Russia Relations: Towards an Increasingly Geopolitical Paradigm' (2017) Henrich Boll Stiftung publications, p. 5 <https://eu.boell.org/sites/default/files/uploads/2017/07/eu-russia-relations_towards-an-increasingly-geopolitical-paradigm.pdf> accessed 12 April 2019.

159 'Ukraine suspends preparations for EU trade agreement' (BBC News, 21 November 2013) <http://www.bbc.com/news/world-europe-25032275> accessed 17 July 2016.

protests in Ukraine and to a revolution which forced President Yanukovich to flee to Russia. New government was formed which went ahead and signed the deal with the EU. Russia subsequently used force in the Crimean peninsula of Ukraine and Crimea was annexed to Russia[160]. Russia's annexation of Crimea resulted in massive economic and political sanctions by the EU and its allies which included freezing of Russia's membership in the G8 platform, suspension of the accession negotiations of Russia to the OECD, freezing of some assets of Russia abroad, visa bans, restrictions on financial transactions. In retaliation, Russia also adopted an embargo for some agricultural goods originating from countries that had economic sanctions against Russia, as well as travel bans for a list of people.

The relation between Russia and the EU was further complicated over the geopolitical situation in Syria, as well as with Salibury and Amesbury incidents where the UK claimed that Russia used a chemical weapon to silence former GRU member residing in the UK.

iv. Other International Players

Turkey

The relations of Russia and Turkey have for a long time been as "politics separately, economics separately", which meant that the two states could cooperate on economic and trade track, while having completely different outlook on political agenda such as Syria, Iraq, "Arab spring" and other contemporary questions[161].

Turkey, with the motivation of allying Turkish states in the Caucasus and Central Asia region have been actively pursuing its foreign policy and presence in these countries, especially in early 1990s[162] . Turkey was the first country to recognize the independence of the post-soviet Turkic republics[163] and open up its diplomatic representatives. In this period, Turkey signed a number of political and economic agreements with these countries. Economic Cooperation

160 'Ukraine crisis timeline' (BBC News, 13 November 2014) <http://www.bbc.com/news/world-middle-east-26248275> accessed 17 July 2016.

161 Maria Bezchastnaya 'SShA-RF: peretyaqivanie turechkoqo Kanata' (USA – RF: tugging of Turkish war}(4 August 2016), < http://www.centrasia.ru/news2.php?st=1470337140> accessed 6 August 2016.

162 Azerbaijan, Turkey, Kazakhstan, Kyrgyz Republic, Turkmenistan and Uzbekistan are Turkish states, their language descend from the same language tree, with Azerbaijan, Turkmenistan and Turkey being almost the same language.

163 Azerbaijan, Kazakhstan, Turkmenistan and Kyrgyz Republic.

Organization was formed in 1992 comprising the Turkic states, as well as Iran, Pakistan and Afghanistan. Yet, Turkey's intensification of relations with these Turkic states was not perceived as friendly by Russia, because of Turkey's growing educational, cultural and religious presence in the Caucasus and Central Asian countries[164]. When Russia started to gain strength and revive after the dissolution of Soviet Union, Turkey was forced to diminish its presence in the Caucasus and Central Asia. However, establishment of Turkic Speaking States Council combining Turkey, Kazakhstan, Azerbaijan, Kyrgyz Republic together is still viewed as a threat by Russia to its interests in the region[165].

Yet, today Turkey is more and more concerned with its problem of escalation of relations with ethnic Kurds in its eastern borders, state of war in Syria and flow of refugees, its fight against terrorism and separatism in light of a series of terrorist attacks occurred in the last couple years. These problems have taken away the focus of Turkey from becoming more active in the region. The "coup" attempt in Turkey in July 2016 was the last drop which lead the government to declare a war against "parallel state" structures within the country, to close educational establishments operated by the "parallel state" abroad[166], as well as in to engaged in domestic "cleansing process" related to the attempted military coup.

This process, followed by USA's denial of extradition of the religious leader of the coup attempt, EU's backing from its promise to Turkey on extending a visa-free regime and halting EU membership negotiations with Turkey, overflow of refugee crisis has lead Russia – Turkey rapprochement. Moreover, Russia and Turkey's current close relations are also due to the strong trade and economic relations between two countries[167].

---

164 Stephen Flanagan 'The Turkey-Russia-Iran Nexus: Eurasian Power Dynamics' (2012) 36 The Washington Quarterly 1.

165 Ekaterina Mixaylenko 'Slojnosti Postroenie Rosiyskoqo Reqionalizma na Post-Sovetskom Prostranstve' (Challenges of establishment of Russian regionalism in post-Soviet space) (2015) Vestnik Tomskoqo Qosudarstennoqo Universiteta 400 <https://cyberleninka.ru/article/v/slozhnosti-postroeniya-rossiyskogo-regionalizma-na-postsovetskom-prostranstve> accessed 26 December 2018.

166 Ebu Sipahiu 'Attack on Gülen Movement Increasingly a Cornerstone of Turkey's Foreign Policy in the Balkans' (Eurasia Daily Monitor, 3 August 2016), <http://www.jamestown.org/programs/edm/single/?tx_ttnews%5Btt_news%5D=45708&tx_ttnews%5BbackPid%5D=27&cHash=ca7589d4943c47c7eb8f21b17da772da#.V6Wsz_l97Dc> accessed 6 August 2016.

167 Ivan Starodubcev 'Rossiysko-Tureckoe Sotrudnicestvo: Sovremennoe Sostayanie I Perspektivi' (Russian-Turkish cooperation: current situation and prospects)

All in all, it can be said that although Turkey has a great interest in the region and vast potential to develop relations and conclude RTAs with the countries in the region, however it pursues a balanced and cautious policy towards Russia vis-a-vis its relationship with the EU and the USA[168].

China

China is mostly present in the Central Asia region. China's presence is growing in this part especially because of Russia's cold relations with the EU and USA. The impact of China's presence is mostly seen in Tajikistan and Kyrgyz Republic. The presence is reinforced through economic expansion, such as purchase of industrial enterprises, rental of agricultural lands and extension of its financial resources[169]. Chinese also account for the largest labor power in these economies[170].

Notwithstanding Chinese economic expansion, Russia continues to be dominant in political and security field in the Central Asia. Russia and China have been supporting each other in the political arena, to counter-balance the US influence in the region[171]. This can be seen in formation of Shanghai Cooperation

---

(2012) 1 Vestnik MQIMO, p. 190 <https://cyberleninka.ru/article/v/rossiysko-turetskoe-sotrudnichestvo-sovremennoe-sostoyanie-i-perspektivy> accessed 25 December 2018.

168 It should be noted that Turkey has a Customs Union with the EU and follows the practice of concluding bilateral free trade agreements with those countries with which EU has free trade agreements. In the region, Turkey has bilateral free trade agreement only with Georgia. See: Free Trade Agreement Between the Republic of Turkey and Georgia (21 November 2007) <https://www.trade.gov.tr/free-trade-agreements/georgia> accessed 13 April 2019.

169 Paul Goble 'China quietly displacing both Russia and US from Central Asia' (Eurasia Daily Monitor, 2 August 2016) <http://www.jamestown.org/programs/edm/single/?tx_ttnews%5Btt_news%5D=45704&tx_ttnews%5BbackPid%5D=27&cHash=535d07b3dea1e3ee152e0af0ae7ddc29#.V6XWYfl97Dc> accessed 6 August 2016.

170 For instance, in Tajikistan more than 80% of foreign labor forces belong to Chinese, while non-official data show that this figure is much more. See: Arkadi Baraev 'Tixaya ekspansiya. Kitaizachiya Tajikistana' (Slow expansion. Making Tajikistan China} (21 July 2016) < http://www.centrasia.ru/news.php?st=1469122500> accessed 6 August 2016.

171 Nabi Ziyadullayev 'Qosudarstva Centralnoy Azii v Usloviax Qlobalizacii: Sovremennie Tendencii i Perspektivi' (Central Asian states in the globalization conditions: current tendencies and prospects) (2006) 6 (48) Centralnaya Aziya I Kafkaz, p. 149 <https://cyberleninka.ru/article/v/

Organization, which is a multilateral security organization, similar to NATO, consisting of Russia, Central Asian countries and China[172].

Iran

Historically, Russia and Iran have diverse interests in the region. They are both competing in the energy markets, they have dispute over the delimitation of Caspian Sea and its resources, as well as they pose threat to each other's stability[173]. However, confronting a common threat – USA – has made these two countries allies[174]. For Russia, cooperation with Iran is also an opportunity to balance Turkic presence in Caucasus and Central Asia[175].

Iran is neutral to the processes in Central Asia, as long as the USA has no major influence over there. For Iran, dominance of China and Russia is preferable to the dominance of the USA[176]. Russia and Iran's friendship is also strengthened through economic cooperation which consists mainly of the sale of missiles by Russia to Iran[177].

The USA

The USA's current involvement in Eastern Europe, Central Asia and the Caucasus region is limited. However, the region has been interesting for the USA from security and geo-strategic aspects, because two of the countries with which

gosudarstva-tsentralnoy-azii-v-usloviyah-globalizatsii-sovremennye-tendentsii-i-perspektivy> accessed 23 December 2018.

172 According to Omelicheva, Russia invited Iran to join Shanghai Cooperation Organization to assert Russia's presence in the Middle East through alliance with Iran and to confront USA. See: Mariya Omelicheva 'Russia's Foreign Policy Toward Iran: A Criticial Geopolitics Perspective' (2012) 14 (3) Journal of Balkan and Near Eastern Studies, p. 336.

173 ibid

174 Guli Yuldasheva 'Iran v Centralnoy Aziatskoy politike Rossii' (Iran in the Central Asian politics of Russia) (2014) 17 (3) Centralnaya Aziya I Kavkaz, p. 129.

175 Stephen Flanagan 'The Turkey-Russia-Iran Nexus: Eurasian Power Dynamics' (2012) 36 (1) The Washington Quarterly, p. 174.

176 Steven Rice 'Iran's strategic position' (Fordham Political Review) <http://fordhampoliticalreview.org/irans-strategic-position/> accessed 7 August 2016.

177 Mariya Omelicheva 'Russia's Foreign Policy Toward Iran: A Criticial Geopolitics Perspective' (2012) 14 (3) Journal of Balkan and Near Eastern Studies, p. 336.

the USA has cold relations – Russia and Iran are both present in the region, as well as the region's proximity to Middle East and Afghanistan[178].

Central Asia became a center of interest for USA after September 11, 2001 attacks, when the USA established military bases in Uzbekistan and Kyrgyz Republic as a gateway to Afghanistan[179]. However, Russia did not welcome the engagement of the USA in the region, which led to the military base in Uzbekistan being shut down by Uzbek government in 2005[180]. In 2014, the military base in Kyrgyz Republic was also shut down, shortly after Russia granted a 2.1 billion USD aid to Kyrgyz government[181].

Conclusions

Having examined the general geopolitical setting of the region, it can be concluded that there is a clearly two trends in the region when it comes to the RTA conclusion: pro-Russia and pro-EU. Pro-EU countries are Georgia, Moldova and the Ukraine. It is also observed that, all the pro-EU countries are those who have somewhat tensed relations with Russia in the geopolitical setting. In the case of Georgia, the root of tensions is 2008 Georgia-Russia war which resulted in annexation of part of its territories. In the case of Ukraine, it is annexation of Crimea in 2014 by Russia. In the case of Moldova, it is protracted Transnistria conflict where Russia supported separatist regime[182]. The other post-Soviet countries display a cautious policy and have so far chosen either to maintain only bilateral RTAs with Russia and each other or to integrate further within the

178 Mahir Xalifazade 'Amerikanskaya Politika 'Perezaqruzki' Otnosheniy s Rossiyey i Yujniy Kafkaz' (American policy of reloading relations with Russia and South Caucasus) (2014) 17 (3) Centralnaya Aziya I Kavkaz, p. 90.

179 Nikolay Kuzmin 'Centralnaya Aziya Posle Operatsiy v Afqanistane' (Central Asia after the operations in Afghanistan) (2003) 1 "Centralnaya Aziya i Kafkaz" Jurnal Socialno Politiceskix Issledovaniy <http://www.fergananews.com/articles/1406> accessed 31 October 2018.

180 Murat Laumulin 'Strateqiceskie Interesi Rossii v Qosudarstvax Centralnoy Azii na Sovremennom Etape' (Strategic interests of Russia in Central Asian countries in current stage) (2009) 3 (63) Centralnaya Aziya I Kafkaz, p. 118 <https://cyberleninka.ru/article/v/strategicheskie-interesy-rossii-v-gosudarstvah-tsentralnoy-azii-na-sovremennom-etape> accessed 26 December 2018.

181 ibid

182 Eugene Rumor 'Moldova Between Russia and the West' (2017) Carnegie Endowment for International Peace <https://carnegieendowment.org/2017/05/23/moldova-between-russia-and-west-delicate-balance-pub-70056> accessed 13 April 2019.

Eurasian Economic Union. Any negotiations or attempts by other powers for RTAs are so far have been unsuccessful.

3. The Main RTAs of Eastern Europe, Central Asia and the Caucasus Region

This sub-section will give a context and background about the following integration in the region: The Eurasian Economic Union (EAEU), Commonwealth of Independent States (CIS) and Association Agreements of the EU with Moldova, Georgia and the Ukraine.

i. The EAEU

Context

The first idea of the establishment of an integration union like the EAEU dates back to 1994[183]. However, this idea could not substantialize at that time, as the circumstances and timing was not ripe. Thus, the EAEU was preceded with various mechanisms[184] which became non-functional later on for several reasons. Firstly, these integration mechanisms were drafted in a way which benefitted mostly Russia, while providing limited economic benefits to other parties (the case of Eurasian Economic Community of 2000)[185]. Secondly, integration was

183 General Information: History (Eurasian Economic Union) <http://www.eaeunion.org/?lang=en#about-history> accessed 1 July 2016.

184 1995 Treaty on the Customs Union between Russia, Belarus and Kazakhstan; 1996 Treaty on Deepening Economic and Humanitarian Integration between Russia, Belarus, Kazakhstan, Kyrgyz Republic to which Tajikistan subsequently joined; 1999 Treaty on Customs Union and Single Economic Space between Russia, Belarus, Kazakhstan, Kyrgyz Republic and Tajikistan; 2000 Decision on the Establishment of Eurasian Economic Community to promote formation of Customs Union and Single Economic Space; 2003 Treaty on the Establishment of Single Economic Space between Russia, Belarus, Kazakhstan, Ukraine; 2006 Decision on Intensification of work between Russia, Belarus and Kazakhstan to create Customs Union and subsequent accession of Kyrgyz Republic and Tajikistan. See: General Information: History (Eurasian Economic Union) <http://www.eaeunion.org/?lang=en#about-history> accessed 1 July 2016.

185 David Tarr 'The Eurasian Economic Union Among Russia, Belarus, Kazakhstan, Armenia and Kyrgyz Republic: Can It Succeed Where Its Predecessor Failed?'(29 September 2015) World Bank Publications, p. 3 <http://as.vanderbilt.edu/gped/documents/DavidTarrEurasianCustomsUnion--prospectsSept282015.pdf> accessed 1 April 2018.

not priority in foreign policy of Russia early in 1990s, because during this period Russia was still recovering from the collapse of Soviet Union and going through painful economic crisis, coupled with hardship of Chechen wars[186]. It was only in 2000 with the election of Putin as President, Russia started to regain their strength, claim its role as a super-power and former economic power[187]. Thirdly, post-Soviet countries had different levels of interests towards integration in the post-Soviet space[188]. While Armenia, Belarus and Kazakhstan were more pro-Russia integration, countries like Azerbaijan, Georgia, Ukraine, Moldova were viewing any integration as attempt to restore former Soviet Union and therefore were not fully committed to the integration[189].

The major steps in the establishment of the EAEU were taken in 2000s between Russia, Kazakhstan and Belarus. They were already enjoying bilateral free trade as a result of CIS free trade agreement of 1994 (updated in 2011)[190]. In 2007, Treaty on the Establishment of the Customs Union was signed between Russia, Kazakhstan and Belarus which lead to launch of the customs union in 2010[191]. The single economic space between them was launched in 2012[192]. The three countries established Eurasian Economic Commission to oversee matters arising from single economic space and to prepare for the next level of integration[193].

186 Chechnya was a part of Russian territory which proclaimed its independence and waged war against Russia. There were 2 Chechen wars: 1994–1996, 1999–2000. There was a insurgence phase in 2000–2009.

187 Andrey Shleifer, Daniel Tresiman 'A Normal Country: Russia After Communism' (2005) 19 (1) Journal of Economic Perspectives, p. 154.

188 Selda Atik 'Regional Economic Integrations in post-Soviet Eurasia: An Analysis of Causes of Inefficiency' (2014) 109 Procedia-Social and Behavioral Sciences, p. 1333.

189 ibid

190 CIS Free Trade Agreement (15 April 1994) <https://www.wipo.int/edocs/lexdocs/treaties/en/ftacis/trt_ftacis.pdf>
CIS Free Trade Agreement (18 October 2011) <http://cis.minsk.by/reestr/ru/printPreview/text?id=3183>

191 Treaty on the Establishment of the Customs Union between Russia, Belarus and Kazakhstan (6 October 2007).

192 2010 Declaration of the Single Economic Space between Russia, Belarus and Kazakhstan, as well as 2011 Declaration of Eurasian Economic Integration between Russia, Belarus and Kazakhstan which outlined the successful operation of the Customs Union, as well as declared the will of the countries to move to the single economic space.

193 Treaty on the Eurasian Economic Commission (18 November 2011) <docs.eaeunion.org> accessed 30 October 2016.

During this period, more than twenty basis documents were adopted to prepare for the next economic integration[194].

The Treaty on the establishment of the EAEU was signed on May 29, 2014 and came into force on January 1, 2015[195] . Thus, the EAEU officially came into being from January 1, 2015. The original signatories were Russia, Belarus and Kazakhstan. However, Armenia and Kyrgyz Republic requested joining the EAEU and they became members within a year of establishment of the EAEU[196] .

Currently, the EAEU is a potentially effective link to unite Europe and Asia-Pacific region[197]. It is the most advanced and highest level of economic integration in the post-Soviet space.

Structure

The EAEU is an international organization for regional economic integration and is governed by 5 main bodies[198]. The highest decision making body is the Supreme Eurasian Economic Council. This is the council of the presidents of the member states where they determine integration course and strategy of the EAEU. The Eurasian Intergovernmental Council is the second highest decision making body consisting of the prime ministers of the member states. It meets at least twice a year, controls the implementation of the EAEU Treaty and instructs the other EAEU bodies with relevant tasks.

The Eurasian Economic Commission is the permanently functioning body of the EAEU and is headquartered in Moscow. The Commission develops proposals for integration and lays ground for effective functioning of the EAEU. The Eurasian Economic Commission itself consists of the Council and the Board. The Council is where the deputy heads of the states convene. It regulates general integration issues in the EAEU and overall governance of the Eurasian Economic Commission. The Board is the executive arm of the Commission. It consists of

---

194 Murat Laumulin 'Diskussiya Po Problemam Evraziyskoy Inteqracii' (Discussion on the problems of Eurasian integration) (2014) 17 Centralnaya Aziya I Kavkaz 3.

195 Treaty on the Establishment of the Eurasian Economic Union (29 May 2014) <docs.eaeunion.org>

196 Armenia signed the EAEU treaty on October 10, 2014 and Kyrgyz Republic signed it on December 23, 2014.

197 Foreign Policy Concept of Russian Federation, adopted by the Decree of President of Russia on 12 February 2013, paragraph 44.

198 Governance (Eurasian Economic Union) < http://www.eaeunion.org/?lang=en#about-administration> accessed 28 August 2016.

departments such as foreign trade, customs cooperation, technical regulation, integration and macroeconomics and others.

The EAEU also has its own dispute settlement mechanism – the EAEU Court. The Court functions permanently and is located in Minsk, Belarus. It is responsible for ensuring uniform application of the EAEU Treaty, other international treaties within the EAEU and the decisions of the EAEU bodies[199]. Every member appoints 2 judges to the Court for the duration of 9 years[200]. Only members and economic entities (legal persons or individuals registered as entrepreneurs) have standing before the EAEU court and thus, physical persons do not have a right to challenge treaties or decisions of the EAEU institutions before the court[201]. In particular, regarding the applications lodged by member states, the Court has a jurisdiction to check compatibility of other treaties of the EAEU with the EAEU Treaty, compliance of another members with the commitments arising from the EAEU treaties, compatibility of the decisions of the EAEU Commission with the EAEU treaties and challenge the decisions of the EAEU Commission[202]. Regarding the complaints lodged by economic entities, the Court has a jurisdiction to rule whether decision or action/inaction of the EAEU Commission violates rights and legitimate interests of the applicant[203]. The Court also can provide clarification to provisions of the EAEU treaties[204].

The court's rulings are mandatory to implement. However, the EAEU court does not have a mandate to create new norms or change/cancel any existing norms[205]. Only the EAEU Commission or Council have the right to do so.

Most of the cases lodged at the EAEU Court concern clarification of the provisions of the EAEU treaties and documents, as well as complaints lodged by the economic entities regarding actions/inactions of the EAEU Commission. Only

199 Statute of the Court of Eurasian Economic Union, Annex 2 to the EAEU Treaty, Article 2.

200 ibid, Article 7.

201 Maksim Karliuk 'The Eurasian Economic Union: An EU-like Legal Order in the Post-Soviet Space? (2015) National Research University Higher School of Economics research papers, p. 17 < https://wp.hse.ru/data/2015/09/23/1075393178/53LAW2015.pdf> accessed 22 July 2017.

202 Statute of the Court of Eurasian Economic Union, Annex 2 to the EAEU Treaty, Article 39.

203 ibid.

204 ibid, Article 45.

205 Statute of the Court of Eurasian Economic Union, Annex 2 to the EAEU Treaty, Article 101.

in one instance, a member challenged the compliance by another member of its commitments arising from the EAEU[206].

The EAEU Treaty also envisages establishment of the financial body of the EAEU by 2025.

Common Market

The EAEU Treaty provides for establishment of common goods, services and labor market, as well as stipulates for common capital market and common energy market to come into being by 2025.

Common goods market has mostly been established, apart from some exceptions[207] . Common labor market is also established. However, formation of the common services market has not been completed yet. This is due to the fact that, the EAEU Treaty stipulates gradual liberalization of the services within the EAEU. The EAEU Treaty sets stage-by-stage liberalization of services sector which would be completed by 2025[208].

Despite the achievements in common goods, services and labor market, formation of common energy or common capital market has not been smooth. Common energy market has been key motivation for Armenia, Belarus and Kyrgyz Republic in joining EAEU. The EAEU Treaty provides for the establishment of the single electricity market by July 1, 2019, and single oil and gas market by January 1, 2025. Having access to single energy market means access to energy infrastructure, free movement of energy resources within the territory of member countries, access to energy services on an equal footing, having unified energy tariff policy. The EAEU countries, mainly Russia and Kazakhstan have

---

206 This was the case which Russian Federation filed against Belarus regarding Belarusian customs restricting the transit of certain goods. The court in its judgment accepted this as being partly against the EAEU Treaty.

207 Common external tariff of the EAEU has been adjusted to Russia's WTO commitments. This in turn violates the WTO commitments of Kazakhstan, Armenia and Kyrgyz Republic, whose "bound tariffs" are in some instances lower than Russia's "bound tariffs". Therefore, Armenia, Kazakhstan and Kyrgyz Republic have been allowed to apply tariffs according to their WTO commitments, as long as they make sure that those goods do not cross the borders of other EAEU members without paying the difference between the tariffs. Armenia, Kyrgyz Republic and Kazakhstan are having negotiations within the WTO to change their "bound tariffs".

208 Protocol on Trade in Services, Establishment, Functioning and Implementation of Investments, Annex No16, EAEU Treaty.

large reserves of oil and gas[209]. However, the process is complicated, as Armenia and Belarus have been pushing for the talks on single energy market, yet Russia and Kazakhstan has not been willing to put this topic on the table yet. As a result, the formation of common electricity market was postponed until 2025.

The EAEU Treaty sets the timeline for the establishment of the common capital market to be completed by 2025. By that time, it is planned that EAEU would have its own financial regulatory body located in Kazakhstan. Common capital market provisions on the EAEU Treaty provides for the mutual recognition of the licenses for banks, insurance and securities firms, development of common requirements for financial market, possibility of provision of financial services without establishment of legal bodies, as well as exchanging of financial information.

Expansion

The EAEU has been actively pursuing the policy of enlargement. Creation of a market where goods and services moves without barriers in the whole Eurasia region has been voiced as a vision for the EAEU. The Foreign Policy Concept of Russia lists the creation of common economic and humanitarian space from Atlantic to Pacific Ocean as the key agenda of the relations between European Union and Russia[210]. However, due to current cold relations between the EU and Russia over annexation of Crimea, as well as over Russia's involvement in Salisbury and Amesbury incidents, any cooperation between the EAEU and the EU does not seem feasible.

Currently, the EAEU is focused mainly on the Asian countries. In 2016, first FTA of EAEU with Vietnam came into force. Thailand, Singapore, Cambodia, South Korea, Indonesia, India are among the Asian partner countries with the possibility of having free trade with the EAEU in the future[211]. A trade deal was

---

209 'Жертвой интеграции энергорынков ЕАЭС может стать "Газпром"?' {Jertvoy inteqrasii enerqorinkov EAES mojet stat "Qazprom"?, The victim of integration of energy markets could be "Gasprom"?}(DW, 18 September 2015), <http://dw.com/p/1GYQf> accessed 2 July 2016.

210 Foreign Policy Concept of Russia, adopted by the Decree of President of Russia on 12 February 2013, 56.

211 'Евразийский экономический союз. Досье' {Yevraziyskiy ekonomiceskiy soyuz. Dosye, Eurasian Economic Union. Dossier} (TACC, 18 May 2016) <http://tass.ru/info/2545319> accessed 1 July 2016.

signed with China[212]. A FTA with Iran was signed, where parties reduced tariffs on several groups of goods[213].

ii. Association Agreements of the EU with Moldova, Georgia and the Ukraine

Context

Association Agreements are the products of the Eastern Partnership framework of the EU with its eastern neighbors. The Eastern Partnership framework targeted 6 countries (Ukraine, Moldova, Belarus, Georgia, Armenia, Azerbaijan) with EU's assistance to develop rule of law, democratization, good governance, resilience and market economy. Association Agreements were offered to these countries which promised free trade and visa free regime in exchange for reforms in other areas of economy. However, the EU progressed with only 3 countries out of 6 in signature of the Association Agreements.

Association Agreements were signed in 2014. EU-Georgia and EU-Moldova Association Agreement entered into force on 1 July 2016, EU Ukraine Association Agreement was partly provisionally applicable since 2014 (deep and comprehensive free trade agreement only from 1 January 2016), however the agreement fully entered into force on 1 September 2017.

They are the documents that lay the ground for political association and economic integration[214]. As European Commissioner for Enlargement and

---

212 'Комментарий: Путин позвал Европу в Большую Евразию' {Kommentariy: Putin pozval Yevropu v Bolshuyu Yevraziyu, Commentary: Putin invited Europe to the Great Eurasia} (DW, 17 June 2016), <http://dw.com/p/1J8tk> accessed 2 July 2016.

213 'Iran's membership in Eurasian Economic Union may serve as an "economic bridge"'(Tehran Times, 14 June 2016) <http://www.tehrantimes.com/news/403405/Iran-s-membership-in-Eurasian-Economic-Union-may-serve-as-economic> accessed 7 July 2016.

214 Association Agreement between the European Union and the European Atomic Energy Community and their Member States, of the one part, and the Republic of Moldova, of the other part (27 June 2014), Official Journal of the European Union L 260, 30 August 2014.
Association Agreement between the European Union and the European Atomic Energy Community and their Member States, of the one part, and the Republic of Georgia, of the other part (27 June 2014), Official Journal of the European Union L261, 30 August 2014.
Association Agreement between the European Union and the European Atomic Energy Community and their Member States, of the one part, and the Republic of

Neighborhood Policy Stefan Füle puts it, they are "reform agenda" for the Eastern Partnership countries. They provide for key reforms in sectors such as justice, freedom, security, foreign and security policy, trade and trade related matters, economic and sector cooperation, financial cooperation and institutionalization.

Deep and Comprehensive Free Trade Agreements (DCFTA) constitute integral parts of the Association Agreements and contain provisions on trade remedies, TBT, SPS, customs and trade facilitation, services, e-commerce, competition, IP, procurement, transparency, energy, sustainable development and general provisions.

Differences

It should be noted that Association Agreements of the EU with Moldova, Georgia and the Ukraine are very similar in structure, market access and the substance. This is because they were modeled on the EU Association Agreement with the Ukraine, as well as because of the same historical context, policy framework and negotiations that took place between these countries and the EU preceding the agreements[215]. However, there are a few differences in areas such as frozen conflicts, military-defense cooperation, approximation level of the legislation, as well as exceptions in tariffs liberalization[216].

For this research, the following differences in trade in goods are relevant. First of all, there are different transitional periods for the implementation of tariff commitments. Article 25 and Article 143 of the relevant Association Agreements with Ukraine and Moldova envisage gradual tariff liberalization within 10 years, whereas the EU provided faster market access to Ukraine and Moldova with shorter transitional periods and more coverage. Georgia, on the other hand did not have transitional periods, as Georgian tariffs were already quite low before the DCFTA[217];

Ukraine, of the other part (27 June 2014), Official Journal of the European Union L278, 20 September 2014.

215 Guillaume van der Loo 'The EU's Association Agreements and DCFTAs with Ukraine, Moldova and Georgia: A Comparative Study' (2017) <http://www.3dcftas.eu/system/tdf/Comparitve%20GVDL%2024.6.17_final_0.pdf?file=1&type=node&id=360&force=> accessed 27 August 2018.

216 ibid.

217 Association Agreement between the European Union and the European Atomic Energy Community and their Member States, of the one part, and the Republic of Ukraine, of the other part, Article 25 (27 June 2014), Official Journal of the European Union L278, 20 September 2014.

Secondly, coverage of the goods which are liberalized are different. Moldova and Georgia use negative tariff elimination lists, where they undertook to liberalize everything except those tariff lines mentioned in the annex to the DCFTA. Whereas Ukraine's DCFTA with EU envisaged positive lists, meaning that Ukraine liberalized only those tariff lines mentioned in the DCFTA[218];

Thirdly, Agreement with the Ukraine has more concessions from the EU side. Unlike Georgia and Moldova, Ukraine has concessions such as transitional periods for phasing out export duties, as well as safeguard measures for passenger cars[219].

Fourthly, the EU included a cautious attitude towards agriculture export from Moldova and Georgia. These DCFTAs include a provision that the EU may suspend agricultural imports from these countries if they exceed import of trigger volume[220].

Association Agreement between the European Union and the European Atomic Energy Community and their Member States, of the one part, and the Republic of Moldova, of the other part, Article 143 (27 June 2014), Official Journal of the European Union L 260, 30 August 2014.

218 See, Annex XV to Association Agreement between the European Union and the European Atomic Energy Community and their Member States, of the one part, and the Republic of Moldova, of the other part (27 June 2014), Official Journal of the European Union L 260, 30 August 2014.
Annex IA to Association Agreement between the European Union and the European Atomic Energy Community and their Member States, of the one part, and the Republic of Ukraine, of the other part (27 June 2014), Official Journal of the European Union L278, 20 September 2014.

219 Association Agreement between the European Union and the European Atomic Energy Community and their Member States, of the one part, and the Republic of Ukraine, of the other part, Article 31 and Annex II (27 June 2014), Official Journal of the European Union L278, 20 September 2014.

220 Annex XVC to Association Agreement between the European Union and the European Atomic Energy Community and their Member States, of the one part, and the Republic of Moldova, of the other part (27 June 2014), Official Journal of the European Union L 260, 30 August 2014.
Annex II-C to Association Agreement between the European Union and the European Atomic Energy Community and their Member States, of the one part, and the Republic of Georgia, of the other part (27 June 2014), Official Journal of the European Union L261, 30 August 2014.

Structure

Institutionally, Association Agreements have established 4 main bodies: Association Councils, Association Committees, Parliamentary Association Committees and Civil Society Platforms.

Association Councils is the main structure that monitor implementation and application of the EU Association Agreements with Georgia, Moldova and the Ukraine[221]. Moreover, they periodically review the agreements in light of their objectives. These Councils also discuss any bilateral or international issues of mutual interest, as well as serve as a platform for discussion of major issues arising from Association Agreements. Association Councils meet once a year and are comprised of one minister from each party.

Association Committees consist of senior officials of the members and are the subsidiary to Association Councils[222]. They also have sub-committees. Parliamentary Association Committee consist of parliamentarians of European Parliament and Georgia, Ukraine and Moldova. Civil Society Platforms consist of civil society representatives[223].

Ukraine's cooperation with the EU is also strengthened with the presence of bilateral summits, in contrast to Georgia and Moldova. The 19th summit between the parties were held in 2017.

iii. The CIS

Context

The CIS is the oldest regional integration in the post-Soviet space. The establishment of the CIS coincide with the collapse of the Soviet Union. It was established on December 8, 1991 between Russia, Ukraine and Belarus. Soon after, Azerbaijan, Armenia, Kazakhstan, Kyrgyz Republic, Tajikistan, Uzbekistan,

221 EU-Ukraine Association Agreement, Article 460.
EU-Georgia Association Agreement, Article 403.
EU-Moldova Association Agreement, Article 433.

222 EU-Ukraine Association Agreement,Article 464.
EU-Georgia Association Agreement, Article 407.
EU-Moldova Association Agreement, Article 438.

223 EU-Ukraine Association Agreement,Article 469.
EU-Georgia Association Agreement, Article 412.
EU-Moldova Association Agreement, Article 442.

Turkmenistan, Georgia, Moldova joined the CIS[224]. Ukraine and Turkmenistan are not considered de-jure members of the CIS, because they did not sign the Statute of the CIS in 1993[225].

Based on its economic potential, the CIS is the third largest integration in the world after the EU and NAFTA[226]. It joins together countries which collectively have 30% of world's energy, 36% of uranium, 20% of precious metals, 10% of ferrous metals resources[227]. Economically, there is a huge potential lying in the region.

The organization's main driving force is the leadership of Russia[228]. Russia is the main power ensuring the integration within the CIS. However, for many the CIS is seen as purely "a civilized divorce" of the Soviet Union[229].

It should be noted here that the goal of establishment of the CIS was not to deepen integration of former Soviet Union countries, but rather, to act as a "civilized divorce" of the Soviet Union and to diminish the negative consequences of Soviet Union integration stage-by-stage within the region[230]. One of the principles advanced within the CIS is therefore "different-speed-integration"[231]. Based on this principle, the CIS parties who are willing to integrate more, can do so

---

224 Georgia left CIS in 2008 as a result of the Georgia – Russia war which ended with the proclamation of independence in South Ossetia and Abkhazia regions of Georgia.

225 See: CIS Executive Committee official web-site: <http://www.cis.minsk.by/page.php?id=174> accessed 29 October 2018.

226 Andrey Kushnirenko, Andrey Spartak 'Dvadcatiletniy Yubiley SNQ: Itoqi I Perspektivi Razvitiya' (Twentieth anniversary of the CIS: Outcomes and prospects) (2011) 10 Rossiyskiy vneshnoekonomimceskiy vestnik, p. 3 <https://cyberleninka.ru/article/v/dvadtsatiletniy-yubiley-sng-itogi-i-perspektivy-razvitiya> accessed 25 December 2018.

227 ibid.

228 Magda Leichtova, *Misunderstanding Russia: Russian Foreign Policy and the West* (2016, Routledge, Abington).

229 Oleq Arestov 'Osobennosti I Protivorechiya Ekonomiceskoy Inteqraciyii Stran SNQ' (Specificities and challenges of economic integration of the CIS) (2009) 2 Finansi: Teoriya I Praktika, p. 72 <https://cyberleninka.ru/article/v/osobennosti-i-protivorechiya-ekonomicheskoy-integratsii-stran-sng> accessed 25 December 2018.

230 Andrey Volinchuk 'Rossiya v Evrazii: Balans Qeoekonomiceskix i Qeopoliticeskix Instrumentov Inteqracii' (Russia in Eurasia: Balance of geo-economic and geo-political instruments of integration) (2018) 1(99) Rossiya I ATR, p. 53 <https://cyberleninka.ru/article/v/rossiya-v-evrazii-balans-geoekonomicheskih-i-geopoliticheskih-instrumentov-integratsii> accessed 26 December 2018.

231 ibid.

without prejudice to the functioning of the CIS. As such, different integration levels, including Customs Union, Single Economic Space and consequently Eurasian Economic Union was established.

Through its existence, CIS has drafted more than dozens of agreements in various sectors. These sectors cover not only economic, but social, security, political, cultural and other areas.

The free trade area within the CIS was attempted to be established first by CIS Free Trade Agreement of 1994. This agreement envisaged adoption of additional documents, which was not completed by all signatories. As a result, free trade among the CIS countries was to a big extent regulated by numerous bilateral Free Trade Agreements of the member states. This created a "spaghetti bowl" of free trade provisions. In 2010 the CIS, under the leadership of Russia, attempted to conclude Free Trade Agreement, which would substitute all the bilateral FTAs in the region. This attempt was successful and unlike its predecessor, this CIS Free Trade Agreement came into force in 2011[232].

The CIS is the only integration which unites most of the countries in the region. All the countries in the EAEU also participate in the CIS. However, effectiveness of the CIS is limited for a number of reasons. First of all, member states of the CIS have conflicting interests with each other: Armenia – Azerbaijan, Russia – Ukraine are a few examples[233]. Secondly, not all the members of the CIS have the same desire to integrate. Turkmenistan and Uzbekistan for instance have a limited willingness to integrate[234]. Thirdly, members are not fully committed to its ideas. Not surprisingly, many agreements drafted within the CIS have not become operational due to the often contradictory policies of its member states[235].

---

232 CIS Free Trade Agreement (15 April 1994) <https://www.wipo.int/edocs/lexdocs/treaties/en/ftacis/trt_ftacis.pdf>
CIS Free Trade Agreement (18 October 2011) <http://cis.minsk.by/reestr/ru/printPreview/text?id=3183>

233 Ikboljan Koraboev 'Ot Reqionalnoy Inteqracii Centralnoy Azii k Evraziyskomu Interacionnomu Prostranstvu? Menyayushaya Dinamika Postsovetskoqo Reqionalizma' (From regional integration of Central Asia to Eurasian Integration Space? Changing dynamics of post-Soviet regionalism) (2010) 3 (8) Evraziyskoe Ekonomiceskaya Inteqraciya, p. 15 <https://cyberleninka.ru/article/v/ot-regionalnoy-integratsii-tsentralnoy-azii-k-evraziyskomu-integratsionnomu-prostranstvu-menyayus chayasya-dinamika-postsovetskogo> accessed 26 December 2018.

234 ibid.

235 Qlazyev S.Y., Chuskin V.I., Tkachuk S.P., *Yevropeyskiy soyuz i Yevraziyskoe ekonomicheskoe soobshestvo: sxodstvo i razlicie processov inteqrachionnoqo stroitelstvo,*

Structure

One of the distinctive elements of the CIS is that institutionally it has the highest number of structures. To be precise, the CIS has 84 bodies, out of which 66 are for sectoral cooperation. Despite the high number of institutional structures, the integration within the CIS in its 28 years of existence has not advanced deeper than free trade area.

According to the Charter of the CIS, the highest institutional structure within the CIS is the Council of Heads of States. It is the meetings of the heads of states which decides principal matters of interest for the CIS[236]. Council of Heads of Governments coordinates the activities of the executive bodies of the CIS in all fields[237].

The CIS Economic Council, located in Minsk, Belarus, is the main executive body. It is the permanently functioning and coordinating secretariat of the CIS[238]. The CIS also has Inter-parliamentary Assembly where the parliamentarians of the members have consultations. The meetings of line ministries regularly take place to discuss sectoral issues. For instance, ministries of foreign affairs meet to discuss foreign policy issues.

It should be mentioned that the CIS has also established a special judicial body to oversee economic disputes[239]. However, the dispute settlement procedure within the CIS is rather weak for several reasons. Although the cooperation within the CIS is multidimensional covering from human rights, social projects, defense, border management and so on, the CIS Economic Court can only oversee disputes arising from implementation of economic commitments[240]. The Court also looks whether the treaties and other documents on economic issues are compatible with other CIS treaties and norms. Secondly, despite its

---

(European Union and Eurasian Economic Community: similarities and differences of the process of integration building) (2013, Vikor Media, Moscow), *p. 116.*

236 Charter of the Commonwealth of Independent States, Article 21 (22 January 1993) <http://cis.minsk.by/reestr/ru/index.html#reestr/view/text?doc=187> accessed 15 April 2019.

237 ibid, Article 22.

238 CIS Executive Committee official web-site: <http://www.cis.minsk.by/page.php?id=11216> accessed 29 August 2018.

239 Charter of the Commonwealth of Independent States, Article 32 (22 January 1993) <http://cis.minsk.by/reestr/ru/index.html#reestr/view/text?doc=187> accessed 15 April 2019.

240 ibid.

economic nature, the Court only considers applications lodged by the states and not economic entities or individuals[241]. The CIS Economic Court only determines the violations by the members and recommendations for remedies for such violations. It is the member states who have to implement the recommendation, however there is no oversight mechanism within the CIS[242].

Another distinctive characteristics of the CIS is that all decisions are adopted with consensus[243]. As it was mentioned earlier there are conflicting interests between the members of the CIS. Therefore, in practice this undermines the efficiency of integration, as the treaties end up being too general to accommodate every country's common interests. This is one of the reasons why the CIS was never able to advance to customs union.

4. Summary of the Chapter

This chapter elaborated the importance of Eastern Europe, Central Asia and the Caucasus region for the trade analysis. It concluded that transition from socialism to capitalism, diverse engagement with the WTO, presence of rich natural resources, existence of frozen conflicts and abundant number of RTAs make the region interesting from RTA analysis perspective. As one of the regions with the highest number of the RTAs in the world, the chapter noted that the RTA provisions in the region were dictated by the economic and foreign relations of the major players, such as Russia and the EU; that the RTAs of the region were concluded mostly with the neighbors and traditional trading partners; that the RTAs in the region were concluded not only based on the economic reasons, but also based on political and security considerations and that despite the fact that the region contained economies rich in hydrocarbon resources, energy provisions of the RTAs had a narrow scope.

The chapter gave a context about the geopolitical situation of the region and policies of the main key players such as Russia, EU, post-Soviet countries, Iran,

241 Rules for the CIS Ecoomic Court, Article 3 (6 July 1992) <http://www.sudsng.org/competence/statut/> accessed 15 April 2019.

242 The CIS Economic Court also gives interpretations of the CIS norms. See: Rules for the CIS Economic Court, Article 4-5 (6 July 1992) <http://sudsng.org/download_files/docs/dk17s021p_01.pdf> accessed 23 August 2018.

243 Charter of the Commonwealth of Independent States, Article 23 (22 January 1993) <http://cis.minsk.by/reestr/ru/index.html#reestr/view/text?doc=187> accessed 15 April 2019.

USA, Turkey and China. It concluded that the economic policies in the region are currently shaped by confrontation of the EU/USA with Russia.

General background information was given for the EAEU, CIS and the EU Association Agreements with Moldova, Georgia and the Ukraine. The analysis showed that the CIS was a foundation for the birth of the EAEU. The CIS started with existence of all post-Soviet countries who shared conflicting interests and had different goals of integration and therefore could not advance beyond free trade agreement. That was the reason why EAEU was established with a narrow scope of countries, who shared equal determination of integration. This factor assisted in acceleration of integration within the EAEU, which advanced from customs union to economic union within 5 years. Despite its deficiencies, the CIS is still an important platform with regards to the post-Soviet countries, who share large economic ties with each-other, as it is the only platform where all post-Soviet countries (except for Georgia) are joined together.

With regards to the Association Agreements of the EU with Moldova, Georgia and the Ukraine, they are drafted to bring economies of Moldova, Georgia and the Ukraine closer to those of the EU. These documents not only shape economic relations, but also foreign relations of these countries, as it shows their move towards the EU, rather than Russia.

Chapter 3 Traditional Sectors in the Regional Trade Agreements in Eastern Europe, Central Asia and the Caucasus and Multilateralization of Regionalism

This chapter gives background information on the traditional and most common sectors of the RTAs and how they are reflected in the RTAs of Eastern Europe, Central Asia and the Caucasus region[244]. Also, the chapter elaborates on whether the traditional provisions in these RTAs could be multilateralized.

This chapter consists of four sub-sections: rules of origin, technical barriers to trade and sanitary and phytosanitary measures, transparency and trade facilitation and intellectual property. The reason for choosing these sections is because they are the most frequently found areas in the RTAs of the region.

This chapter compares relevant provisions of the EAEU, CIS and Association Agreements with WTO agreements and elaborates their relationship. In particular, this chapter aims to elaborate how certain provisions in these RTAs affect the trade liberalization, if there are any innovative or progressive elements in these RTAs and, if so, whether they can be taken as a basis of multilateral negotiations. Finally, the chapter will analyze whether any element of the RTAs could be used in multilateralization of regionalism and the costs and gains of this process.

1. Rules of Origin Provisions of the RTAs in Eastern Europe, Central Asia and the Caucasus

i. Definition and the Importance of the Rules of Origin

Rules of Origin (RoO from hereinafter) are important and indispensable elements in current trade negotiations, because they determine the place of origin

244 Here traditional and most common sectors are considered as those which are in some or other way are found in all the RTAs analyzed in the research.

of products in order for a product to qualify for a preferential treatment[245] . Determining RoO when a good is wholly produced in a single country is relatively simple. In contrast, the situation changes when inputs for a product are sourced from different countries, as sometimes inputs can reach up to 60–70% of a final product[246]. Then a question arises as to what extent the country of final production/manufacture can be named as the origin of the good. RoO requirements of RTAs differ in conferring preferential treatment in such scenarios.

Problems around RoO exacerbate because states apply different RoO to their different trading partners[247]. This causes "spaghetti or noodle bowl" effect, a term popularized to characterize the chaotic nature of the RoO[248]. Since RoO are discriminatory in their nature, they are also perceived as non-tariff barriers to trade. The most notable negative impact of RoO is that they limit the freedom of the producer to outsource from the most efficient countries and force them to utilize inefficient production just to qualify for a preferential treatment[249].

In the field of RoO, two organizations work hand by hand: the WTO and World Customs Organization (WCO). The main multilateral legal documents covering rules of origin are International Convention on the Simplification and Harmonization of Customs Procedures (Kyoto Convention hereinafter)[250], WTO

245 Preferential treatment can be conferred in three scenarios: (1) If a country applies GSP or GSP+ system, having the origin from GSP / GSP+ beneficiaries makes the product qualify for a preferential treatment. (2) The same is true if a country is in the RTA which applies zero or reduced tariffs to its parties. Bearing the country of origin from such party confers a preferential treatment to a product. (3) The last is true if a certain country is in the WTO and applies MFN treatment to WTO members and higher tariffs to non-WTO members. In such a case, a product qualifies for preferential treatment if it originates from WTO member territory.

246 Vivian C. Jones, Michael F. Martin 'International Trade: Rules of Origin' (2011) 4 (3) Journal of Current Issues in Globalization, pCRS5.

247 Won-Mog Choi, 'Defragmenting Fragmented Rules of Origin of Regional Trade Agreements: A Building Block to Global Free Trade' (2010) 13 Journal of International Economic Law, p. 111.

248 The term spaghetti bowls was introduced by Jagdish Bhagwati, *Termites in the Trading System: How Preferential Agreements Undermine Free Trade* (2008, Oxford University Press, Oxford), p. 63. The term spaghetti bowls have been used as noodle bowls in Asia. The term was introduced by ADB President Haruhiko Kuroda in 2006 in South Korea.

249 WTO Survey "Rules of Origin Regime in Regional Trade Agreements" WT/REG/W/45, 5 April 2002.

250 The following countries in the analyzed region are party to the revised Kyoto Convention: Armenia, Azerbaijan, Russia, Kazakhstan, Ukraine, Belarus See: International Convention on the Simplification on the Simplification and Harmonization of

Agreement on Rules of Origin[251], as well as WTO Bali and Nairobi Ministerial Decisions on Preferential Rules of Origin for Least-Developed Countries[252].

Historically, when GATT was introduced in 1947, it did not contain any provisions on RoO. However, when RTAs started to proliferate, a need for criteria on RoO surfaced. Definition of the RoO was first introduced in Kyoto Convention of World Customs Organization as "*the country in which the goods have been produced or manufactured, according to the criteria laid down for the purposes of application of customs tariff, of quantitative restrictions or of any other measure related to trade*"[253]. Kyoto Convention also determined standards for the various RoO determinations.

Later, based on the definitions of Kyoto Convention, GATT contracting parties developed Agreement on Rules of Origin during the Uruguay Round[254]. In this agreement RoO were classified into preferential and non-preferential categories. This agreement dealt mainly with non-preferential RoO, because it was not possible to achieve consensus among members regarding preferential RoO. Therefore, only limited common understanding on the elements of preferential

---

Customs Procedures (Kyoto Convention), Specific Annex K (1974) <www.wcoomd.org>.

251 Agreement on Rules of Origin (15 April, 1994), Marrakesh Agreement Establishing the World Trade Organization, Annex 1A, <http://docsonline.wto.org> accessed 11 January 2017.

252 Bali Decision puts forward the elements for the preferential rules of origin that WTO members could apply for the goods from LDC countries. Nairobi Decision further elaborates on the requirements for preferential rules of origin for LDCs. Since, none of the countries in the region are LDCs, these decisions will not be further analyzed. See: WTO Ministerial Decision on Preferential Rules of Origin for Least-Developed Countries (7 December 2013) <http://docsonline.wto.org> accessed 20 January 2017 and WTO Ministerial Decision on Preferential Rules of Origin for Least Developed Countries (19 December 2015) <http://docsonline.wto.org> accessed 20 January 2017.

253 International Convention on the Simplification on the Simplification and Harmonization of Customs Procedures (Kyoto Convention), Specific Annex K, E1/F2 (1974). This agreement was updated in 1999 which entree into force on 3 February 2006 <http://www.wcoomd.org/en/topics/facilitation/instrument-and-tools/conventions/pf_revised_kyoto_conv.aspx> accessed 7 March 2017.

254 Vladimir Mixaylovich Shumilov, *Pravo Vsemirnoy Torqovoy Orqanizachii* (World Trade Organization Law) (2017, Yurayt, Moscow).

RoO, which were based on the Kyoto Convention, were inserted in the Annex II of the Agreement on Rules of Origin[255].

Non-preferential RoO are used in conferring origin for the most-favored nation treatment, application of anti-dumping and countervailing duties, safeguard measures, origin marking requirements, discriminatory quantitative restrictions, tariff quotas, trade statistics and government procurement"[256]. A harmonizaton process for non-preferential RoO has been ongoing jointly by the WTO and WCO.

Preferential RoO are applied for preferences that go beyond the MFN principle[257]. In other words, preferential RoO are applied to confer privileges to the RTA partners. As such, they tend to be more restrictive to limit free-riding by non-parties to RTAs[258]. In contrast to non-preferential RoO, preferential RoO have been far away from harmonization efforts. This chapter focuses on preferential RoO.

ii. The Preferential RoO

There are two criteria to determine RoO. The first is wholly obtained criterion. It applies to natural products that are wholly obtained, harvested or produced in one country, for instance agriculture produce, live animals, harvested plants and anything that is produced solely from such products. Revised Kyoto Convention defines the minimum thresholds for products that can be considered as wholly-obtained[259]. The second is substantial transformation criterion. It applies if a good is produced in more than one country and determines the country where the good underwent such transformation so as to confer on it the place of origin[260] .

---

255 Agreement on Rules of Origin, Article 1.1 (15 April, 1994), Marrakesh Agreement Establishing the World Trade Organization, Annex 1A, <http://docsonline.wto.org> accessed 11 January 2017.

256 ibid, Article 1.2.

257 ibid, Article 1.1.

258 This is called as "trade deflection". See: Jong Bum Kim and Joongi Kim 'The Role of Rules of Origin to Provide Discipline to the GATT Article XXIV Exception' (2011) 14 (3) Journal of International Economic Law.

259 International Convention on the Simplification on the Simplification and Harmonization of Customs Procedures (Kyoto Convention), Specific Annex K, 2.Standard (1974) <www.wcoomd.org>.

260 ibid, 3. Recommended Practice.

Substantial transformation criterion can be determined by the application of three different rules and most of the countries use combinations from all three:

(1) *Change in tariff classification rule* is the most wide-spread rule. It confers the origin only when non-originating materials are added to the product and a change in tariff classification (Harmonized System of Tariff Nomenclature – HS) of a final product occur[261]. The degree of the change required differs from RTA to RTA. The change can be in chapter (HS 2 digit), heading (HS 4 digits), sub-heading (HS 6 digits) or item (HS 8 digits)[262,263]. Requiring a change in chapter classification is the most restrictive, while requiring a change only in item classification is the least restrictive[264]. A country can require different changes in tariff classification with regards to different product categories[265]. That creates a lot of complexity in application.
(2) *Ad valorem percentage share rule* determines permissible threshold of non-originating material in a final product. Countries can apply either maximum or minimum thresholds for the addition of such non-originating material. The more the permissible share of the non-originating material, the less restrictive is the rule. For instance, LDC countries in Bali Ministerial were lobbying for 75% ad valorem percentage share, because they were

261 Harmonized System or HS in short is the commodity description and coding system adopted by World Customs Organization and applied by 207 countries. The 2017 edition consists of 97 chapters and some 5000 commodity groups. See more: http://www.wcoomd.org/en/topics/nomenclature/overview> accessed 6 February 2017.

262 Antoni Estevadeordal, Kati Suominen 'Rules of Origin: A World Map and Trade Effects' (2004) 7th Annual Conference on Global Economic Analysis: Trade, Poverty and Environment, p. 4.

263 An example of a very restrictive change in tariff heading can be bread and flour which are categorized in different headings. For bread to receive preferential treatment under the Association Agreements of the EU they need to be prepared with anything other than flour. Another example is preparations of meat or fish or other crustaceans, which requires that the meat, fish or crustaceans should be wholly-obtained for the preparations of them to receive preferential treatment.

264 World Customs Organization, Rules of Origin Handbook, p. 9 <http://www.wcoomd.org/-/media/wco/public/global/pdf/topics/origin/overview/origin-handbook/rules-of-origin-handbook.pdf> accessed 18 April 2019.

265 Paul Brenton & Hiroshi Imagawa 'Rules of Origin, Trade and Customs' (2005) The Customs Modernization Handbook, World Bank, p. 192 <https://siteresources.worldbank.org/INTEXPCOMNET/Resources/Customs_Modernization_Handbook.pdf> accessed 6 February 2017.

arguing that LDCs did not have necessary potential to produce all the parts and elements of a product[266].

(3) *Manufacturing/processions operations rules* determines a list of operations, which makes a product considered as transformed[267]. This could entail prohibition of certain operations or application of certain operations. An example for specific processes criterion could be the EU electronic product RoO. Based on this RoO, the origin of an electronic device is considered to be to the country of origin of its transistors[268].

Certain exceptions apply to the substantial transformation criterion. These exceptions have been found to limit the negative effects of the stringent RoO provisions and make them less restrictive[269]. They are as following: (1) Countries usually determine list of minimal operations that are necessary in the production of a good, which do not affect the origin[270]; (2) Some countries also apply tolerance or "de minimis" rule under which addition of a certain percentage of non-originating materials is tolerated[271]; (3) Roll-up/absorption principle: When this principle is applied, non-originating inputs of the intermediate product are disregarded when determining origin of the final product[272]; (4) Notably, the most important exception in the context of RTAs is cumulation rule. Cumulation rule

---

266 This provision became a part of the Bali Ministerial Decision, however has not binding power. See: WTO Ministerial Decision on Preferential Rules of Origin for Least-Developed Countries (7 December 2013) <http://docsonline.wto.org> accessed 20 January 2017.

267 World Customs Organization, Rules of Origin Handbook, p. 10 <http://www.wcoomd.org/-/media/wco/public/global/pdf/topics/origin/overview/origin-handbook/rules-of-origin-handbook.pdf> accessed 18 April 2019.

268 Dylan Geraets, Colleen Carroll, Arnoud R.Williems 'Reconciling Rules of Origin and Global Value Chains: The Case for Reform' (2015) 18 (2) Journal of International Economic Law, p. 6.

269 Antoni Estevadeordal, Kati Suominen 'Rules of Origin: A World Map and Trade Effects' (2004) 7th Annual Conference on Global Economic Analysis: Trade, Poverty and Environment, p. 6.

270 International Convention on the Simplification on the Simplification and Harmonization of Customs Procedures (Kyoto Convention), Specific Annex K, 6. Recommended Practice (1974) <www.wcoomd.org>.

271 Antoni Estevadeordal, Kati Suominen 'Rules of Origin: A World Map and Trade Effects' (2004) 7th Annual Conference on Global Economic Analysis: Trade, Poverty and Environment, p. 5.

272 ibid.

allows to source non-originating inputs from other countries as if these materials are originated in the country of the final product and reduces the negative impacts of rules of origin.

There are 3 types of cumulation based on their scope from the narrowest to widest.

(1) The first cumulation is bilateral cumulation, which is minimum threshold. In bilateral cumulation, an input originated in one RTA partner can be considered to be originated in the other RTA partner when determining the origin of the final product. Let's say, Country A imports all components for an automobile from Country B and assembles it in Country A. In bilateral cumulation, the car can be exported duty-free to Country B, as if all the components were from Country A.
(2) The second cumulation type is diagonal /regional cumulation[273] . It is applied to RTAs among more than two countries. In this cumulation system a country is permitted to use non-originating raw materials from all the RTA partners without the product changing its origin. Let's imagine, Country A has a RTA with Country B and Country C. Country B and C also have RTA among themselves and in all 3 RTAs diagonal cumulation is in place. In this scenario, Country A produces cars, by importing components from Country C. Country A does not add any value to the car production, it only assembles the components and afterwards, exports it to Country B. Will the care considered to be produced in Country A or B? If diagonal cumulation is in place, the car would be considered as produced in Country A. Under this cumulation, all the components are considered to be originating from Country A, because all three countries have diagonal/regional cumulation.
(3) The third cumulation is full cumulation. It is applied in customs unions, where the preferential trade zone is taken as a whole for RoO and not only input, but also all the operations processed in the trade zone are counted as originating in the country of final product[274]. Let's imagine that the RoO requirement for an automobile is that non-originating inputs cannot be more than 30% of the product. There is a full cumulation in place between

273 Some sources differentiate between diagonal and regional cumulation system. However, we are taking as a basis the approach of World Customs Organization in this matter.

274 World Customs Organization, Rules of Origin Handbook, p. 17 <http://www.wcoomd.org/-/media/wco/public/global/pdf/topics/origin/overview/origin-handbook/rules-of-origin-handbook.pdf> accessed 18 April 2019.

Country A, B and C, but not with Country D. Country A imports components from Country D, then assembles it, colors in Country B and polishes it in Country C. For the calculation of RoO for this car, all the manufacturing/processing that were done in Country A, B and C will be added together and considered as if all were done in Country A.

Lately, there have been more and more cases of cross-cumulation. Cross-cumulation is similar to diagonal cumulation, because it allows third party inputs, but in contrast to diagonal cumulation, countries do not need to have the same RoO arrangements and harmonize their RoO. In this cumulation, they just conclude mutual recognition agreements[275].

In the area of RoO, certain concepts exist, which overall make rules of origin even more stringent. Complexity of certification, prohibition of duty drawback and development of lists of operations that are considered to be insufficient to confer origin are among such concepts[276]. Among them, most frequent is the prohibition of duty drawback. Duty drawback is a concept that is used to define refund or exemption of tariffs for non-originating input when they are used in a final product and exported to a preferential country[277]. In general, RTAs will not allow for duty drawback, even though this is seen as a way to increase investment in developing countries[278]. Duty drawbacks are mainly used in Asian and African countries with the trend being to phase out and eliminate.

WTO Agreement on Rules of Origin has the following requirements for preferential RoO[279]: (i) when change in tariff classification rule is applied, it should specify the specific heading/subheading that should be changed, (ii) when ad valorem percentage share criterion is applied, calculation method should be

---

275 Rohini Acharya, *Regional Trade Agreements and the Multilateral Trading System* (2016, Cambridge University Press, Cambridge), p. 66.

276 Antoni Estevadeordal, Kati Suominen 'Rules of Origin: A World Map and Trade Effects' (2004) 7th Annual Conference on Global Economic Analysis: Trade, Poverty and Environment, p. 6.

277 World Customs Organization, Rules of Origin Handbook, p. 18 <http://www.wcoomd.org/-/media/wco/public/global/pdf/topics/origin/overview/origin-handbook/rules-of-origin-handbook.pdf> accessed 18 April 2019.

278 Antoni Estevadeordal, Kati Suominen 'Rules of Origin: A World Map and Trade Effects' (2004) 7th Annual Conference on Global Economic Analysis: Trade, Poverty and Environment, p. 6.

279 Agreement on Rules of Origin (15 April, 1994), Marrakesh Agreement Establishing the World Trade Organization, Annex 1A, <http://docsonline.wto.org> accessed 11 January 2017.

included, (iii) when manufacturing or processing operations criterion is applied, the process that confers origin should be clearly shown, (iv) RoO shall be based on positive standard, (v) they shall be published, (vi) new RoO or any change shall not be applied retroactively, (vii) upon request, assessment of RoO is to be issued, (viii) administrative decisions should be reviewable, (ix) respect for confidentiality should be honored.

iii. RoO Models

There are a number of different RoO models applied in the world such as Pan-Euro-Mediterranean model, NAFTA model, ASEAN model, Latin America Integration Agreement model[280]. Basically, the over-lapping RTAs around these regions use the same RoO and thus the models are created. Among these models the most prominent ones are Pan-Euro-Mediterranean model and NAFTA model.

Pan-Euro-Mediterranean model is employed by the EU to EFTA countries (Switzerland, Liechtenstein, Luxembourg, Norway), Turkey, Faroe islands, the Western Balkans, Algeria, Egypt, Israel, Jordan, Lebanon, Morocco, Syria, Tunisia, Palestinian Authority. Among these countries Regional Convention on pan-Euro-Mediterrenean Preferential Rules of Origin apply[281]. The EU applies mostly diagonal or full cumulation system allowing for inputs to be cumulated in wider region. However, even in Pan-Euro-Mediterranean model, use of the different rules (ad valorem percentage, specific processing, change in tariff classification) makes the whole system complicated.

In the Americas two models are more popular. The first one is Latin America Integration Agreement model which uses one rule across the board for all of the tariff lines: either change in the tariff chapter or at least 50% value-added[282]. This is mostly used in South American countries. The other most wide-spread model is NAFTA model. In terms of restrictiveness NAFTA model is quite stringent,

---

280 Won-Mog Choi, 'Defragmenting Fragmented Rules of Origin of Regional Trade Agreements: A Building Block to Global Free Trade' (2010) 13 Journal of International Economic Law, p. 111.

281 Regional Convention on pan-Euro-Mediterrenean Preferential Rules of Origin (26 March 2012) L54/3<https://eur-lex.europa.eu/legal-content/GA/TXT/?uri=CELEX:32013D0094> accessed 18 April 2019.

282 Antoni Estevadeordal, Kati Suominen 'Rules of Origin: A World Map and Trade Effects' (2004) 7th Annual Conference on Global Economic Analysis: Trade, Poverty and Environment, p. 8.

as it might require satisfaction of not only one, but two criteria, such as both value-added criterion and change in tariff classification criterion[283]. The NAFTA model is also characterized with multiplicity of use of different rules across the board, such as requirement of change in tariff chapter, heading, subheading, value-added criterion and a lot of exceptions[284].

The ASEAN model is characterized with simpler RoO compared to NAFTA and Pan-Euo-Mediterrenean model. A simple 40% value added change is required here, even though there is a tendency nowadays to include different RoO to different areas such as textiles[285].

iv. Way Forward

Studies have pointed that preferential RoO are hindering trade facilitation and becoming more and more a constraint on trade[286]. Not only are they complex, but administration of them, as well as compliance can be quite costly. The estimates are that the cost of compliance of a good to RoO can be up to 6% of its export value[287]. When most of the world countries are entering into different and sometimes overlapping RTAs, the cost of this creates an unnecessary burden for trade[288]. Not surprisingly, sometimes traders prefer to bypass the tariff preferences because of the complexity of the RoO provisions.

---

283 Philippe de Lombaerde, Luis Jorge Garay 'Preferential Rules of Origin and the Multilateral Trading System: Pro-Development Policy Options' (2007) UNU-CRIS Working Paper W2007-14, p. 4.

284 ibid.

285 Erline Medalla, Jenny Balboa 'ASEAN Rules of Origin: Lessons and Recommendations for Best Practice' (2009) ERIA Discussion Paper series ERIA-DP-2009-17, p. 11 <http://www.eria.org/ERIA-DP-2009-17.pdf> accessed 19 April 2019.

286 Paul Brenton & Hiroshi Imagawa 'Rules of Origin, Trade and Customs' (2005) The Customs Modernization Handbook, World Bank, p. 184 <https://siteresources.worldbank.org/INTEXPCOMNET/Resources/Customs_Modernization_Handbook.pdfd> accessed 6 February 2017.

287 Philippe de Lombaerde, Luis Jorge Garay 'Preferential Rules of Origin and the Multilateral Trading System: Pro-Development Policy Options' (2007) 42 (5) Intereconomics, p. 263.

288 Olivier Cadot and Jaime de Melo analyze this situation and come to a conclusion that rules of origin in many RTAs are designed so that less-developed countries use intermediate products of developed countries in their final product, also developed countries gain most of the rules of origin compliance costs. See: Olivier Cadot, Jame de Melo 'Why OECD Countries Should Reform Rules of Origin' (2008) 23 The World Bank Research Observer 1.

Development of global value chains have necessitated different segments of production and manufacturing to shift to different countries. This in return made harmonization of preferential RoO more urgent than ever[289]. Which segment of the global value chain confers the country of origin becomes an issue when different trade agreements define different rules. The challenge is to somehow merge differentiated RoOs into one global framework or to find a way to reduce the discriminatory effect of preferential rules of origin.

The WTO and WCO together have been progressing in harmonization of non-preferential RoO. However, the work for the harmonization of preferential RoO lags behind. In fact, the only arena for harmonization of preferential RoO has been not the WTO, but RTAs[290]. The EU has been able to harmonize its fragmented rules of origin in Pan-Euro-Mediterranean system. A single convention within the EU on preferential ROO is underway[291].

There are several issues that could be harmonized in a single multilateral trade agreement: (1) common guidelines and methodology for determination of preferential RoO (2) facilitating administration and application of RoO; (3) common principles regarding transparency of RoO.

v. RoO Provisions within the RTAs of Eastern Europe, Central Asia and the Caucasus

(a) Association Agreements of the EU with Ukraine, Georgia and Moldova[292]

The RoO provisions of the EU – Georgia, EU – Ukraine and EU – Moldova Association Agreements appear to be more restrictive in their terms when compared to other FTAs of the EU, such as EU – South Korea FTA or EU – Singapore

289 Paul Brenton, Miriam Manchin 'Making EU Trade Agreements Work: The Role of Rules of Origin' (2003) 26 (5) World Economy, p. 12.

290 John J. Barcelo III 'Harmonizing Preferential Rules of Origin in the WTO System' (2006) Cornell Law Faculty Publications, p. 5 <https://www.peacepalacelibrary.nl/ebooks/files/CLFP_Barcelo_Harmonizing_Preferential.pdf> accessed 11 March 2017.

291 EU Commission website <ec. europa.eu> accessed 11 March 2017.

292 EU – Ukraine Association Agreement, EU – Georgia Association Agreement, EU – Moldova Association Agreement Protocol 1 "Concerning the definition of the concept of "originating products" and methods of administrative co-operation" (29 May 2014) <trade.ec.euorpa.eu/doclib/docs/2016/November/tradoc_155103.pdf> accessed 23 January 2017.

FTA. The restrictiveness of the RoO is specifically seen in scope of cumulation, substantial transformation criteria and documentary requirements.

Cumulation: Bilateral cumulation is in place in all three agreements. As it was explained previously, bilateral cumulation is the most restrictive cumulation where only inputs originating from the parties can be considered as originating inputs. It has to be noted here that the EU does not have bilateral cumulation with all its RTA partners. In fact, in many instances diagonal or even full cumulation is in place. For instance, Pan – Euro – Med cumulation of the EU allows for diagonal cumulation between the EU, Turkey, EFTA and a number of countries[293]. Full cumulation is in place between the EU and Algeria, Morocco and Tunisia[294]. It is also worthwhile to note that having bilateral cumulation in these agreements is not advantageous for Georgia, Ukraine and Moldova, as the EU is more capable to outsource its inputs within its territory (all 28 countries) and export it to Georgia, Ukraine and Moldova duty-free. In contrast, Ukraine, Georgia and Moldova would face more challenges in exporting their products duty-free to the EU.

When it comes to other flexibilities, the de minimis rule has been set at 10%[295]. Roll-up or absorption principles are allowed, in other words if a product is considered to be originated and used as an input to a final product, the non-originating materials in the first product will be disregarded in the final calculation. The Association Agreements prohibit drawback of customs duties, which as was mentioned in the previous section is a practice which is gradually eliminated worldwide[296].

The agreement contains list of operations that will not confer origin. For instance, if fruit is exported to a country where it is unshelled or peeled and then exported to RTA parties, it will not confer origin[297]. Another

293 Algeria, Egypt, Israel, Jordan, Lebanon, Morocco, Palestine, Albania, Bosnia and Herzegovina, Macedonia, Montenegro, Serbia, Kosovo, Switzerland, Norway, Iceland, Liechtenstein, EU, Turkey.

294 European Commission Web-site <ec.europa.eu> accessed 13 March 2017.

295 EU – Ukraine Association Agreement, Protocol 1, Article 2 (a) "Concerning the definition of the concept of "originating products" and methods of administrative co-operation" (29 May 2014) <trade.ec.euorpa.eu/doclib/docs/2016/November/tradoc_155103.pdf> accessed 23 January 2017.

296 For instance in EU – South Korea FTA, duty drawback is allowed, while the parties acknowledge to review their schemes after transitional period.

297 EU – Ukraine Association Agreement, EU – Georgia Association Agreement, EU – Moldova Association Agreement Protocol 1 "Concerning the definition of the concept

example is simple slaughter of animals which does not make it an originating product[298].

Substantial transformation criteron: In terms of determining sufficient transformation of a product, the Association Agreements apply a combination of criteria, mainly change in tariff classification and ad valorem percentage share. Change in tariff classification is expressed in 4 digits (tariff heading) with occasional exceptions. The Special Annex lists all the product based criteria for goods to qualify for preferential treatment. For instance, in the case of articles of apparel and clothing in Chapter 61, the rule of origin requires manufacture from yarn – famous restrictive rules of origin among both NAFTA and the EU countries. This rule means that merely sewing of fabric together does not confer the place of origin. Thus, the agreement requires two stages of manufacturing to take place within the preferential zone – weaving the fabric and sewing it into a garment[299] .

Another example is the cocoa and cocoa preparations listed in chapter 18 of HS Nomenclature. For such products to qualify for preferential treatment, two rules should be complied with: (i) The inputs should not contain anything from the same heading (ii) value of the sugar (chapter 17) should not exceed 30% of the ex-works price of the product. In practice, that means that if chocolate preparations were made using imported cocoa powder, it would not qualify for preferential treatment. Moreover, even if the imported cocoa powder was not used, but the value of the sugar within the chocolate preparation were more than 30%, the product would still not qualify for preferential treatment.

In some examples, Association Agreements offers two alternatives. For instance, for turbo-jets (HS8411) there are two alternatives[300]: (i) the requirement that the materials from HS 8411 (turbo jets, gas turbines, turbo-propellers)

---

of "originating products" and methods of administrative co-operation", Article 6 (h) (29 May 2014) <trade.ec.euorpa.eu/doclib/docs/2016/November/tradoc_155103.pdf> accessed 23 January 2017.

298 ibid, Article 6 (q).

299 Association Agreement between the European Union and the European Atomic Energy Community and their Member States, of the one part, and the Republic of Georgia, of the other part (27 June 2014), Official Journal of the European Union L261, 30 August 2014.

300 EU – Ukraine Association Agreement, Annex II "List of working or processing required to be carried out on non-originating materials in order that the product manufactured can obtain originating status" (29 May 2014) <trade.ec.euorpa.eu/doclib/docs/2016/November/tradoc_155103.pdf> accessed 23 January 2017.

should not be used and the requirement that the materials for the final products should not exceed 40% of value of the final product. (ii) the value of all the materials should not exceed 25% of the value of the final product. In this example, the first alternative uses combination of both change in tariff classification and ad valorem percentage share criteria, while the second alternative uses only ad valorem percentage share criterion. The exporter chooses the best fitting alternative according to his needs.

Documentary requirements: In terms of certification of the proof of origin, the EU has used two types of certification methods in the Association Agreements. First one is the certification issued by the competent authority[301]. In this certification, a movement certificate and application form are filled by the exporter or exporter's authorized representative and together with accompanying documents they are submitted to the customs authority of the exporting country[302]. This type of certification system is more burdensome than the second type. The second type of certification is self-certification (declaration by exporter) which is applied to exports not exceeding 6000 euros in value or to "approved exporters"[303]. Approved exporter is the status granted by the customs authorities to frequent exporters[304].

In contrast with the EU's Association Agreements with Georgia, Ukraine and Moldova, EU for instance employed only the self-certification (declaration by exporter) in its FTA with South Korea[305]. The same is true with the EU-Singapore FTA. This type of certification facilitates handling of the trade, as the trader does not need to obtain certificate of origin from the competent authority. Merely expressing the origin in an invoice or other document is enough in such cases. This attests to higher degree of liberalization of the trade relations of the EU with these countries in contrast to Association Agreement counterparts – Georgia, Ukraine and Moldova.

Considering that the EU consists of 28 countries which collectively produce all kinds of agricultural and industrial products, while Moldova, Georgia and

301 EU – Moldova Association Agreement Protocol 1 "Concerning the definition of the concept of "originating products" and methods of administrative co-operation", Article 15 (29 May 2014) <trade.ec.euorpa.eu/doclib/docs/2016/November/tradoc_155103.pdf> accessed 23 January 2017.

302 ibid, Article 16.

303 ibid, Article 21.

304 ibid, Article 22.

305 EU – South Korea FTA (15 October 2009) <eur-lex.europa.eu> accessed 22 February 2017.

Ukraine are sourcing a considerable share of the inputs necessary for the manufacture of their export products, RoO provisions of DCFTAs can limit the trading potential of Moldova, Georgia and Ukraine to a certain extent[306]. However it should also be noted that, the EU has adopted a "Trade for all" strategy in 2015 which envisages simplification and modernization of RoO and aiming to conclude one regional PanEuroMed convention on RoO[307]. Based on this strategy, there is a possibility that the RoO of the EU with regards to these countries would be simplified in the future.

(b) The CIS

RoO provisions in the CIS region are regulated through the CIS Treaty on Rules of Origin[308]. The treaty is applicable to the goods in circulation in the CIS area to which the CIS Free Trade Agreement of 1994 applies[309]. This treaty is valid only for the trade between the CIS parties and does not regulate the import/export of the goods from CIS members to third countries, which is a matter of national legislation.

As customary, the Treaty discerns between wholly obtained and sufficiently transformed criteria. Wholly obtained criterion of the Treaty corresponds for the most part to the standard prescribed in revised Kyoto convention. However, in contrast to RTAs of the EU, wholly obtained criterion encompasses also high technology products obtained in the spacecraft of the country in outer space[310]. It should be noted that, NAFTA also has a similar provision. However, the language used in NAFTA and CIS is different. The difference lies with the fact that NAFTA defines this rule as "*goods taken from outer space*", while CIS defines it as "*high technology products obtained in the spacecraft of the country in outer space*"[311]. To be precise, NAFTA refers to a process of "taking", while CIS refers

306 export.Gov <https://www.export.gov/article?series=a0pt00000000PjMAAU&type=Country_Commercial__kav> accessed 19 February 2018.

307 'Trade for All – Towards a More Responsible Trade and Investment Policy' (2015, Luxembourg, Publications Office).

308 Treaty on the Rules of Origin of the Goods in Commonwealth of Independent States (20 November 2009). <docs.eaeunion.org>.

309 Treaty on the Establishment of the Free Trade Area in Commonwealth of Independent States (15 April 1994).

310 Treaty on the Rules of Origin of the Goods in Commonwealth of Independent States, Article 2.2 (20 November 2009) <docs.eaeunion.org>.

311 North-American Free Trade Agreement (17 December 1992) <www.sice.oas.org/trade/nafta/naftatce.asp> accessed 15 March 2017.

to a process of "obtaining". Though "taking" and "obtaining" can be seen as synonyms, in this context there are differences. The process of "obtaining" encompasses the process of production, as well as taking. On the other hand "taking" cannot refer to the process of production[312].

It should be noted that, similar provision exists also among other RTAs in the region to which Russian Federation is a party, such as the EAEU – Vietnam FTA, Treaty on the Rules of Origin among Customs Union members, Russia-Serbia FTA.

<u>Cumulation:</u> The Treaty allows diagonal cumulation among the Treaty parties[313]. In other words, notwithstanding that inputs and materials are originated from other CIS parties, final products are considered as originating[314]. Allowance of diagonal cumulation is a positive feature of the CIS RoO.

The Treaty is silent about the duty drawback or roll up/absorption principles. A de minimis/tolerance rule is 5% of the value of ex-works. There is a pre-condition that the input should be a necessary component of the good[315] .

Specific characteristic feature of the CIS rules of origin is the residency rule. Based on this residency rule, a product would be considered as originating if it is imported by a resident and exported by a resident from a CIS customs territory[316]. This limits duty-free treatment within the CIS only to the residents of CIS, effectively limiting all non-residents from applying for duty-free treatment[317]. This is a feature that is not present in other RTAs in the world. In essence, if a non-CIS resident produces a product in a CIS country and exports it to another CIS country, it will not enjoy duty-free treatment, because of his non-residency. Effectively, this feature excludes companies from other countries to reap the fruits of CIS duty-free regime. This feature of the CIS Treaty seems to be more politically motivated, rather than economical, as it does not take into account the global role of transnational companies and global value chains.

---

312 Products from the outer space in our analysis refers to the research facility of International Space Station that is operated by 15 countries, including Russia.

313 Treaty on the Rules of Origin of the Goods in Commonwealth of Independent States, Article 2.4 (20 November 2009) <docs.eaeunion.org>.

314 ibid, Article 2.5.

315 Ex-works is the term used to imply the good which comes from the factory of its production/substantial transformation.

316 Treaty on the Rules of Origin of the Goods in Commonwealth of Independent States, Article 5.1 (20 November 2009) <docs.eaeunion.org>.

317 Rohini Acharya, *Regional Trade Agreements and the Multilateral Trading System* (2016, Cambridge University Press, Cambridge), p. 64.

Substantial transformation criteria: Substantial transformation of the good could be determined through application of one or combination of the following criteria[318]: (i) change of tariff classification in the first 4 digits; (ii) specific manufacturing/processing operations; (iii) ad valorem percentage share criterion.

Change in the tariff classification is the priority rule. It should be noted that change in tariff classification within the CIS region, even in the bilateral RTAs, are determined in 4 digits (change in tariff heading)[319]. As previously noted, this is more liberal than change in tariff chapter (2 digit), but is more restrictive than change in 6 digits (change in tariff sub-heading). This criterion applies to all products, except a list of goods to which specific manufacturing/processing operations rule or ad valorem percentage share rule should be applied.

Having compared CIS Treaty on Rules of Origin and EU Association Agreements with Moldova, Georgia and Ukraine, one can reach the conclusion that EU Association Agreements are more stringent in conferring origin. For instance, if milk and cream is analyzed which is reflected in HS 0402, the CIS RoO allow for the foreign inputs of any tariff line. The only condition is that foreign inputs from HS 0402 should be no more than 40% of the value of the final product. In contrast, the EU Association Agreements require that all the inputs of Chapter 4 to be wholly obtained. In other words while the CIS allows any foreign inputs in the production of milk and cream, the EU is stricter in this regard and requires all Chapter 4 (dairy produce, bird's eggs, natural honey, edible products of animal origin) to be wholly produced, which means they should originate from preference granting country.

Again, the same comparison goes in the production of clothing. While EU DCFTAs require manufacture from yarn, CIS Treaty has no specific RoO for clothing and requires only change in HS tariff heading (4 digit). This means that, for instance, a woman's blouse that is produced from foreign lace will comply with the CIS rules of origin, because sewing of lace into a blouse will change the classification of the tariff heading. But sewing of the same lace into a blouse in EU Association Agreements will not be compliant with origin requirements. In

318 Treaty on the Rules of Origin of the Goods in Commonwealth of Independent States, Article 2.4 (20 November 2009) <docs.eaeunion.org>.

319 Vladimir Storojcuk 'Opredelenie strain proisxojdeniya tovarov na usloviyax soqlasheniy o svobodnoy torqovle, zaklyuchennix Ukrainoy so stranami SNQ' (Determination of rules of origin of goods on the conditions of the agreements of free trade, concluded by Ukraine with the countries of CIS) (2014) Viunik 45 <http://www.visnuk.com.ua/ru/pubs/id/7829> last accessed 15 December 2017.

the Association Agreement cases, in order to get a preferential origin, the lace should be sewed from yarn and then made into a blouse.

If bread, pastry, cakes, biscuits in HS 1905 are compared again, the CIS Treaty applies ad valorem percentage share rule, based on which the value of all the inputs should not exceed 50% of the final product. In comparison, the EU Association Agreements require that inputs should not come from Chapter 11 (products of the milling industry, malt, starches, wheat gluten). In other words, flour for making of bread should not be foreign input in the EU Association Agreements, while CIS Treaty allows foreign ingredients, as long as they do not exceed 50% of the value of the good.

Documentary requirements: It is possible to submit a mere declaration on the origin of goods not exceeding value of 5000 USD. However, in practice this is hardly possible and the CIS countries require CT-1 certificate of origin to be issued by the respective national government[320]. Moreover, unlike the EU Association Agreements with Georgia, Ukraine and Moldova, there is no concept of authorized exporter in the CIS Treaty. This makes the trade within the CIS region more burdensome for traders in comparison with the self-certification systems applicable in many developed countries. Although, individual CIS countries, such as Russia, Kazakhstan, Azerbaijan are exploring the possibility of applying the authorized economic operators concept within their trading system, the CIS Treaty has no provision regarding it. Currently, there are negotiations going on upgrading this Treaty. Perhaps, the new treaty will have provisions on this matter as well.

In conclusion, after comparing and analyzing RoO applied by CIS and EU Association Agreements with Georgia, Ukraine and Moldova, this analysis shows that CIS rules for calculation of RoO are more liberal. However, the common regulation on administration and governance of RoO, specifically the residency rule and lack of the concept of authorized exporter in CIS Treaty makes it more obsolete in contrast to the EU Association Agreements.

320 'Usloviya oformleniya tovarov vvozimix iz stran SNQ i Qruzii, bez uplati tamojennoy poshlini' (Conditions of administration of goods imported from the CIS countries and Georgia without payment of customs duties) (2016) <https://custom.by/vvoz-iz-sng> last accessed 15 December 2017.

(c) The EAEU

The EAEU has recently adopted a new Customs Code which also regulates RoO[321]. The Code governs both preferential and non-preferential rules and mainly deals with documentary requirements.

Specificities of RoO are handled through specialized treaties of the EAEU. There are two sets of RoO in the EAEU: RoO applied to imports from third countries, except for developing and least-developed countries; and RoO applied to imports from developing and least-developed countries[322]. In addition, the EAEU has a special treaty that harmonizes the RoO for goods exported from the EAEU territory[323].

Similar to the CIS, the EAEU applies the concept of "high technology products obtained in the spacecraft in outer space" in determination of wholly-obtained goods. For such goods, the spaceship should be registered by the country producing the good[324].

Substantial transformation criterion: Treaty "On Unified Rules of Origin of Goods" is the main document that is applied to imports from third countries, except for the developing and least-developed countries[325]. Change in tariff classification rule is the key rule here with occasional implementation of specific manufacturing/processing operations. The EAEU RoO are almost identical to the CIS RoO. Therefore, CIS RoO section of this book can be taken as a reference.

RoO to developing and least-developed countries are governed through Treaty on Rules of Origin of Goods from Developing and Least Developed Countries[326]. The de minimis rule on this treaty is 50–60% compared to 10%

---

321 The Customs Code of the EAEU (26 December 2016) <www.eurasiancommission.org> accessed 16 March 2017.

322 Svetlana Starix 'Osobennosti osushestvleniya tamojennoqo dela v ramkax Evraziyskoqo ekonomicheskoqo soyuza' (Characteristing of customs formalities in the framework of the Eurasian Economic Union) (2016) 1 Mejdunarodniy jurnal qumanitarnix I yestestvennix nauk, p. 46 <https://cyberleninka.ru/article/n/osobennosti-osuschestvleniya-tamozhennogo-dela-v-ramkah-evraziyskogo-ekonomicheskogo-soyuza> accessed 29 November 2018.

323 Treaty on harmonized system of confirmation of the origin of goods, exported from customs territory of the Eurasian Economic Union (22 mart 2016) <https://docs.eaeunion.org> accessed 31 January 2017.

324 Treaty on Unified Rules of Origin of Goods (25 January 2008) Article 2.10 <https://docs.eaeunion.org> accessed 30 January 2017.

325 ibid.

326 Treaty on Rules of Origin of Goods from Developing and Least Developed Countries (14 June 2018) <https://docs.eaeunion.org> accessed 07 November 2018.

to other countries[327]. The treaty allows cumulation of inputs from all the developing and least-developed countries to which preferential regime applies. The EAEU also applies formula for calculation of non-originating materials in the production of final product.

Documentary requirements: The EAEU Customs Code discerns between declaration on the origin of the good and certificate of the origin of the good[328]. Certificate is a document issued by competent authority, while declaration is a document declared by a producer, seller or importer of a good. Thus, the EAEU makes it legally possible to accept a mere declaration of the importer, which simplifies the handling of trade and business. In the EAEU-Vietnam FTA, imports of goods which value do not exceed 200 USD are exempt for submitting certificate of origin[329]. In RoO to developing and least-developed countries, the threshold is 5000 euro for a similar case.

The Customs Code also brings a new concept on preliminary decision on RoO in order to expedite the customs processing[330]. This concept was not utilized in the CIS treaties. According to this concept, importers could apply for the customs authorities to issue decisions on RoO in advance, which would help them know the decision of the customs on RoO before actual importation of the goods.

In certain cases, such as in FTA with Vietnam, the parties undertook to develop and implement "electronic origin certification and verification system" to facilitate the procedure[331]. Based on this system, submission of original certificate of origin is not required, as long as there is an electronic customs declaration submitted by the applicant[332].

---

327 Treaty on Rules of Origin of Goods from Developing and Least Developed Countries, Article 6 (14 June 2018) <https://docs.eaeunion.org> accessed 07 November 2018.

328 The Customs Code of the EAEU, Article 30 and 31 (26 December 2016) <www.eurasiancommission.org> accessed 16 March 2017.

329 EAEU – Vietnam Free Trade Agreement, Article 4.17 (29 May 2015) <https://docs.eaeunion.org> accessed 30 January 2017.

330 The Customs Code of the EAEU, Article 33 (26 December 2016) <www.eurasiancommission.org> accessed 16 March 2017.

331 EAEU – Vietnam Free Trade Agreement, Article 4.29 (29 May 2015) <https://docs.eaeunion.org> accessed 30 January 2017.

332 ibid.

vi. Key Findings

This sub-chapter presented short information on the general principles of application of preferential RoO and analyzed the main features of the RTAs in Central Asia, Caucasus and Eastern Europe on RoO. Based on the analysis, the following common features of the RoO provisions of all the RTAs in the region have been compiled:

Firstly, there is not a single RoO model in the region. While the CIS and the EAEU RoO are almost identical, Ukraine, Moldova and Georgia apply different RoO in their trade with the EU. Neither of the RTAs in the region uses a single RoO determination method, such as change in tariff classification or ad-valorem percentage share rule. In fact, all of them use a combination of these rules and they vary across the board of the products. As it was explained in the previous sub-sections, ASEAN model or Latin America Integration Agreement model prescribes mostly one single RoO determination rule. However, this is not the case in this region and this makes the whole of RoO compliance quite difficult for importers. The more diverse the rules, the less chances there are for multilateralization.

Secondly, RoO are not overall too restrictive in the region. Change in tariff classification rule is mostly expressed in HS 4 digit level. The overall analysis shows that the RoO provisions in the region are not too restrictive in comparison with the existing RoO models of the world, such as NAFTA model, but at the same time they are not too liberal.

Thirdly, the administration of RoO is complex in the region. This was clearly seen when compared to the leading RTAs of the other regions where administration was much simpler such as RTAs of the EU with the Asian countries. Compliance with the RoO schemes requires in-depth knowledge of the RoO in order to qualify for a preferential treatment. This in its turn necessitates additional resources for the trader in order to qualify for preferential treatment. However, there are less differences in the field of administration between the countries of the region, than the substance of the RoO. Therefore, administration of RoO can be a potential area for multilateralization.

Fourthly, the documentary requirements tend to be relaxed depending on the year when the RTA is negotiated. While, for instance, the EAEU-Vietnam RTA documentary requirements are the most flexible, the CIS documentary requirements are the hardest in terms of compliance. But the general trend shows that the RoO documentary requirements will eventually become less of a burden on the importers.

Fifthly, there are certain flexibilities unitized in the region for RoO. For instance, self-certification is allowed in some RTAs which facilitates the trade in the region. However, this is also permitted to a certain extent. In the Association Agreements the extent is 6000 euros, while the EAEU-Vietnam FTA is 200 USD. CIS does not allow self-certification at all. Considering that the most advanced RTAs in the world between the developed countries allow for complete self-certification in all situations, the extent of permission of self-certification in this region demonstrates the tight government control over the trade and the degree of trust to the traders. Another flexibility is cumulation principle. Cumulation principle is utilized which allows the importers some flexibilities in outsourcing their inputs. However level of cumulation within the RTAs in this region is quite different. While, the EAEU and CIS tend to utilize diagonal/regional cumulation, Association Agreements utilizes more restrictive bilateral cumulation. However, EU's future agenda shows that bilateral cumulation could be replaced with a less restrictive cumulation method in the future;

Lastly, duty drawback is prohibited in all agreements. Duty drawback is a scheme which allows importers to get the duties paid by them when they export the product. The concept behind the allowance of duty drawback is to encourage trade and investment. Though there is a general trend to eliminate duty drawback schemes, some developing countries, as well as USA are still offering it. However, the region analyzed in this sub-chapter has completely eliminated this feature.

It is necessary to say that RoO provisions can affect the multilateral trade in this region in two ways: in production and administration aspects. From production point of view, firms operating within the RTA region tend to establish their production based on the RTA's RoO in order to receive preferential treatment. For instance, trade with Vietnam has increased 28% in the first year after the effect of the EAEU-Vietnam FTA, because firms in the EAEU and Vietnam started to export more to each other goods which complied with the ROO provisions of the FTA[333]. Here, certain flexibilities in the RoO schemes are quite beneficial for the importers. These are: de minimis rules, allowance of extended level of cumulation such as full/cross/diagonal cumulation, utilization of simpler rules of

333 Vietnam WTO Center <http://wtocenter.vn/other-agreement/vietnam-eaeu-fta-gives-boost-economic-trade-ties> last accessed 26 February 2018.

origin determination method. Although, RoO schemes can be quite complex to comply, these flexibilities within the RTAs soften this process.

From the administrative aspect, when RoO are complex to comply with, firms tend to forego the RoO in order to get an expedited release. However, in this region, this has not been the case. For instance, textiles is the most difficult to comply section for the RoO, however trade in textiles has increased 41% since the conclusion of the EU-Moldova Association Agreement[334].

Examining the innovative and progressive elements of such RTAs on RoO, one can conclude that overall there are few innovative or progressive aspects. However, there are two aspects of these RTAs that we can regard as distinctive. (1) The first distinctive aspect lies in the field of documentary requirements. To be precise, based on the relevant provision of EAEU – Vietnam FTA, encouraging institution of electronic origin certification and verification system is a way forward in the era of globalization and use of high technologies. (2) The second distinctive element is inclusion of products originated in the spacecraft in the list of wholly originating products. This eliminates legal ambiguity regarding any goods that could be produced in outer space, by determining the origin of it.

The last question is to discuss whether any of these provisions can be used in multilateralizing regionalism and what are the costs and gains of this. First and foremost, RoO softening mechanisms such as allowance of diagonal/full cumulation, high share of de minimis which in its turn will facilitate the liberalization of trade can be a part of the multilateralization process. Secondly, documentary requirements, especially practical possibility of self-certification, as well as electronic certification could be employed. This could be done by operationalizing concepts of authorized economic operators. This will reduce the time necessary for import and export, which is a considerable gain for the trade and business handling in the region[335]. The EU Association Agreements have this option, but the analysis showed that EU had less restrictive terms on this matter with the RTAs with its eastern partners, such as Korea and Singapore. A multilateral agreement promoting best practices for conclusion of RTAs could share

---

334 EU – Moldova DCFTA <http://dcfta.md/eng/in-2016-moldova-s-exports-to-european-union-countries-held-a-share-of-over-65-of-total-exports> last accessed 26 February 2018.

335 Olga Biryukova 'Qlobalnie Tsepokci Stoimosti I Voprosi Torqovoy Politiki' (Global value chains and trade policy issues) (2016) 6 Economy and business, p. 6 <https://cyberleninka.ru/article/v/globalnye-tsepochki-stoimosti-i-voprosy-torgovoy-politiki> accessed 22 December 2018.

minimum thresholds for such RoO softening mechanisms which might include easier certification procedures, use of electronic means, promotion of full /diagonal cumulation, allowance of higher share of de minimum, utilization of authorized economic operators. Countries could still choose their implementation method, but existing minimum thresholds would make RoO requirements already easier than it is. Another possible multilateralization could be by adopting a model framework for the whole region, while bilateral RTAs could just adjust to the multilateral framework. In other words, multilateralization of regionalism here would not mean multilateralization of all aspects of RoO, but it would entail multilateralization of best practices, and rules that actually promote trade, as well as have positive impact on the overall trade of the parties.

The main issue for the RoO provisions in this region remains their complexity. There is a necessity is to streamline and simplify the specific RoO for goods. This seems to be the most difficult task in order to reach a consensus among the various states. Eastern European countries are adapting their RoO to EU's Pan-Euro-Med Convention which will guarantee application of the same RoO within the European region. On the other hand, the EAEU RoO and the CIS RoO are quite similar and almost identical. So, it is safe to assume that, there will eventually be 2 models for the RoO in the region analyzed: the EAEU model and the EU model. This would result in partial multilateralization of RoO within the regions.

The reason behind the adoption of RoO is twofold: on the one hand to avoid free-riders, on the other hand to protect local businesses (note the case of RoO for tomato ketchup in NAFTA: the rule requires that ketchup could be tariff free if it is made from fresh tomatoes, but not tomato paste, which effectively protects USA farmers). From this aspect, it should be noted that simplification of RoO, such as allowance of flexible documentary requirements, simpler administration or allowance of diagonal / full cumulation still achieves the main goal of RoO – avoidance of free-riding by non-members, but it also eases the burden on traders. The only remaining issue is the protection of local businesses. In other words, the cost could be loss of the local business which was benefitting from stricter RoO. This can hamper =competition within the market, while more liberal RoO would open the market to more competition. However, even in this scenario, the gains outweigh the costs. Hence, in the long run, higher competition brings know-how, better consumption products and adds to the creativity within the economy.

2. Technical Barriers to Trade (TBT) and Sanitary and Phytosanitary (SPS) Provisions of the RTAs in Eastern Europe, Central Asia and the Caucasus

i. TBT and SPS in the Multilateral Trade

Definition: For many decades, tariffs were considered to be the main barriers to trade. But with conclusion of the GATT and advancement of tariff negotiations, more and more countries started liberalizing their tariffs. This eventually led to the decrease of the protectionist policies caused by high tariffs[336]. In this context, the role of non-tariff measures, including SPS and TBT, started to increase.

TBT: In general, TBT measures are adopted by a country to ensure protection of national security, prevention of deceptive practices, protection of human health and safety, animal and plant health and life and the environment[337]. They consist of 3 elements: (1) technical regulations (2) standards and (3) conformity assessment procedures. Technical regulations are specifications that are mandatory for a certain product to comply. For instance, in most of the countries cigarette packaging should include the health risks that smoking entails and not conforming with this regulation prevents the product from entering the market. Standards, on the other hand, are voluntary to comply with. For instance, production of a good based on "fair trade" principles and putting the "Fair trade" label on it is a voluntary standard which some exporters choose to comply with in order to win certain segment of consumers. Conformity assessment is the sum of procedures necessary to verify whether a product complies with certain technical regulations and standards before it is placed in the market for sale. Conformity assessment procedures include testing, certification, sampling, evaluation and inspection.

SPS: SPS measures are adopted to protect human, animal, plant life and health from SPS risks such as spread of pests, additives, contaminants, diseases, disease-carrying or disease-causing organisms and toxins[338]. The distinction between SPS and TBT measures are in their protection aims. For instance, if a packaging and labeling requirement for an agricultural product is considered to be a TBT

---

336 Qalina Vladimirovna Kuznetsova, *Mejdunarodnaya torqovlya tovarami i usluqami* (International trade of goods and services) (2017, Yurayt, Moscow).

337 ibid.

338 WTO Agreement on Sanitary and Phytosanitary Measures, Art 2 (April 15, 1994) Marrakesh Agreement Establishing the World Trade Organization, Annex 1A <docs.wto.org> accessed 14 November 2017.

measure, then the rule for permitted fertilizer residue in agricultural product is an SPS measure.

Principles: SPS and TBT rules are covered in the respective WTO Agreements on SPS and TBT. These agreements mainly ensure the goals of introduction of SPS and TBT measures, in other words the goals of protection of human, plant, animal health, national security, prevention of deceptive practices and so on are not disguised protectionism. In this context, certain basic principles regarding the TBT and SPS have been incorporated in these agreements: (i) The two main principles of the WTO – MFN and national principle need to be applied to both TBT and SPS measures; (ii) These measures need to be based on international standards. With the SPS, there are 3 sister organizations where SPS measures are encouraged to be based on: Codex Alimentarius, International Office of Epizootics and International Plant Protection Convention. When an SPS measure is based on an international standard, which is accepted by the above mentioned organizations, it is deemed to be based on scientific principles. Requiring higher degree of protection than the international standard is allowed when there is a scientific justification for it. Technical regulations should also be based on international standards when they exist, except when such standards are ineffective or inappropriate to fulfill the legitimate objectives[339]. However, the TBT Agreement does not reference a specific organization for standard setting as was the case with the SPS Agreement. When a technical regulation is based on the international standards and pursues legitimate objectives, it is assumed that this technical regulation does not create an unnecessary burden on international trade. If a technical regulation is not based on international standard, then the country shall publish a notification about it at an early a stage as possible and an interval of time shall exist between adoption and implementation of the technical regulation[340]. (iii) Though protection of health and safety is deemed to be a legitimate object, members must use the least trade-restrictive measure to achieve the SPS protection that they aim at; (iv) Different processes can lead to the protection that is equal to member's own protection level. In such cases, members are required to accept equivalency of SPS and TBT measures of other members, even when these measures are different, as long as they achieve the same level of protection. TBT Agreement also encourages mutual recognition of conformity assessment. When concluding mutual recognition agreements, countries recognize each other's conformity assessment procedures and equivalency of their

339 ibid.
340 ibid.

own standards. Equivalency is unilateral approach, while mutual recognition agreements are reciprocal. A country may just recognize another country's standards and regulations equivalent to its own or may choose to enter into mutual recognition agreement where both parties recognize equivalency of each other[341] . (v) Members notify proposed changes to SPS and TBT regulations to WTO SPS and TBT Committee thus ensuring transparency and predictability of their SPS and TBT policies.

Areas for further development: Current problematic areas within the global trade community regarding the SPS and TBT concern a number of areas:

First of all, although the SPS and TBT measures positively impact the trade, developing countries are struggling to reap gains of these measures[342]. This issue is somewhat more aggravated when they are confronted with private standards. Private standards are standards required by private companies or civil society organizations[343]. Although not mandatory, they need to be complied with if a company wants to access consumers of the said private standard imposing body. For instance, small farmers who want to have their produce to be sold in the big supermarket chains of a neighboring country, have to comply not only with the SPS and TBT measures of that country, but also private standards imposed by the said supermarket chain. Private standards become increasingly important with the development of global value chains, as compliance with them might impose financial and administrative constraints of value chain players[344]. How private standards can be streamlined so that they would not hamper the trade has been an ongoing discussion within the WTO for more than a decade, yet there has been no agreement to this day[345]. Some recent RTAs , such as Canada – EU Free Trade Agreement has

341 Roberta Piermartini and Michele Budetta "A Mapping of Regional Rules on Technical Barriers to Trade." (2009) In A. Estevadeordal, K. Suominen, and R. Tech, eds., Regional Rules in the Global Trading System. (Cambridge: Cambridge University Press).

342 Jong Woo Kang, Dorothea Ramizo 'Impact of Sanitary and Phitosanitary Measures and Technical Barriers on International Trade' (2017) Asian Development Bank Paper 82352, p. 22 <https://mpra.ub.uni-muenchen.de/82352/1/MPRA_paper_82352.pdf> accessed 28 April 2019.

343 Fabrizio Meliado 'Private Standards, Trade and Sustainable Development: Policy Options for Collective Action' (2017, ICTSD, Geneva), p. 1.

344 ibid, p. 11.

345 ibid, p. 25.

been successful in providing a set of principles for businesses when they adopt private standards[346].

Secondly, although countries should notify new or changed SPS and TBT regulations to the WTO, there are complaints in the WTO regarding the lack of early warnings and transparency[347]. Not all of the countries are notifying or publicly informing about their changes in the SPS and TBT legislation, which results in unexpected disruption of exports of other members confronted by new SPS/TBT regulations.

Thirdly, regionalization is not always implemented. Regionalization means that when there is a SPS issue in one part of the country, trade regulations should affect only that specific region, bearing in mind that other regions of the country can be free from SPS concerns[348]. This is especially true for large countries, such as the EU, USA, Canada, Russia. However, sometimes countries just use blank SPS bans for the whole country. Though the WTO has developed the guidelines for regionalization, it is still a frequently confronted area in the SPS. For instance, in 2017 Russia raised a trade concern within the WTO regarding EU's non-recognition of regionalization of avian influenza in Russia by banning poultry products from Russia[349]. This is just one of the many instances where issues regarding regionalization is brought within the WTO.

Fourthly, equivalence is rarely recognized and mutual recognition agreements are not easily concluded[350] . Though, in theory it is recognized that the same SPS protection can be achieved by different processes which are deemed to be equivalent, in practice implementation of it has been challenging. This is true especially for developing countries which are not always able to be accepted as equivalent by their trading partners in terms of their SPS and TBT policies. It rarely happens that a country accepts another other country's quality assurance system. It is more often the case that an importer has to go through the

---

346 ibid, p. 29.

347 WTO web-site <https://www.wto.org/english/tratop_e/sps_e/sps_issues_e.htm> accessed 28 April 2019.

348 WTO Committee on Sanitary and Phytosanitary Measures G/SPS/GEN/1552, 16 June 2017.

349 WTO sanitary and Phytosanitary Information Management System <http://spsims.wto.org/en/SpecificTradeConcerns/View/420> accessed 28 April 2019.

350 Roberta Piermartini and Michele Budetta "A Mapping of Regional Rules on Technical Barriers to Trade." (2009) In A. Estevadeordal, K. Suominen, and R. Tech, eds., Regional Rules in the Global Trading System. (Cambridge: Cambridge University Press).

testing, inspection and other procedures in the market where it is importing its goods[351]. If a trader imports to several markets, it will probably have to go through these procedures in several markets as well. Lack of mutual recognition agreements thus leads to burdensome procedures for exporters.

ii. SPS and TBT in the RTAs

The WTO treaties include only general principles and provisions such as the rules on non-discrimination, adherence to international standards, prior publication of regulations before their entry into force. The WTO does not regulate the substance of the SPS or TBT rules. However, it ensures that such rules do not create unnecessary burden to the international trade. In practice, this means that countries all over the world have different rules on SPS and TBT. As such, TBT and SPS rules remain fragmented and chaotic across the globe. Against this background, the role of the RTAs increase, because these agreements lead to harmonization and convergence of the variable rules and regulations across specific regions and groups of countries. This facilitates the work of traders, as well as the governments which control adherence to these rules.

Many RTAs around the globe have now provisions on TBT and SPS issues that go beyond what is already enshrined in the WTO, as they want to capture more of what is already achieved in multilateral arena[352]. There is a trust issue between the WTO members for further liberalization of TBT and SPS[353]. In other words, it requires certain trust between the countries to be able to trust the quality assurance system of the other country. This, however, can be more easily achieved in a smaller environment like RTAs. Moreover, the complexity of the content of SPS and TBT issues, as well as the geographical and cultural differences of the

351 WTO Agreement on Sanitary and Phytosanitary Measures, Art 2 (April 15, 1994) Marrakesh Agreement Establishing the World Trade Organization, Annex 1A <docs.wto.org> accessed 14 November 2017.

352 Andrew Stoler 'TBT and SPS Measures in Practice" chapter in "Preferential Trade Agreement Policies for Development: A Handbook" (2011) World Bank Resources, p. 217 <http://siteresources.worldbank.org/INTRANETTRADE/Resources/C11.pdf> accessed 16 November 2017.

353 Richard Baldwin, Simon Evenett and Richard Low 'Beyond Tariffs: Multilateralising Deeper RTA Commitments' (2007) p. 8 <https://www.wto.org/english/tratop_e/region_e/con_sep07_e/baldwin_evenett_low_e.pdf> accessed 26 March 2018.

countries adopting them make it almost impossible to have one common SPS and TBT system around the world[354].

In general, there are two common RTA models for dealing with problems associated with the diverse nature of TBT and SPS measures across the globe[355]. The first model calls for harmonization of standards, as well as conformity assessment procedures with those of the hub country. This model is widely used by the EU. It should be mentioned here that the EU's rules are somewhat more stringent than the WTO. For instance, while the WTO requires introduction of SPS measures when there is a scientific basis for them, the EU's SPS regulations are not merely based only on scientific basis, but also on caution. It means that if there is an uncertainty with regard to a product, the EU can still prohibit the imports[356].

The second model is where RTAs call for the use of international standards, conclusion of mutual recognition agreement or recognition of equivalence. This system is mostly used with the partners of the USA and in Asia-Pacific region[357]. It should be noted that conclusion of mutual recognition agreements is most widely used TBT liberalization among the developed world[358]. While, the large countries tend to not conclude such agreements with their small and less developed partners, it is very common across the industrial world. However, when such agreement is concluded, neighboring countries also benefit from it. For instance, when the US and the EU concluded mutual recognition agreement and US testing facilities were recognized as equivalent to EU testing facilities, Canadian and Mexican firms were able to use US facilities to export their goods to the EU.

Yet, the scope of SPS and TBT commitments across the RTAs are divergent. While some of the RTAs are merely repeating WTO commitments, there are also a number of RTAs that go beyond the WTO in their scope. For instance,

---

354 ibid.

355 Andrew Stoler 'TBT and SPS Measures in Practice" chapter in "Preferential Trade Agreement Policies for Development: A Handbook" (2011) World Bank Resources, p.217 <http://siteresources.worldbank.org/INTRANETTRADE/Resources/C11.pdf> accessed 16 November 2017.

356 Stephen Wolcock 'EU Policy Towards Free Trade Agreements' (2007) ECIPE Working Paper No 03/2007.

357 ibid.

358 Richard Baldwin, Simon Evenett and Richard Low 'Beyond Tariffs: Multilateralising Deeper RTA Commitments' (2007) p. 8 <https://www.wto.org/english/tratop_e/region_e/con_sep07_e/baldwin_evenett_low_e.pdf> accessed 26 March 2018.

requiring establishment of Joint SPS Committee to resolve the problems arising from SPS matters, or recognizing one country's SPS body as competent authority to allow goods to enter the market of the another country are beyond WTO measures that are present in the current RTAs of the world[359]. In some instances, RTAs also allow for participation of its parties in each other's national standard setting procedures[360].

While usually any liberalization of TBT and SPS laws and regulations effect all trade partners simultaneously, RTAs can also opt that some parts of TBT and SPS liberalization remain purely towards the RTA partners[361]. For instance, they may require that certain measure not to be applied to trade from RTA partners, while the country could apply it towards other trade partners.

iii. SPS and TBT Provisions within the RTAs in Eastern Europe, Central Asia and the Caucasus

(a) The EAEU

In general, the EAEU merely reiterates provisions of the WTO TBT and SPS Agreements with slight differences. However, the legitimate basis for adoption of technical regulations in the EAEU Treaty are wider than the WTO TBT Agreement. For instance, protection of property is a legitimate objective for adoption of relevant technical regulation in the EAEU Treaty, but the TBT Agreement does not mention it. Another example is that the EAEU Treaty uses energy efficiency and resource saving as two legitimate goals[362]. On the contrary, the TBT Agreement specifies protection of environment as a goal for adoption of technical regulation. As it can be seen, environment is a much wider concept compared to energy efficiency and resource saving.

The EAEU Commission approves a list of products to which technical regulations are applicable. Apart from this list, no other goods can be subject to technical regulations. This means that members cannot adopt separate technical

359 OECD (2015), "Regional Trade Agreements and Agriculture", OECD Food, Agriculture and Fisheries Papers, No. 79, OECD Publishing, p. 18.

360 Linda Fulponi, Matthew Shearer and Juliani Almeida 'Regional Trade Agreements – Treatment of Agriculture' (2011) OECD Food, Agriculture and Fisheries Papers, No. 44, OECD Publishing, p. 38.

361 Tracy Ebbs, Michael Trebilcock, *Research Handbook on WTO and Technical Barriers to Trade* (2013, Edward Edgar, UK).

362 EAEU Treaty, Article 52 <www.eaeunion.org> accessed 17 November 2017.

regulations. The technical regulations adopted by the EAEU are directly applicable in all the member countries and are equally equivalent in all of them.

When it comes to the conformity assessment, the EAEU Treaty provides for common rules and methods for analysis, tests and measurements[363]. In general, the EAEU calls for harmonization of legislation on these matters. It also recognizes mutual accreditation of bodies of conformity assessment.

There is a slight difference in the adoption of SPS measures. As mentioned earlier, members cannot adopt their separate technical regulations. It is different with regards to SPS. While the EAEU Commission adopts the common SPS policy, the members keep the right of adopting temporary SPS measures[364]. The Treaty even goes further by allowing temporary veterinary and sanitary measures, if the members receive information from international organizations, member-states and third countries about the deterioration of epizootic situation, but they do not possess scientific evidence about it or they do not have time to present such an evidence in the determined timelines[365]. It shows that the EAEU members can adopt temporary SPS measures without scientific justification, only on the basis of caution. By inserting this measure it seems that the EAEU members did not want to lose control of SPS policy as a whole.

It is interesting to note that the EAEU members, especially Russia, have been using the above-mentioned provision a lot, not only towards third countries, but also towards each other. For instance, Belarus had been complaining that Russia was blocking the import of some Belarusian products, especially foodstuff to its markets[366]. Kazakhstan also stopped imports of several Russian goods on grounds such as non-compatibility with technical regulations or SPS requirements[367].

---

363 ibid, Article 51.

364 ibid, Article 56.

365 ibid, Article 58.

366 Andrey Gurkov 'Цели, средства, результаты торговых войн России' {Tseli, sredstva, rezultati torqovix voyn Rossii, Aims, means and results of the trade wars of Russia} (DW, 28 September 2016) < http://dw.com/p/2Qdo2 > accessed 5 November 2016.

367 'Trade war mounts between Kazakhstan and Russia' (The Moscow times, 13 April 2015) < https://themoscowtimes.com/articles/trade-war-mounts-between-kazakhstan-and-russia-45711> accessed 9 November 2016.

(b) *Association Agreements of the EU with Moldova, Georgia and the Ukraine*

In general, Association Agreements of the EU with Georgia, Moldova and the Ukraine cover the same level of commitments as the SPS and TBT Agreement, but they go in details in providing specific timelines, lists, definitions and procedures.

Association Agreements call for the harmonization of Georgia, Moldova and Ukraine's legislation to that of the EU gradually, by incorporation of necessary regulations, performance of administrative and institutional reforms, provision of transparent and efficient administrative system[368]. These agreements create unilateral commitments for Ukraine, Moldova and Georgia by requiring them to take necessary steps for approximation of their TBT systems with that of the EU. This also includes transposition of the European standards as national standards and letting go of the GOST (regional standards under the Commonwealth of Independent States) standards[369].

With regards to labeling and marking, Association Agreements go into specific details in contrast with the TBT Agreement, which just generally mentions that the technical regulations shall not be disguised restrictions on international trade. The Association Agreement provides for minimization of requirements for labeling and marking and elimination of approval, certification and registration of labels[370].

Once Ukraine, Georgia and Moldova align their legislation on TBT with the EU, special Agreement on Conformity Assessment and Acceptance of Industrial Products will form part of the annexes of the Association Agreements. This agreement will bring trade in goods between the EU and Georgia, Moldova and Ukraine under the same conditions existent between the EU members. This means that the Association Agreements do not recognize equivalency of the conformity assessment of Georgia, Moldova and Ukraine yet. Though free trade agreement have been concluded with these countries, there are still unilateral commitment for the latter parties to incorporate the EU's technical regulation and standard system. Only when they have done that, agreement on

368 EU – Ukraine Association Agreement Article 56 (29 May 2014) <http://trade.ec.europa.eu/doclib/docs/2016/november/tradoc_155103.pdf> accessed 21 November 2017.

369 ibid.

370 ibid, Article 58.

conformity assessment will be concluded paving way to the facilitation of trade in industrial goods.

The same applies for the SPS chapters in the Association Agreements. There are unilateral calls for approximation of legislation of Moldova, Ukraine and Georgia to SPS acquis of the EU. The parties also establish Sanitary and Phytosanitary Management Sub-Committee which monitors the approximation process[371].

The concept of regionalization is further developed in the Association Agreements. The Association Agreements state specific time-frames for application of regionalization decision. For instance, if an exporting country applies for disease-free areas and the importing country has no objections or raises no request for consultation, then after 15 days this status is considered to be accepted[372]. For the pest-free areas, this time frame is 3 months[373].

Section on notification of serious risks for animal, human and plant life and health are also beyond the WTO provisions. They have specific procedures to comply with. For instance, serious risks should be notified within 2 days and notification shall be in writing, consultations for the risks to animal, human or plant health should be held within 15 days, whereas consultations for the risks to animal welfare should be conducted within 20 days of notification of risks[374].

(c) The CIS

The CIS has its own standards setting organization, which is called Euro-Asian Council for Standardization, Metrology and Certification. This organization has adopted several treaties on conformity assessment procedures. One of these treaties provides for recognition of equivalency among the parties[375]. Therefore, among the CIS countries, equivalency of conformity assessment systems are ensured.

The CIS Treaty on Free Trade Area of 2011 gives reference to WTO Agreements on TBT and SPS when regulating these issues and provides that TBT and SPS rules within the free trade area should correspond to these agreements. Thus in theory, SPS and TBT measures within the CIS are compliant with the WTO.

---

371 ibid, Article 63.

372 ibid, Article 182.

373 ibid.

374 ibid, Article 185.

375 Treaty on mutual recognition of the results of accreditation work on conformity assessment procedures (May 21, 2003).

However, in practice, it is not the case, as existence of standards and technical regulations which are remnants of the Soviet Union are a major problem in this region. That is to say, Soviet GOST-standards are applicable throughout the region. These standards, in nature not voluntary, are not compatible with the relevant WTO agreements[376]. They are not based on scientific evidence and lack transparency[377]. Therefore, the CIS countries, especially those that acceded to the WTO, have been in the process of converting GOST standards into international standards and differentiating between voluntary standards and mandatory technical regulations. This system also makes it challenging for these countries to import into EU and other international markets because of the conformity assessment procedures.

iv. Key Findings

This sub-chapter analyzed the SPS and TBT provisions of the RTA in Eastern Europe, Central Asia and the Caucasus and their relationship with respective WTO agreements. During this process, the following main trends regarding the SPS and TBT in the RTAs of the region were observed.

Firstly, both TBT and SPS are an important part of these RTAs. Special attention has been dedicated to these topics in the Association Agreements, CIS and the EAEU Treaty. In comparison, the older bilateral RTAs in the region do not include any provisions on SPS and TBT.

Secondly, most of the provisions in these RTAs are mere repetition of the WTO provisions. These treaties refer to the SPS and TBT Agreements of the WTO. Nonetheless, in contrast with these agreements, the language used in the RTAs are more detailed, specific and mandatory.

Thirdly, harmonization is the main method used in the region. Usually RTAs have 3 type of commitments: harmonization of norms, mutual recognition of norms and mutual recognition of certification procedures[378]. The RTAs in this region call for harmonization of the norms. In the case of the Association Agreements, Ukraine, Georgia and Moldova are supposed to harmonize their norms

---

376 'Food Safety and Agricultural Health Management' (2007) World Bank Report No.40069-RU.

377 ibid.

378 Roberta Piermartini and Michele Budetta "A Mapping of Regional Rules on Technical Barriers to Trade." (2009) In A. Estevadeordal, K. Suominen, and R. Tech, eds., Regional Rules in the Global Trading System. (Cambridge: Cambridge University Press), p. 291.

to that of the EU. In the case of the EAEU, Russia is taken as a model for harmonization. As it can be seen, bigger trading partners usually urge their smaller trading partners to harmonize their norms to that of bigger party. Equivalency of norms and certification procedures are not guaranteed in the Association Agreements. However, the mutual recognition of the certification procedures is present in the EAEU and CIS.

Fourthly, TBT and SPS policy in the RTAs is institutionalized. Association Agreements have specific Committees on this matter, the EAEU has specific section within the EAEU Commission dealing with this matter, and the CIS holds regular meetings on SPS and TBT. Disputes or trade concerns can be brought within these mechanisms, as well as within the EAEU or the Economic Court of the CIS.

The provisions on SPS and TBT positively affect the trade in the region by transposing Soviet GOST standards to internationally accepted standards. In doing so, both Association Agreements and the EAEU make it possible for the companies from the former Soviet Union countries to reach further markets and thus they further develop multilateral trade. Moreover, these RTAs ensure the harmonization of the SPS and TBT systems in the region. Availing of harmonized system reduces transaction costs for the companies operating in the region. By harmonizing the legislation, most of the changes affect not only the RTA partner, but also all the trade partners. So, effects of SPS and TBT liberalization in the RTAs can be seen on non-RTA partners as well.

Although most of the provisions of these RTAs are merely repetition of the WTO Agreement on TBT and SPS, there are some areas in the SPS and TBT sections of the Association Agreements with Georgia, Ukraine and Moldova that further developed WTO law. For instance, the concept of regionalization is more elaborated in the Association Agreements. As was elaborated earlier, this is one of the issues that is tackled more and more often in multilateral negotiations. Association Agreements further developed WTO law also by providing minimization of labeling and marking requirements for products. However, the subchapter failed to find any innovative or progressive elements among the SPS and TBT provisions of these RTAs. Nonetheless, the concept of regionalization and the minimization of labeling and marking requirements can still be used in the multilateralization of regionalism.

The main gain of the multilateralization of TBT and SPS policy of the region will be simplification of trade and business handling in the region and thus increase of trade and investment. In this road the main barrier so far seems to be the governments' willingness to liberalize. There are still a number of problematic areas that are still present in the region regarding the TBT and SPS policies.

For instance, inclusion of protection of property as legitimate basis for introduction of technical regulation in the EAEU limits the trade freedom. Secondly, it is possible to adopt SPS measures, even though temporary, on the basis of caution, but not scientific evidence. Lastly, there are still some CIS countries utilizing GOST standards and it is necessary for them pave way for the standards and technical regulations that are internationally recognized.

When it comes to the cost of multilateralization of SPS and TBT policy, there are a couple of points to take into account. SPS and TBT policies of the region are harmonized either to that of the EU or of Russia. However, the EU and Russia's SPS and TBT policies are not fully compatible with each-other. This in essence means that the best way forward in multilateralization of SPS and TBT policies in the region is through mutual recognition of SPS and TBT policies. Furthermore, chances are high that it might not be feasible for all the countries in the region to have the same technical regulations, SPS measures and standards. So, multilateralization process should not aim for harmonization and having the same SPS and TBT policy across the region. It should rather aim at achieving mutual recognition and equivalence system, in which each country would recognize as equivalent the other country's SPS and TBT policy, albeit the difference. This will allow for co-existence of EU and Russia's own SPS and TBT policies. It will also take into consideration of differences in geographical and cultural characteristics of countries when they are designing their SPS and TBT policies.

3. Transparency and Trade Facilitation Provisions of the RTAs in Eastern Europe, Central Asia and the Caucasus Region

i. Trade Facilitation and Transparency Harmonization across the Globe

In the global framework, there are a number of agreements that deal with transparency and trade facilitation. For instance, the WCO Revised Kyoto Convention, International Maritime Organization Guidelines for the Use of Electronic Certificates and Amendments to the Annex to the Convention on Facilitation of International Maritime Traffic, United Nations Centre for Trade Facilitation and Electronic Business Recommendations and Guidelines are all important instruments that impact global trade relations[379] . But these documents have not been

379 See: Amendments to the Annex to the Convention on Facilitation of International Maritime Traffic (7 July 2005) <www.imo.org> accessed 5 April 2017. These

sufficient for harmonizing the trade facilitation and transparency provisions, because some of them are merely recommendations and have no binding force, while the others have a limited membership and do not apply to a wide range of countries.

Trade facilitation topic was added to the WTO negotiations mandate during Singapore Ministerial[380]. However, for many years, the WTO could not make any progress on this topic. Up until recently, the WTO rules on trade facilitation comprised of three articles of the GATT. Namely, Article V (Freedom of transit), Article VIII (fees and formalities connected with Importation and Exportation) and Article X (Publication and administration of trade regulations). In Bali Ministerial Conference, the WTO members managed to adopt Trade Facilitation Agreement which came into force on 22 February 2017[381]. This was a landmark agreement that encompassed all the above-mentioned GATT provisions, as well as a vast area of other provisions for trade facilitation and transparency. It is estimated that if all the provisions in this agreement are implemented, then the world GDP could be increased by 4.7%[382].

It is also the first agreement that categorizes its provisions according to the needs of developing and least-developed countries[383]. In fact, there are three

amendments are for facilitating clearance and release of cargo and persons. International Maritime Organization Guidelines for the Use of Electronic Certificates (20 April 2016) <www.imo.org> accessed 5 April 2017. These guidelines encourage use and acceptance of electronic certificates.
United Nations Center for Trade Facilitation and Electronic Business (UN/CEFACT) Recommendation and Guidelines on establishing a Single Window (Recommendations 33) (July 2005) and United Nations Center for Trade Facilitation and Electronic Business Recommendation on Establishing a Legal Framework for International Trade Single Window (Recommendation 35) (December 2010) <www.unece.org> accessed 5 July 2017. These recommendations focus on improving policies and practices for establishment and operation of single window.

380 Elisha Tsume 'Soqlasheniye ob uproshenii prosedur torqovli: vozmojnosti i uqrozi dlya chastnoqo sektora s tochki zreniiya razvivayushixsya stran' (Trade Facilitation Agreement: opportunities and threats for the private sector from the point of view of the developing states) (2014) Tamojenniy nauchniy journal 2.

381 WTO Trade Facilitation Agreement (7 December 2013), Bali Ministerial Decision <http://docsonline.wto.org> accessed 03 April 2017.

382 Tatyana Isachenko 'Soqlasheniye po uprosheniyu procedur torqovli otkrivaet novie vozmojnosti' (Agreement on Trade Facilitation opens new opportunities) (2014) 7 (1) Mosti, p. 10.

383 WTO Trade Facilitation Agreement, Article 13 (7 December 2013), Bali Ministerial Decision <http://docsonline.wto.org> accessed 03 April 2017.

categories of commitments: Category A – where a member undertakes to implement within 1 year after the entry of the Agreement, Category B – where a member needs a transition period for implementation of commitments and Category C – where a member needs not only a transitional period, but also assistance and support. The only commitment that cannot be categorized is the obligation to establish national trade facilitation committee intertwined in Article 23.2.

What does "facilitating trade" encompass? There are a number of definitions across the trade literature. WTO defines it as "simplification, harmonization and modernization of import and export procedures"[384]. According to the OECD, which is one of the main institutions that has researched extensively trade facilitation, trade facilitation is a compilation of measures that smoothes the flow of trade[385]. In a narrow sense, it encompasses measures that make goods pass through borders more easily. However, in today's global trade transactions, trade facilitation is more than that. It is not only easing of customs procedures and logistics across borders, but it also encompasses facilitation of all other non-tariff barriers (for instance the ability to pay electronically or ability to comment the laws before they are adopted). In this sense, trade facilitation measures can be categorized in four sections: port infrastructure, customs environment, regulatory environment and e-business infrastructures[386].

Based on the gradual transformation of global academia and practitioners thinking on this issue, UN Center for Trade Facilitation and Electronic Business (UN/CEFACT) now defines trade facilitation as "*the simplification, standardization and harmonization of procedures and associated information flows required to move goods from seller to buyer and to make payment*"[387]. This appears to be the most precise definition developed so far.

---

384 WTO <https://www.wto.org/english/tratop_e/tradfa_e/tradfa_e.htm> accessed 18 June 2017.

385 OECD Policy Brief 'Trade Facilitation: The Benefits of Simpler, more Transparent Border Procedures' (OECD Observer, 2003) <www.oecd.org/trade/facilitation/8920454.pdf> accessed 8 April 2017.

386 John S. Wilson, Catherine L. Mann & Thunehiro Otsuki 'Assessing the Benefits of Trade Facilitation: A Global Perspective' (2005), 28/6 World Economy, p. 841 <www.researchgate.net/profile/Tsunehiro_Otsuki/publication/4997218_Assessing_The_Benefits_Of_Trade_Facilitation_A_Global_Perspective/links/02e7e52308a1ac8ef8000000.pdf> accessed 8 April 2017.

387 Mario Apostolov 'Mexanizmi uprosheniya procedure torqovli v reqionalnoy torqovoy inteqracii' (Mechanisms of facilitation of trade procedures in regional trade integration), Eurasian Commission publication p. 5 <http://www.eurasiancommission.org/

When it comes to the definition of the transparency, it should be noted that these are intertwined concepts. Trade facilitation and transparency are so interrelated that UN/CEFACT defines transparency as the fundamental principle of trade facilitation[388]. Transparency ensures that countries make their foreign trade policies and regulations available for all the interested trade parties. It is essential for any party to be able to get the full picture of all practices and regulations before they make a decision to enter the market. This is the reason why trade facilitation and transparency are examined together in this sub-chapter.

In today's trade literature, it is generally accepted that trade facilitation and transparency ease the trade. Estimates show that, revenue loss from inefficient border management can add up to 5% of GDP sometimes[389]. Every time security measures in international trade and transport are increased by 1%, the global welfare is reduced by 75 million USD[390]. So, facilitating trade and enhancing transparency benefits both the exporters and importers, as well as increases GDP. Moreover, the OECD predicts that trade costs which result from non-flexible customs procedures and non-tariff barriers could be reduced by 14.5% with full implementation of trade facilitation measures[391].

ii. Trade Facilitation and Transparency and the RTAs

The following conclusions can be put forward based on the trade facilitation and transparency measures in the RTAs. Firstly, trade facilitation and transparency are new topics in the context of multilateral trade. Therefore, not surprisingly the older RTAs have barely any provisions on such measures. Yet it should also be noted that WTO Agreement on Trade Facilitation has benefitted from trade facilitation and transparency measures contained in different RTAs of the world. The

---

ru/act/integr_i_makroec/dep_makroec_pol/seminar/Documents/article%20on%20MA%20presentation%20v3%20clean.pdf> accessed 19 December 2017.

388 See UN/CEFACT 'Trade facilitation – principles and benefits' <www.tfig.unece.org/details.html> accessed 8 April 2017.

389 OECD Policy Brief 'Trade Facilitation: The Benefits of Simpler, more Transparent Border Procedures' (OECD Observer, 2003) <www.oecd.org/trade/facilitation/8920454.pdf> accessed 8 April 2017.

390 Yuriy Vasilevic Kosov, Andrey Vasilevic Toropiqin, Aleksandr Anatolevic Marishev 'Uprosheniye prosedur mirovoy torqovli: problema i puti resheniya' (Simplification of global trade procedures: problems and solution ways) (2014) Управленческое консультирование 8.

391 David Shark 'Benefits of WTO's Trade Facilitation Agreement' (Speech delivered in Tajikistan, 1 June 2015).

commitments enshrined in this landmark WTO agreement was a result of compilation of best practices across RTAs and national experiences. However, before the WTO Agreement on Trade Facilitation was concluded, the approaches of the RTAs for trade facilitation and transparency differed. So, WTO Agreement was successful in multilateralization of regionalism in trade facilitation and transparency, as it introduced a single approach to follow.

As a result of WTO Agreement on Trade Facilitation, there are more and more trade facilitation and transparency provisions being included in the RTAs[392]. Neufeld in her research analyzes the scope of the 28 trade facilitation measures of the WTO Agreement on Trade Facilitation that have been included in the RTAs. In her analysis, she finds that while Russia, Azerbaijan, Central Asian Countries and Armenia have quite low coverage (approximately 5 out of 28 commitments), the highest share is the EU (25 commitments) and in the context of Eastern Europe it is Georgia, Ukraine and Moldova (20). This sub-chapter would partly agree with this conclusion, while partly disagree. Indeed it is true that Azerbaijan, Turkmenistan Uzbekistan have quite low coverage of these measures, yet the EAEU (Russia, Belarus Kazakhstan, Kyrgyz Republic, Armenia) in its newly drafted Customs Code have covered many of these provisions, so currently they have as much coverage as Georgia, Ukraine and Moldova. More information on this topic is given in the next section.

Secondly, some governments tackle trade facilitation and transparency issues unilaterally and not through RTAs or multilateral front. However, this tendency is changing in favor of the multilateral approach. This is true especially for landlocked countries, as they depend on their neighbors for efficiency of the trade facilitation measures[393] . The WTO Agreement on Trade Facilitation is quite young and have been in force since 2017. So, it is understandable that at this point, the WTO law seems to be more developed than the RTA law. However, it is also true that RTA law played its part on development of the Trade Facilitation Agreement. Moreover, considering the vast potential of this field, the positive

392 Nora Neufeld 'Trade Facilitation under the Regional Trade Agreement Umbrella: Origins and Evolution', in *Regional Trade Agreements and the Multilateral Trading System*, edited by Rohini Archaya, (2016, Cambridge University Press, Cambridge).

393 Bernard Hoekman 'The WTO Trade Facilitation Agreement: Milestone, Mirage or Mistake?' (2014) Prepared for a Columbia University/John Hopkins University conference on the world trade system, Washington DC, October 1–2, 2014.

effects of the trade facilitation and transparency on the increase of the trade[394], the dynamics of the integration of this field in the RTAs, it would be logical to assume that in the near future, this field in the RTAs might outgrow the WTO law itself.

Thirdly, when trade facilitation and transparency measures are included in RTAs, they usually apply not only to the RTA counterparts, but in general to all trade partners. For instance, if a state publishes all import/export related documents, it will benefit everyone. This is the reason why some scholars have questioned whether there is a point in including such provisions in the RTAs. Of course, this is not always true. Certain provisions, such as mutual recognition systems, agreement to exchange paperless documents between the RTA parties only, exchange of information within single windows, cooperation within the customs authorities and etc. can be applied narrowly only to the RTA parties. Duval, Neufeld and Utoktham have looked at the question of the impact of inclusion of trade facilitation measures in RTAs[395]. They measured the trade costs after the conclusion of RTAs and pointed out that these trade facilitation measures in the RTAs, especially provisions on transit, transparency and aid-for-trade, have indeed positively impacted on the reduction of the trade costs.

Finally, most trade facilitation and transparency provisions in the RTAs do not have a precise enforcement mechanism. In other words, most of the language used is mainly "endeavor to" instead of "shall" and there is no specific details how the parties undertake to implement certain commitments[396]. Most of the RTAs do not have a dispute settlement procedure to which a counterpart can take the country if it is in breach of this measure[397]. In such circumstances,

394 WTO estimates that full implementation of the trade facilitation measures can increase the global trade by 1 trillion USD each year. See: <https://www.wto.org/english/tratop_e/tradfa_e/tradfa_e.htm> accessed 12 November 2018.

395 Yann Duval, Nora Neufeld, Chortip Utoktham 'Do Trade Facilitation Provisions in Regional Trade Agreements Matter? Impact on Trade Costs and Multilateral Spillovers' (2016) Asia-Pacific Research and Training Network Series Working Paper No164, p. 24.

396 Tom Cachet 'The World Trade Organization Trade Facilitation Agreement: Legal Consequences and Impact on Union Customs Code' (2017) 12 (2) Global Trade and Customs Journal, p. 74.

397 Yann Duval, Nora Neufeld, Chortip Utoktham 'Do Trade Facilitation Provisions in Regional Trade Agreements Matter? Impact on Trade Costs and Multilateral Spillovers' (2016) Asia-Pacific Research and Training Network Series Working Paper , No164,, p. 8.

WTO rises above the RTAs. Though WTO Trade Facilitation Agreement does not always use binding language, unlike RTAs, it has dispute settlement and enforcement mechanisms for Trade Facilitation Agreement, which the members can use when they find their counterpart is in breach.

iii. Core Trade Facilitation and Transparency Measures

There are 12 core trade facilitation and transparency commitments included in the WTO Trade Facilitation Agreement. The first 11 commitments expand and improve GATT Article V (freedom of transit), Article VIII (fees and formalities connected with importation and exportation), Article X (publication and administration of trade regulation), while the last 12th commitment is novel[398]. Each commitment also combines several elements (in total 28). Commitments can be classified in 3 groups, such as mandatory commitments, "best endeavour" commitments and commitments that can become mandatory when a condition is met (using words such as when applicable, as appropriate)[399].

First core commitment is regarding publication and availability of information[400]. It requires all the rules and regulations related to the trade to be published and some of this information to be placed on the internet[401]. Furthermore, this provision requires establishment of Enquiry Points to provide information to the interested parties[402].

Second core commitment is opportunity to comment information before entry into force and consultations[403]. This is a "best endeavor" provision and it enables the traders and interested parties to access the draft laws and regulations related to the trade in goods for commenting purposes. It also ensures that certain time period is made available between introduction and entry of the force of the regulation.

398 Robert McDougall 'Evaluating the Implementation Obligations of the Trade Facilitation Agreement in the Context of Existing Multilateral Trade Rules' (2017) International Center for Trade and Sustainable Development publication, p. 3 <https://www.ictsd.org/sites/default/files/research/evaluating_the_implemenation_of_the_tfa.pdf> accessed 21 April 2019.

399 Antonia Eliason 'The Trade Facilitation Agreement: A New Hope for the World Trade Organization' (2015) 14(4) World Trade Review, p. 653.

400 WTO Trade Facilitation Agreement, Art 1 (7 December 2013), Bali Ministerial Decision <http://docsonline.wto.org> accessed 03 April 2017.

401 ibid, Article 1.2.

402 ibid, Article 1.3.

403 ibid, Article 2.

Third core commitment is advance rulings[404]. Advance rulings are the written decisions that traders and other stakeholders can request the government to issue. For instance, a trader can ask the customs in advance under which tariff heading she or he should classify certain good before the trader imports this good into the territory. It facilitates the clearance of the good and expedites the process. The Trade Facilitation Agreement makes it obligatory for the government to issue advance rulings in a "time-bound and reasonable manner" when the traders and other interested parties have submitted all necessary information. This is a relatively new commitment[405]. Under the agreement, advance rulings are obligatory for the cases of the origin of the good and good's tariff classification[406]. Other cases, such as quotas, exemption from customs duties are not obligatory; however parties are encouraged to do so[407]. In general, advance rulings are binding, unless the government discovers that the information provided by the applicant was false or otherwise misleading and in that case the government can retract its advance ruling[408].

Fourth core commitment relates to procedures for appeal or review[409]. This provision ensures that importers/exporters and other parties enjoy the right to appeal from the customs decisions. This entails not only administrative appeal, but also judicial appeals.

Fifth core commitment is measures to enhance impartiality, non-discrimination and transparency[410]. This commitment concerns mainly SPS measures and is relatively new commitment[411]. It ensures that any enhanced control or inspections

404 ibid, Article 3.

405 Robert McDougall 'Evaluating the Implementation Obligations of the Trade Facilitation Agreement in the Context of Existing Multilateral Trade Rules' (2017) International Center for Trade and Sustainable Development publication, p. 8 <https://www.ictsd.org/sites/default/files/research/evaluating_the_implemenation_of_the_tfa.pdf> accessed 21 April 2019.

406 Trade Facilitation Agreement, Article 3.9 (a).

407 Ibid, Article 3.9 (b).

408 Ibid, Article 3.4 and 3.5.

409 ibid, Article 4.

410 ibid, Article 5.

411 Robert McDougall 'Evaluating the Implementation Obligations of the Trade Facilitation Agreement in the Context of Existing Multilateral Trade Rules' (2017) International Center for Trade and Sustainable Development publication, p. 8 <https://www.ictsd.org/sites/default/files/research/evaluating_the_implemenation_of_the_tfa.pdf> accessed 21 April 2019.

in the border in relation with food, beverages and feedstuff to protect health of human, animals of plants is carried out based on risk and is notified[412]. In cases when the goods are detained, this provision requires that the trader should be notified promptly[413].

Sixth core commitment is disciplines on fees and charges imposed on or in connection with importation and exportation and penalties[414]. This provision further elaborates GATT Article VIII (fees and formalities connected with Importation and Exportation) and eliminates questions of interpretations[415]. It provides that charges and fees associated with import and export of a good should be published, an adequate time should be allocated between their publication and entry into force, they should be periodically reviewed and fees for customs processing should be limited to the cost of the services rendered[416]. Any penalty for the breach of customs law should be based on the facts and circumstances of the case and shall be commensurate with the breach, moreover these breaches should apply only to the person who breached it and should be explained to him in writing[417].

Seventh core commitment is release and clearance of goods[418]. This is the most comprehensive provision and it entails several procedures for expediting processing and release of goods. First of all, members are obliged to accept documents prior to the arrival of the goods[419]. This is the provision that expedites the shipment and clearance of goods. Thus, the trader can submit the documents prior to the actual arrival of the goods and cut the wait time. Secondly, based on the agreement, customs shall allow the release of the goods before the final determination of customs duties, provided that the trader ensures a guarantee[420]. Thirdly, for further expediting the release of the goods, countries have to apply risk management, which implies that not every good should undergo customs checks[421]. Instead, only the goods that are deemed to be high risk based on their

---

412 Trade Facilitation Agreement, Article 5.1.

413 Ibid, Article 5.2.

414 ibid, Article 6.

415 Antonia Eliason 'The Trade Facilitation Agreement: A New Hope for the World Trade Organization' (2015) 14(4) World Trade Review, p. 658.

416 Trade Facilitation Agreement, Article 6.1 and 6.2.

417 Ibid, Article 6.3.

418 ibid, Article 7.

419 ibid, Article 7.1.

420 Ibid, Article 7.3.

421 Ibid, Article 7.4.

nature, origin and etc. should be checked, which facilitates customs processing and release. Fourthly, maintaining post clearance audit is another commitment. This is a procedure in which customs chooses a person/consignment based on the risk assessment and audits it to ensure that they comply with the customs rules and regulations[422]. Fifthly, though the agreement does not make it obligatory, it encourages the parties to accept electronic payments as much as possible[423]. It is also encouraged to publish average release times[424]. In connection with authorized economic operators, the Agreement specifies that, members shall provide at least three facilitating measures for such operators. These measures are requiring lesser documents, deferral of duties, lesser inspections, rapider release, single customs declaration, ease of guarantees, specific premises for clearance[425]. Lastly, members are obliged to provide expedited release for goods. The article specifies that this treatment have to be offered to at least to those shipments arrived by air cargo[426]. In such cases, the documentation has to be lesser and the release should be rapid[427]. Countries are encouraged to specify the minimal value or dutiable amount to qualify for such expedited shipment[428]. Perishable goods are to be accorded priority[429]. The agreement even states that, if possible, member countries should process these goods outside the normal business hours[430].

Eighth core commitment is border agency cooperation[431]. This is a commitment for agencies on the border dealing with import/export and transit procedures to cooperate with each other. Where countries have common borders, they need to coordinate their border procedures.

Ninth core commitment is movement of goods intended for import under customs control[432]. This is a commitment allowing goods to move freely from port of entry to customs point of release, provided that all formalities are met. This

422 Ibid, Article 7.5.
423 Ibid, Article 7.2.
424 Ibid, Article 7.6.
425 ibid, Article 7.7.
426 Ibid, Article 7.8.
427 Ibid, Article 7.8.
428 Ibid, Article 7.8.
429 Ibid, Article 7.9.
430 Ibid, Article 7.9.
431 ibid, Article 8.
432 ibid, Article 9.

provision usually concerns the countries which have dry port or inland container depots, where the goods enter and release from different customs points.

Tenth core commitment is formalities connected with importation, exportation and transit[433]. This trade facilitation measure aims for minimizing documents and formalities, and thus reviewing them periodically and removing when no necessity arises. These formalities and documents in essence must aim to expedite trade procedures, facilitate trade, in particular for perishable goods, and cut down the time and costs. Therefore, paper and electronic copies of the documents are encouraged to be accepted as much as possible. Use of international standards are encouraged. The core commitment is establishment of a single window, where traders submit all the documents in one place. For instance, instead of submitting sanitary certificate to health agency, customs and origin declaration to customs officials, phitosanitary declaration to agriculture agency, the trader can submit everything in one place which could disseminate relevant information in between the line agencies. The Trade Facilitation Agreement forbids the use of pre-shipment inspection for valuation and tariff classification purposes (leaves space for using the inspection for other purposes)[434]. Mandatory use of customs brokers are also eliminated with the adoption of the Trade Facilitation Agreement[435].

Eleventh core commitment is freedom of transit[436]. This is a commitment that transit should be free from fees and charges (except those related to service

433 ibid, Article 10.

434 Pre-shipment inspection is when the importing country makes it mandatory to check the quality of the goods before they are being imported. The rationale behind this inspection is to avoid low quality goods from entering the market. There are only a handful of countries in the world that implement pre-shipment inspection and some of them apply a minimum value threshold to do so. In the region that we are analyzing, only Uzbekistan makes use of pre-shipment inspection. The WTO has Pre-shipment Agreement which contains detailed rules on obligations of members when they require pre-shipment inspection and obligations of exporting members. The Trade Facilitation Agreement is complementing Pre-shipment Agreement.

435 Customs brokers are the intermediaries who submit all the documents on behalf of importers and clear the goods through the customs. Until the entry into force of Trade Facilitation Agreement, some countries required to deal only with specified customs brokers, which resulted in extra costs for importers. So, this article was designed to reduce these costs for the traders.

436 WTO Trade Facilitation Agreement, Article 11 (7 December 2013), Bali Ministerial Decision <http://docsonline.wto.org> accessed 13 May 2017.

charge or administrative costs), any restraints, burdensome documentation and formalities, as well as quality controls.

The twelfth and final core commitment is customs cooperation[437]. This is a similar commitment to border agency cooperation. The only difference is that this commitment specifically requires customs agencies to cooperate and share their best practices.

iv. Trade Facilitation and Transparency Provisions within the RTAs of Eastern Europe, Central Asia and the Caucasus

As trade facilitation and transparency are relatively new topics in the trade literature, many older RTAs do not have provisions on them. However, the more recent RTAs have far more coverage than the WTO Trade Facilitation Agreement. This sub-section will analyze the trade facilitation and transparency measures in the EAEU, EU Association Agreements with Moldova, Georgia and the Ukraine, as well as CIS.

(a) The EAEU

Trade facilitation and transparency are extensively covered in the EAEU Treaty. New Customs Code of the EAEU even further elaborates and specifies trade facilitation measures. While some of these provisions are not fully reflected or not reflected at all in the EAEU, others go beyond what is covered in the WTO Trade Facilitation Agreement.

For instance, publication of trade laws and regulations is one of the trade facilitation measures where EAEU commitment is deeper than the WTO. The EAEU views publication of the measures for the implementation of foreign trade policy as one of the principles of the operation of the foreign trade market[438]. Based on the Article 111 of the EAEU Treaty, it is thus obligatory to publish international treaties within the EAEU, international treaties with third parties and decisions of the union[439]. Not only all the documents have to be published, but the EAEU also requires that all the relevant documents to be placed online. This is not the case with the Article 1 of the WTO Trade Facilitation Agreement, which requires only a limited amount of information to be placed online. Thus, the requirement

---

437 ibid, Article 12.

438 EAEU Treaty, Article 33.2 <docs.eaeunion.org> accessed 05 May 2017.

439 EAEU Treaty, Article 111 <docs.eaeunion.org> accessed 05 May 2017.

of placing all the information online within the EAEU is a measure that goes deeper than the WTO Trade Facilitation Agreement.

Another example is advance submission of documents. Based on the Article 11 of the EAEU Customs Code, advance submission of the documents for the import of a good is mandated[440]. In this way, customs can make necessary risk analysis and choose a relevant control method. While Article 11 of the Trade Facilitation Agreement obliges parties to accept documents when they are submitted in advance, the EAEU makes it obligatory to submit information in advance for the import of goods in all cases. The EAEU also prioritizes electronic customs declarations, which makes it possible to cut the time necessary for the import[441].

On the other hand, certain trade facilitation measures in the EAEU have a limited coverage compared to the WTO Trade Facilitation Agreement. For instance, although Article 111 of the EAEU Treaty contains provision on the right of traders to comment on draft legislation, the exceptions to this rule are quite far-reaching. Generally, Article 111 of the EAEU Treaty requires all legislative pieces to be published at least 30 calendar days before their entry into force[442]. Moreover, they are placed on the official internet web-site of the EAEU. This gives all the interested parties enough time to accustom to the new regulation. However, the exceptions weaken the strong language of the commitment: (i) The first exception is for the decisions of the EAEU which bear urgency for the entry into force. In those instances, the EAEU can determine different proceedings for entry into force. (ii) Second exception is for the documents which are intended for limited circulation. (iii) Third exception is for the decisions of the EAEU Court. The Treaty provides that the Court may determine different entry into force procedures as it may decide so. (iv) The last exception is for the instances when the publication of the document can hinder their implementation or otherwise contradict the public interests. As it can be seen, among these exceptions, the last exception is quite broad and can be loosely interpreted. The EAEU documents do not specify instances when a publication of a normative act of the

440 EAEU Customs Code, Article 11 (26 December 2016) <docs.eaeunion.org> accessed 13 May 2017.

441 Svetlana Starix 'Osobennosti osushestvleniya tamojennoqo dela v ramkax Evraziyskoqo ekonomicheskoqo soyuza' (Characteristing of customs formalities in the framework of the Eurasian Economic Union) (2016) Mejdunarodniy jurnal qumanitarnix I yestestvennix nauk 1 <https://cyberleninka.ru/article/n/osobennosti-osuschestvleniya-tamozhennogo-dela-v-ramkah-evraziyskogo-ekonomicheskogo-soyuza> accessed 29 November 2018.

442 EAEU Treaty, Article 111 <docs.eaeunion.org> accessed 05 May 2017.

EAEU can hinder its implementation. Thus, it gives a broad discretion for the EAEU to determine what to publish and what not to publish.

It should also be mentioned that Article 111 of the EAEU Treaty gives the interested party a right to send their comments and suggestions for the proposed legislation. This does not however mean that they would be taken into consideration. It entirely depends on the EAEU body. The treaty states that collection, analysis and consideration of such comments/suggestions are determined by the body proposing the legislation.

Another example where the EAEU is less liberal compared to the Trade Facilitation Agreement is formalities necessary for the release of the goods. Based on Article 121 of the EAEU Customs Code, release of good before the final determination of customs tariffs and taxes is possible with the condition of the payment of the tariffs and taxes indicated in the customs declaration and provision of the guarantee[443]. However, there is a slight difference in the EAEU Customs Code from the WTO Trade Facilitation Agreement. To be precise, Article 7 of the Trade Facilitation Agreement acknowledges that state parties in return for the release of goods may ask the payment of duties, taxes or provision of guarantee. In other words, the Trade Facilitation Agreement presents options to choose from. In contrast, based on the EAEU Customs Code, importers have to provide both payment of duties and provision of guarantee. The only exception is the authorized economic operators and other cases determined by national legislation of the state-parties[444]. Also, when the customs considers that in relation to the goods concerned, there are possibilities for introduction of a ban, restriction or other measures for the protection of internal market, other than anti-dumping, countervailing or safeguard measures, it will not allow the release of the good before determination of the case details[445]. The latter exception is too broad in its substance. In practice, this gives the customs broad authority to deny the release of the goods upon its will.

Transit is another trade facilitation measure which is reflected to a lesser degree in the EAEU than Article 11 of the Trade Facilitation Agreement. EAEU Treaty does not have any provision on transit, while Customs Code has a whole chapter on the transit movement of the goods[446]. However, unlike the WTO

443 EAEU Customs Code, Article 121 (26 December 2016) <docs.eaeunion.org> accessed 07 May 2017.

444 ibid.

445 ibid.

446 Valentina Vasilyevna Pokrovskaya, *Tamojennoe delo* (Customs work) (2017, Moscow, Yurayt).

Trade Facilitation Agreement, it is more of a procedural nature and it does not elaborate on the rights of the transit holders.

Some of the trade facilitation measures are not per se mentioned in the EAEU normative acts, but they are practically implemented. For instance, The EAEU Treaty is silent on enquiry matters and does not per se create Enquiry Points, however EAEU Commission replies to the enquiries of the interested parties, governments and traders whenever there is a request to do so. So, basically the EAEU Commission performs the function of the Enquiry Point. Here, it should be noted that as a member of the WTO, Russia, the Kyrgyz Republic, Armenia and Kazakhstan already have their own national Enquiry Points on trade facilitation and Belarus is in the process of establishing one. Another example is customs cooperation. Customs cooperation has not been separately reflected in the EAEU Treaty. Nonetheless, the EAEU Commission in its structure has a specific minister in charge for customs cooperation, which specifically deals with this kind of trade facilitation measures.

Some of the trade facilitation and transparency provisions are similar to the Trade Facilitation Agreement, but they are more specific. For instance, advance ruling provision of the EAEU is almost identical to the Article 3 of the Trade Facilitation Agreement and the only difference is the detailed language in contrast to the Trade Facilitation Agreement's general language[447]. For example, while the Trade Facilitation Agreement requires "being time-bound and reasonable" in advance rulings, the EAEU provides specific time-frames for it – 90 calendar days[448]. But, the code also mentions that national customs authorities are free to issue advance ruling earlier if they wish so. The Customs Code has set 3 years for the duration of validity for advance rulings for the tariff classification issues. In case of advance rulings for rules of origin, they are valid by the date of expiration of certificate of origin[449]. Overall, it seems that both 90 calendar days for issuance and 3 years for the duration of validity for advance rulings can fall under the category of "time-bound and reasonable". The grounds for revocation of the advance rulings is similar to the Trade Facilitation Agreement: (i) when the applicant presents false, misleading or incomplete information, (ii) when the customs made mistakes in determining the tariff classification of the good. Like Trade Facilitation Agreement, the EAEU makes it obligatory to issue advance

447 EAEU Customs Code, Articles 21-27, 32-36 (26 December 2016) <docs.eaeunion.org> accessed 07 May 2017.

448 ibid, Article 25.

449 ibid, Article 35.

rulings on tariff classification and rules of origin. It does not make obligatory advance rulings on other matters, but provides for the national authorities to decide the possibility of issuance of advance rulings on other matters, such as customs valuation.

Certain trade facilitation measures are only generally elaborated in the EAEU and the specific details are left to the national authorities. For instance, a whole section of the EAEU Customs Code is dedicated to authorized economic operators, which is a concept that was not present when the EAEU was formed, but it was subsequently adopted[450]. For any importer to be considered as an authorized economic operator, they have to be registered as such by the national customs authorities[451]. So, the matter is left for national authorities to determine who can be classified as an authorized economic operator. Relevant certificate on registration is then issued to such persons. From that moment, the importer is considered to be a low-risk customs control person. The registry of authorized economic operators is put on the respective web-sites of the customs authorities. In order to apply for such status, the importer/exporter should have complied with all the taxes, tariffs, charges by the date of the application, have carried out all his obligations, complied with the time/operation criteria outlined in the Customs Code, lacked any indebtedness or administrative/criminal liability, had relevant financial stability and other criteria determined by the national legislations[452]. Authorized economic operators enjoy the following types of trade facilitation measures[453]: priority customs release, not having to provide the goods for customs declaration, not having to give guarantee for payment of customs duties, taxes, release of goods before declaration, priority status in pilot projects for further trade facilitation measures and so on.

Another example is import, export and transit formalities. Again, the EAEU Treaty provides only some basic understanding and leaves the rest to the national authorities. For instance, on the use of international standards, the EAEU states

---

450 Svetlana Starix 'Osobennosti osushestvleniya tamojennoqo dela v ramkax Evraziyskoqo ekonomicheskoqo soyuza' (Characteristing of customs formalities in the framework of the Eurasian Economic Union) (2016) 1 Mejdunarodniy jurnal qumanitarnix I yestestvennix nauk, p. 46 <https://cyberleninka.ru/article/n/osobennosti-osuschestvleniya-tamozhennogo-dela-v-ramkah-evraziyskogo-ekonomicheskogo-soyuza> accessed 29 November 2018.

451 EAEU Customs Code, Articles 430 (26 December 2016) <docs.eaeunion.org> accessed 07 May 2017.

452 ibid, Article 433.

453 ibid, Article 437.

that intergovernmental standards and technical regulations should be aligned to international or regional standards and technical regulations[454].

In conclusion, some measures such as authorized economic operators, import, export and transit formalities are left to national authorities within the EAEU. Some measures such as transit, enquiry points, release of goods are not fully reflected in the EAEU. However, overall the EAEU has encompassed major trade facilitation measures and in some instances, such as publication of laws and regulations and advance submission of documents, EAEU has even been more liberal than the WTO. It is also observed that, some of the trade facilitation measures, such as authorized economic operators were adopted by the EAEU subsequently. This shows that EAEU has more leverage to adapt to the constantly changing realities of trade and it is easier to introduce a new trade facilitation measure in the EAEU rather than currently in the WTO. So, although at this point of moment the EAEU is less liberal in some trade facilitation measures mentioned above, it is not excluded that they will be adopted in the coming years.

(b) *The Association Agreements of the EU with Moldova, Georgia and the Ukraine*

In general, Association Agreements go beyond and deeper than the WTO Trade Facilitation Agreement in the area of trade facilitation and transparency measures. However, there are still some trade facilitation measures in the Association Agreements that are still lagging behind the multilateral standards.

Association Agreements have a whole chapter on transparency. Even beyond that chapter, in different sections they require specifically publication and availability of various information. The coverage of the measures that are supposed to be published based on these agreements are much broader than the WTO Trade Facilitation Agreement. For instance, Association Agreements require publication of juridical decisions, administrative rulings and any other measure, interpretation or requirement which has impact on trade[455]. As can be seen, this is a much broader approach than the commitment enshrined in the WTO. Association Agreements go further in another point as well. Not only such documents should be published, but also rationale and explanation should be given

454 EAEU Treaty, Articles 51, 54 <www.eaeunion.org> accessed 06 May 2017.

455 EU – Moldova Association Agreement Articles 355 and 357 (29 May 2014) <trade.ec.euorpa.eu/doclib/docs/2016/November/tradoc_155103.pdf> accessed 21 May 2017.

for introduction of them[456]. Unlike the EAEU, the Association Agreements in a written form, authorize creation of Enquiry Points to answer the request for information pertaining to the DCFTAs[457].

Appeal or review right is also enshrined in the Association Agreements[458]. While Article 4 of the WTO Trade Facilitation Agreement only states that the right to appeal has to be non-discriminatory, Association Agreements go further and add that they should be "prompt, effective, easily accessible and costs shall be reasonable". Special attention should be given to the last part[459]. Thus, by using this wording, Association Agreements require that appeal procedure from the customs decisions should not be expensive for traders. This is quite a distinctive aspect of these agreements.

Mandatory use of customs brokers, pre-shipment or destination inspections are eliminated in the Association Agreements[460]. While the WTO Trade Facilitation Agreement eliminates pre-shipment inspection for tariff-classification and customs valuation, in contrast, Association Agreements do not differentiate between the purposes of the pre-shipment inspections and the language calls for elimination of conditions for mandatory use of pre-shipment and destination inspections.

The Association Agreements go really into detail and beyond what is enshrined in WTO Trade Facilitation Agreement on fees and charges associated with import/export and transit. In other words, not only do they provide that fees and charges should be limited to the cost of the service rendered, but also they note that they should not be calculated on ad-valorem basis. Moreover, Association Agreements specify that customs authorities should apply fees and charges only if the declarant asks for services outside normal operation hours, conditions or premises[461]. Thus, it is clear from this provision that customs authorities cannot impose specific duties, nor charge for services if it is within normal operation hours/premises. Since post-Soviet countries usually charged specific fees and charges which were not commensurate with the cost of the services rendered,

---

456 ibid.

457 ibid, Article 358.

458 ibid, Article 193.

459 ibid.

460 EU – Georgia Association Agreement Article 67, 3a,b (29 May 2014) <trade.ec.euorpa.eu/doclib/docs/2016/November/tradoc_155103.pdf> accessed 18 June 2017.

461 EU – Moldova Association Agreement Article 195 (29 May 2014) <trade.ec.euorpa.eu/doclib/docs/2016/November/tradoc_155103.pdf> accessed 5 June 2017.

one can assume that this provision was inserted by the EU to have this matter streamlined. Association Agreements have no penalty provision.

Association Agreements have strong provisions on transit. First of all, they reiterate that the parties are bound by the WTO rules, especially the GATT Article V and any clarification/amendment resulting from the Doha Round[462]. Considering that Trade Facilitation Agreement Article 11 is a part of broader clarification of the GATT Article V resulting from Doha Round, Association Agreements obligate the parties to abide by the relevant provision of the Trade Facilitation Agreement. Moreover, going beyond the WTO, the Association Agreements state that the parties shall pursue "customs transit system interconnectivity"[463]. This interconnectivity is needed for future accession to the common transit system which is currently in place between the EU countries, EFTA members, Turkey, Serbia and Macedonia. The main purpose of the common transit procedure is that relevant duties are suspended when they move from customs point of departure to customs point of destination and thus making transit system much easier for the economic operators[464]. The WTO does not have any provision on this. Even though the Association Agreements merely hint to the future deed at this point, once this becomes practical, it would be a really deep commitment of this given RTA. Even cooperation and coordination provisions of transit agencies in the Association Agreements go beyond the Trade Facilitation Agreement. To be precise, these agreements also call for the promotion of cooperation between government and the private sector in relation to the transit which is something not included in the WTO[465].

Association Agreements also provide the trade facilitation measure which enables the traders with the opportunity to comment on draft laws, albeit with a weaker language. To be precise, the relevant language is "endeavor to publish", "provide reasonable opportunities to comment" and "endeavor to take into account the comments"[466]. However, unlike the EAEU, Association Agreements

---

462 EU – Georgia Association Agreement Article 67, 4a (29 May 2014) <trade.ec.euorpa.eu/doclib/docs/2016/November/tradoc_155103.pdf> accessed 18 June 2017.

463 ibid, 4b.

464 See: EU Transit Manual, (27 April 2016) TAXUD/A2/TRA/003/2016-EN <http://ec.europa.eu/taxation_customs/sites/taxation/files/resources/documents/customs/procedural_aspects/transit/common_community/transit_manual_en.pdf> accessed 18 June 2017.

465 EU – Georgia Association Agreement Article 67, 4c (29 May 2014) <trade.ec.euorpa.eu/doclib/docs/2016/November/tradoc_155103.pdf> accessed 18 June 2017.

466 EU – Moldova Association Agreement Article 357 (29 May 2014) <trade.ec.euorpa.eu/doclib/docs/2016/November/tradoc_155103.pdf> accessed 4 June 2017.

do not provide exceptions for this rule. But, the specific wording used does not make any exception necessary, as Association Agreements make it possible to ground any restriction without in fact breaking the commitment. Thus, it can be concluded that this trade facilitation commitment in the RTAs is almost repeating what the WTO Trade Facilitation Agreement is providing.

Association Agreements provide advance binding rulings for tariff classification and rules of origin[467]. Unlike the EAEU, the Association Agreements do not provide any details for advance rulings, so this matter is left to the national authorities. The only detail is that the ruling can be revoked/annulled only after notification of the importer. Also, only when the ruling is based on incorrect/incomplete information, then it can be retrospectively revoked[468].

Unlike the EAEU, Association Agreements have an established specific mechanism, which is called Customs Sub-Committee. This Sub-Committee deals among other matters with the customs cooperation[469].

Unlike the EAEU, Association Agreements do not have extensive coverage of trade facilitation measures on release and clearance such as detailed rules on accepting documents prior to the arrival of goods, expedited release, releasing the goods before the determination of customs duties, accepting electronic payments, publishing release times. Only authorized economic operator concept is introduced, however even this concept has not been thoroughly explained. Association Agreements only mention that customs and trade legislation should "avoid unnecessary or discriminatory burden" and "provide further facilitation" for economic operators[470]. As such, trade facilitation measures on release and clearance are mainly left to the national authorities, while the EAEU deals with these issues in its Customs Code. This is understandable, because the EAEU is a higher integration unit, while the Association Agreements are merely broad and extensive free trade agreements.

(c) The CIS

The CIS does not have detailed trade facilitation and transit measures as does the EAEU or the Association Agreements and even those that are contained in the

467 ibid, Article 193.

468 ibid.

469 EU – Georgia Association Agreement Article 74 (29 May 2014) <trade.ec.euorpa.eu/doclib/docs/2016/November/tradoc_155103.pdf> accessed 18 June 2017.

470 EU – Moldova Association Agreement Article 193 (29 May 2014) <trade.ec.euorpa.eu/doclib/docs/2016/November/tradoc_155103.pdf> accessed 5 June 2017.

CIS are not as broad and detailed as the WTO Trade Facilitation Agreements. The CIS merely leaves the trade facilitation and transit issues to the national authorities. The reason for this is because trade facilitation is a new agenda in the trade negotiations and as such, when the CIS trade documents were being drafted, these issues were not introduced.

Transit issues are one of the few trade facilitation measures already contained in the CIS. The CIS Free Trade Agreement of 2011 reiterates the main principles of the GATT Article V commitments regarding the transit, but does not have extensive coverage of the Trade Facilitation Agreement[471]. It also mentions that the transit provision does not encompass pipeline transportation.

Another trade facilitation measure that is covered in the CIS is customs cooperation. The CIS Treaty on Cooperation and Mutual Assistance in Customs Issues regulates the exchange of information between the customs authorities of the member states, as well as provides legal grounds for cooperation[472].

The CIS Treaty on Simplification of Customs Formalities and Customs Controls of the Goods Crossing Between Member States of the Treaty on Free Trade Area stipulates that customs formalities should be simplified between the free trade area members, yet the treaty does not go into details of the trade facilitation measures[473].

v. Key Findings

This sub-chapter analyzed the trade facilitation and transparency provisions in the EAEU, Association Agreements of the EU with Moldova, Georgia and the Ukraine, as well as the CIS.

There are certain general features regarding the trade facilitation and transparency measures in the region. First of all, many elements of the EAEU and the Association Agreements on the trade facilitation and transparency go deeper than the WTO Trade Facilitation Agreement. The WTO Trade Facilitation

471 CIS Treaty on Free Trade Area, Article 7 (18 October 2011) <http://cis.minsk.by/reestr/ru/index.html#reestr/view/text?doc=3183> accessed 14 November 2018.

472 CIS Treaty on Cooperation and Mutual Assistance in Customs Issues (15 April 1994) <http://cis.minsk.by/reestr/ru/index.html#reestr/view/text?doc=336> accessed 14 November 2018.

473 CIS Treaty on Simplification of Customs Formalities and Customs Controls of the Goods Crossing Between Member States of the Treaty on Free Trade Area (8 October 1999) <http://cis.minsk.by/reestr/ru/index.html#reestr/view/text?doc=951> accessed 14 November 2018.

Agreement provides a basis framework for trade facilitation across the world, but this region has much broader scope of commitments both in terms of quantity, but also in depth. For instance, the EAEU requires far more measures to be published and made available, and Association Agreements require to publish the reasoning behind the adoption of certain legislation. Right of appeal is another field which is tackled in a more comprehensive way than the WTO. For instance, Association Agreements require that right of appeal to be cost-effective. In disciplines on fees and charges imposed in connection with importation and exportation, Association Agreements again go further than the WTO specifying that fees and charges for services should be requested only if they are provided outside the normal working hours, as well as that they should not be based on ad-valorem percentage share. Another example is regarding pre-shipment inspection. While WTO eliminates pre-shipment inspection for certain category of activities, Association Agreements ban any kind of mandatory pre-shipment inspection. In transit cooperation, again Association Agreements build grounds for the connectivity of the customs check-points. This would allow for cutting time and costs for traders between the RTA partners. This is an issue not covered by the WTO.

Secondly, trade facilitation and transparency provisions in the region have a binding nature. The WTO Trade Facilitation Agreement was drafted by all the WTO members, so a number of provisions in the agreement have a compromised "best endeavor" language, which gives a discretion to its members on the ways to implement them. On the contrary, because RTAs are concluded with a narrow membership, it is easier to come into common ground, so they have used more of a binding language.

Thirdly, the scope of the domain of the national authorities on the formulation and implementation of relevant trade facilitation measures is different across the region. The WTO Trade Agreement gives the broadest discretion to the national authorities in this regard. Association Agreements also have a tendency to leave some issues to the domain of the national authorities, but the EAEU encompasses more matters within its competence. For instance, when it comes to the details of many trade facilitation measures, Association Agreement would only highlight the general lines and leave the rest to the national authorities. But, the EAEU would go into tiny details in its Customs Code. This is due to the fact that EAEU is an economic union – more advanced RTA compared to Association Agreements which are merely free trade agreements.

Fourthly, certain trade facilitation and transparency issues are either left out or not adequately reflected in the RTAs of the region. There are some sections of the Trade Facilitation Agreement that are either not touched upon in the RTAs or they are introduced with certain limitations. For instance, the procedures for expediting the customs release as enshrined in Article 7 of the Trade Facilitation Agreement is almost completely missing in the Association Agreements. The EAEU has included it partially with limitations. Trade facilitation measures related to SPS are very weakly reflected in the RTAs of the region. Transit is another field in the EAEU which is missing many of the components of the Trade Facilitation Agreement.

In general, trade facilitation and transparency is a gateway for access to other trade liberalization measures. For instance, if customs formalities are burdensome, even if the tariffs are very low, it is very difficult to reap the benefits of such liberalization. Therefore, trade facilitation and transparency per se affect trade liberalization positively. Yet, the effects of trade agreements on trade liberalization cannot be entirely measured. However, there are certain indicators that could be examined such as trade growth, lower level of trade barriers coupled with the consistent reforming procedure and effective implementation[474]. If trade growth is examined, it should be noted that, after entry into force of the RTAs, there have been different trade outlooks across the region. For instance, nowadays Ukraine and Moldova exports more to the EU, but Georgia started to export less. From the EU side, EU started to export less to Moldova[475], but more to the Ukraine[476] and Georgia[477]. So, out of 3 countries in the Association agreement, 2 countries showed positive progress. However, there is not enough data to point that the positive growth rate of the exports were due only to the trade facilitation and transparency provisions. When it comes to the EAEU, the situation is different. The internal trade within the EAEU in 2015 decreased by 25.8% compared to 2014. However, since 2016, a positive growth has been experienced within the EAEU[478]. The negative growth rate observed in 2015 could be well due to the falling oil prices, impact of the sanctions of the European countries

474 'Regional Trade Agreements: Effects on Trade' in *Global Economic Prospects: Trade, Regionalism and Development* (2005, Washington, World Bank publications) pp. 72–73 <http://siteresources.worldbank.org/INTGEP2005/Resources/GEP107053_Ch03.pdf> accessed 24 April 2019.

475 European Commission 'Trade in Goods with Moldova' <http://trade.ec.europa.eu/doclib/docs/2006/september/tradoc_113419.pdf> accessed 7 March 2018.

476 European Commission 'Trade in Goods with Ukraine' <http://trade.ec.europa.eu/doclib/docs/2006/september/tradoc_113419.pdf> accessed 7 March 2018.

477 European Commission 'Trade in Goods with Georgia' <http://trade.ec.europa.eu/doclib/docs/2006/september/tradoc_113383.pdf> accessed 7 March 2018.

478 Eurasian Economic Commission <https://docs.eaeunion.org> accessed 8 March 2018.

and the USA on Russia and the devaluation of the Russian currency. However, growth rates observed since 2016 gives an opportunity to assume that it might be the result of the effect of trade liberalization measures, including transparency and trade facilitation. So, although, increase in the trade flow has not been reliable, it also should be taken into account that, impact of the RTA provisions, especially on transparency and trade facilitation take some time to be observed, so their effect might be seen in a long term, rather than in such a short timeframe.

When the second indicator and third indicator is examined – lower levels of trade barriers coupled with reforms, as well as effective implementation – as it was mentioned above, many RTAs in the region have deep and binding trade facilitation and transit provisions. This in turn lowers the trade barriers in the region comprehensively, yet it is still up to the countries to implement them. Association Agreements, the EAEU and the CIS have a monitoring mechanism, yet these mechanisms are not mandated to force the parties to implement their obligations. So in other words, effectiveness of the RTAs lie completely on whether the parties choose to implement and to introduce relevant reforms.

So all in all, it can be summarized that the RTAs in the region provide a solid foundation for positive trade liberalization and it is up to the parties to effectively implement their commitments.

Coming to the question regarding the multilateralization of regionalism on trade facilitation and transparency, as it was earlier mentioned, currently there is no urgent need for further development of the multilateral trade agreement on this matter. However, RTAs can provide a good example to show what worked well and what did not as a reference point for future development of the multilateral law. Some of these RTAs cover issues that are not present in the WTO agreements. In this context, some parts the trade facilitation and transparency measures of the RTAs further developed the WTO Trade Facilitation Agreement because they introduced new elements that were not present in WTO agreements.

The analysis showed that some of the trade facilitation and transparency provisions could indeed be counted as progressive, although not innovative. For instance, the cost-effectiveness of appeal procedure is a progressive element, which would ensure that appeal from the decisions of customs and border agencies is an accessible option for trader. Because, if appealing from a customs decision is too burdensome, time-consuming and expensive, the right itself does not give much to the traders. Another progressive element is the provision in the Association Agreements on building connectivity between the customs check-points. This measure is facilitating the transit of the goods and expediting the overall shipment process. So, these measures could be utilized in the multilteralization of the regionalism.

Regarding the costs and gains of such multilateralization, one must take into account that the complexity in the region regarding trade facilitation and transparency is that law and practice is not always the same. Especially in the case of the EAEU, there have been numerous incidents with the EAEU countries and its neighbors. Notwithstanding the fact that all these countries (except for Belarus) are members of the WTO and accordingly party to the Trade Facilitation Agreement, the results have not been always compliant with it. For instance, at one point Russia put burdensome transit limitations on Belarus[479]. Another example is the case of the Ukraine, which faced obstacles and restrictions in rail and road transport for its goods transiting through territories of the Russian Federation to Kazakhstan and Kyrgyz Republic. Russia asserted that the restrictions were taken for security considerations as a result of tension between Russia – Ukraine relations in 2014 and were according to Article XXIb of the GATT. This case was eventually taken to the WTO Dispute Settlement Body which concluded that the measures taken by Russia satisfied requirements for Article XXIb and therefore transit restrictions were covered by the said article[480].

So, overall, the main barrier in this multilateralization process is the willingness of the countries to make a real, lasting and practical changes in the trade facilitation area. In other words, the main cost of the multilateralization of trade facilitation and transparency measures in the region seems to be lack of political will. The gains seem to be high – increase of trade, simplification of business handling, generation of more business. Whether the gains will outweigh the cost will be seen in the future.

4. Intellectual Property Provisions of the RTAs in Eastern Europe, Central Asia and the Caucasus

i. Intellectual Property and the WTO

Knowledge and innovation have become major assets nowadays and are traded intensively across the borders. With the increased participation of the countries

479 Qalina Petrovskaya 'Kak Rossiya lishila Belarus statusa tranzitnoy strani' (How Russia made Belarus lose its transit country status) (DW, 14 October 2016) < http://dw.com/p/2RDrV> accessed 7 November 2016.

480 Russia – Measures Covering Traffic in Transit – Report of the WTO Dispute Settlement Panel (5 April 2019) WT/DS512/R.

in global supply chains, the need for more efficient protection of knowledge and innovation has also become a necessity. Thus, there is a growing importance attributed to protection of knowledge and innovation across the world. This has been the main driving factor for the RTAs to include more and more provisions on the intellectual property protection.

Intellectual property rights are dealt mainly in two international organizations: The WTO and the World Intellectual Property Organization (WIPO). Both of them are interconnected, as the relevant agreement of the WTO references to the WIPO's multilateral agreements. Though WIPO agreements also regulate protection of intellectual property, they do not address international trade concerns for such protection. Therefore, this sub-chapter will focus on WTO's Agreement on Trade-related Aspects of Intellectual Property Rights (TRIPS), which forms part of the Uruguay Round agreements.

The adoption of the TRIPS was revolutionary at the time because for the first time the WTO focused not primarily what members should not do when goods and services cross the borders, but what policies they should adopt internally to promote fair exchange of trade. For the first time TRIPS created standards and mechanisms as a component of trade agreement to be harmonized by all WTO members, notwithstanding their development status[481].

The TRIPS builds on the WIPO's agreements and is based on the following core principles: (i) It provides minimum standards of protection for intellectual property. The members are free to put in place greater level of protection, if they desire so[482]; (ii) It provides a set of rules, but leaves the implementation to the national authorities. In other words, members are free to choose their own method of implementation of these rules[483]; (iii) it provides for national treatment and most-favored nation treatment of intellectual property rights[484]; (iv) It operates in close cooperation with Paris, Berne, Rome and Washington treaties

481 John M.Curtis 'Intellectual Property Rights and International Trade' 2012 CIGI Papers No 3 <https://www.cigionline.org/sites/default/files/no.3.pdf> accessed 13 March 2018.

482 Jerome Reichman 'Universal Minimum Standards of Intellectual Property Protection under the TRIPS Component of the WTO Agreement' (1995) 29 International Lawyer, p. 351.

483 Peter K.Yu 'The Objectives and Principles of the TRIPS Agreement' (2009) 46 (979) Houston Law Review, p. 1010.

484 Jerome Reichman 'Universal Minimum Standards of Intellectual Property Protection under the TRIPS Component of the WTO Agreement' (1995) 29 International Lawyer, p. 347.

of the WIPO and expands theses treaties. Members cannot derogate from their obligations under these treaties[485]; (v) intellectual property rules are to serve for advancing technological innovation, transfer and dissemination of technology, not to hinder or block trade in any manner[486].

ii. Specific Elements of Intellectual Property

Objects of intellectual property can be classified in two categories: products of creative work, such as books, songs, films, as well as products of differentiations, such as trademarks (making one good or service distinctive from other), geographical indications. The main elements of intellectual property are the following:

Copyright and the Related Rights: Copyright is one of the most complicated and widely used rights within the intellectual property law. Copyright is "the rights that creators have over their artistic and literary works"[487]. In the trade literature, copyright is usually followed by the term of the "related rights". The related rights are the rights of performers, producers of phonograms and broadcasting organizations which are protected to a certain degree by the TRIPS. For instance, in case of performers, TRIPS grants them a right to bar fixation and reproduction of their performance, as well as public broadcasting and communication of their live performance without their authorization[488].

Trademarks: Trademarks are the signs used to distinguish goods or services from each other. These signs could consist of, but are not limited to, words, letters, numbers, names, colors, figurative elements, and combinations of colors[489]. The main criteria for any sign to be registered as a trademark is its distinctiveness. In other words, trademarks cannot be generic signs, incapable of distinguishing goods and services. The nature of the goods/services does not play any role for the signs to be accepted as trademarks[490].

---

485 Huala Adolf 'Trade Related Aspects of Intellectual Property Law and Developing Countries' (2001) 39-1 Developing Economies, p. 62.

486 ibid, p. 61.

487 WIPO web-site <http://www.wipo.int/copyright/en/> accessed 12 August 2017.

488 ibid, Article 14. There are certain differences between the rights of performance, phonogram producers and broadcasting organizations.

489 WTO Agreement on Trade-Related Aspects of Intellectual Property Rights, Art 15 (April 15, 1994) Marrakesh Agreement Establishing the World Trade Organization, Annex 1C <docs.wto.org> accessed 12 August 2017.

490 ibid, Art 15.4.

Geographical indications: The geographical indications are the signs which help to identify the origin of a good in cases where the origin is the essential criteria for the characteristics, reputation or quality of the good[491]. For instance, Cognac or Champagne all identify the alcohol originating from the territory of France.

Industrial Designs: Industrial designs are "aesthetic or ornamental aspects of an article"[492]. For instance, industrial design can be a specific pattern on a cloth in the fashion industry. However, there are certain criteria for any design to be protected as industrial designs. They have to be new or original and independently created.

Patents: Patents can be granted for protection of any invention, in any technological field, without difference to its place, field and origin, as long as these inventions are new, include an inventive step and can be industrially applied[493]. Inventions, use of which should be banned to protect public order or morality, or in order to protect human, animal and plant health and life, as well as environment can be excluded from the patentability[494]. Some areas, such as methods for the treatment of humans or animals, as well as plants and animals other than micro-organism and biological processes for the production of them can also be excluded from patentability[495].

Undisclosed information: Undisclosed information, as well as data submitted to government and government agencies for obtaining approval for marketing of certain products are protected within the TRIPS[496]. In order for an information to be considered as an undisclosed information, it should be secret (not known among the people that normally deal with this kind of information), have commercial value because of its secrecy, as well as should be protected by its owner because of its secrecy[497].

491 WTO Agreement on Trade-Related Aspects of Intellectual Property Rights, Art 22 (April 15, 1994) Marrakesh Agreement Establishing the World Trade Organization, Annex 1C <docs.wto.org> accessed 20 August 2017.

492 World Intellectual Property Organization official web-site < http://www.wipo.int/designs/en/> accessed 20 August 2017.

493 WTO Agreement on Trade-Related Aspects of Intellectual Property Rights, Art 27 (April 15, 1994) Marrakesh Agreement Establishing the World Trade Organization, Annex 1C <docs.wto.org> accessed 20 August 2017.

494 ibid, Article 27.2.

495 ibid, Article 27.

496 ibid, Article 39.

497 ibid, Article 39.2.

This kind of information is protected in order to promote fair commercial practices[498].

Layout-designs (topographies) of integrated circuits: Basically, integrated circuits are "chips" and "micro-chips". In these integrated circuits, all the elements are assembled in a specific order to create it. The three-dimensional design of this layout is therefore protected. TRIPS refers to the Washington Treaty on Intellectual Property in Respect of Integrated Circuits (Articles 2-7, as well as Art 12 and Art 16.3) and provides commitments in addition to that treaty.

WTO's current agenda for negotiations over intellectual property rights cover issues such as: (i) the TRIPS and public health, in other words possibility to produce generic medicines under compulsory licenses for the countries unable to produce them. (ii) relationship of TRIPS and UN Convention on Biological Diversity, protection of traditional knowledge and folklore, agreeing on patentability of plant and life forms, avoiding biopiracy, which is the unauthorized use of genetic resources or traditional knowledge, (iii) extending higher standards for geographical indications and creating a registry for geographical indications, (iv) ways for promoting technology transfer and innovation which is the major goal for the developing countries, (v) discussion over the transitional period and support needed for LDCs in order to implement the TRIPS, (vi) identifying mechanisms for ensuring effective enforcement procedures for the TRIPS provisions, (vii) coming into an agreement on possibility of non-violation complaints under the TRIPS[499].

It should be added here that with regards to the enforcement of TRIPS, in the last decade the Anti-Counterfeiting Trade Agreement (ACTA) was concluded, however this agreement took place outside the WTO, because members were not able to come into consensus on modalities for further strengthening enforcement mechanisms[500]. The treaty does not have extensive membership. It should

498 Anna Konstantinovna Jarova *Zashita intellektualnoy sobstvennosti* (Protection of intellectual property) (2017, Yurayt, Moscow).

499 Non-violation complaint is when a country goes to the Dispute Settlement Body of the WTO not because another party violated any agreement, but because the other parties action or any situation in the other party deprived it a benefit. Non-violation complaints are allowed for goods and services, but are disputed whether they can be lodged for intellectual property.

500 ACTA was signed in 2011 and it targets trade in counterfeit goods, generic medicines and infringement of copyright over the internet.

be noted that though the EU initially took part in the ACTA negotiations and even signed it, later due to wide-spread protests, it rejected this treaty.

iii. The TRIPS versus RTAs on Intellectual Property

There are some issues to keep in mind with regards to the role of intellectual property provisions in the RTAs. Firstly, the transnational companies and businesses in developed countries push for higher intellectual property protection. After the adoption of the TRIPS, developed countries have been pushing for stronger intellectual property protection. The WTO has not been successful in delivering this outcome for these countries, so RTAs have come into play in this regard. While not all RTAs have intellectual property sections, most of the RTAs entered by developed countries tend to have a special chapter dedicated to this. Thus, many recently concluded RTAs have commitments that go much beyond the TRIPS[501]. This may include extension of patent terms, limiting parallel imports for both patented and copyrighted products/works, specifying intellectual property enforcement mechanisms, creation of new intellectual property areas, expansion of subject matters and rights, elimination of exceptions and so on.

Secondly, *protection of intellectual property is a challenge for developing and least-developed countries.* The TRIPS has provided minimum standards for protection of intellectual property rights. But still these minimum standards are considered to be quite high for the developing and least-developed countries. Having even the minimum TRIPS standard of intellectual property protection across the countries with different socio-economical development is therefore quite challenging[502]. It should be noted that, when it comes to RTAs, developing and least-developed countries have lesser leverage point to oppose to higher protection standards for intellectual property than the WTO and oftentimes developed RTA partners provide market access if the other party has adequate intellectual property protection. Therefore, in order to reap the other benefits of the RTAs, developing and least-developed countries tend to accept these standards when they are joining the RTAs.

---

501 Frederick Abbott 'Intellectual Property Provisions of Bilateral and Regional Free Agreements in Light of US Federal Law' (2006) 12 UNCTAD – ICTSD Project on IPRs and Sustainable Development Issue Paper, p.1.

502 Ben Willis 'The Arguments For and Against TRIPS Agreement' (2013) <http://www.e-ir.info/2013/12/23/the-arguments-for-and-against-the-trips-agreement/> accessed 17 August 2017.

Thirdly, intellectual property liberalization is automatically multilateralized. The TRIPS contains very limited exceptions to the MFN principle. With the exception of the agreements that were in force prior to the entry into force of TRIPS, any international agreement on protection of intellectual property has to be multilateralized. In other words, any privilege, favor, advantage granted to the national of one country, should be accorded to the nationals of all WTO members. Thus, it does not make sense to give better terms for just some partners in regards to IP. Any privilege will be automatically granted to all the WTO members[503]. Therefore, when the RTAs include higher standards of intellectual property protection for the RTA parties, they have to apply the same high protection towards all countries, without exception.

Fourthly, the RTAs have more general and detailed language compared to multilateral agreements. In intellectual property field, the TRIPS does not define the key terms used in the agreement. For instance, it says in Article 25 that independently created industrial designs that are new or original should be protected, however the agreement does not define what is new, what is original and what is independently created. This is also true with regards to patents when it says that patents are protected when they are "new, involve an inventive step and are capable of industrial application"[504]. Instead, these are left to national authorities to define. Most of the times, RTAs with intellectual property provisions define these terms to provide for harmonization of laws and regulations.

Fifthly, protection of intellectual property can at times hinder the access to knowledge. Protection of intellectual property rights and promotion of innovation and creativity is important. But, when it comes to patented drugs and medicines and public health, the issue becomes quite sensitive. Certain patented drugs can be quite costly to use in the developing countries which cannot afford it, however these countries are usually in urgent need of these medicines to fight diseases. This issue was somewhat solved with the Doha Declaration on TRIPS and Public Health of 2001 and General Council Decision of 2003 where the countries were allowed to use parallel importing and compulsory licensing

503 David Vivas-Eugui 'Regional and Bilateral Agreements and a TRIPS-Plus World: the Free Trade Area of Americas' (2002) 1 Quaker United Nations Office, TRIPS Issues Papers, p. 5 <http://homepages.3-c.coop/tansey/pdfs/ftaa-a4.pdf> accessed 27 August 2017.

504 Cynthia Ho 'A collision course between TRIPS flexibilities and Investor-State Proceedings' (2016) 6 (3)k UC Irvine Law Review, p. 491.

with regards to medicines. However, still every compulsory licensing/parallel importing case is allowed only on strictly regulated instances.

iv. Regional Trade Agreements of Eastern Europe, Central Asia and the Caucasus on the Intellectual Property Rights

(a) The EAEU

The EAEU provisions on intellectual property, compared to the Association agreements, do not go generally beyond what is covered in the TRIPS and WIPO treaties, except for instances which will be elaborated in this section. They do not bring anything innovative, neither do they go deeper in their substance. In fact, they either reiterate what is already written on the treaties, or they slightly provide lesser protection than the treaties. For instance, if TRIPS provides obligatory protection for geographical indications, the EAEU leaves it to the national authorities of the member parties to provide them. Basically, if national authorities protect geographical indication, then that geographical indication can be protected within the whole EAEU. If geographical indication is not protected, then the EAEU will not confer protection either.

Another example is non-visible trademarks[505]. The TRIPS left it to the national authorities to decide on this matter. In its turn, the EAEU Treaty does not recognize the marks that are not available in a graphic form[506]. So, basically the smell and sound and taste marks are not recognized within the EAEU region.

However, there are some instances where the EAEU differs from the TRIPS. First of all, the EAEU's list of the intellectual property elements are more extensive than those contained in the TRIPS. It encompasses: copyright and related rights, patents, trademarks, geographical indications, appellations of origin, utility models, industrial designs, trade secrets, topography of integrated circuits and plant variety patents[507].

Secondly, duration of protection of the intellectual property elements are different. For instance, if protection of trademark in TRIPS is merely 7 years, in the

---

505 Non-visible trademarks are non-conventional trademarks such as sound, odour or taste trademarks. For instance, cinnamon smell for a furniture, MGM's lion roar and etc.

506 Protocol on the protection and defense of the rights for the objects of intellectual property, Art 14, Annex 26 to the Treaty on the Establishment of the Eurasian Economic Union (29 May 2014) <docs.eaeunion.org> , accessed 15 August 2017.

507 ibid.

EAEU it is minimum 10 years. However, as it was mentioned before TRIPS is a minimum standards treaty and it is perfectly normal for the countries to go beyond these standards. Inventions, industrial designs and utility models are protected by patents. Patents granted to these inventions, designs and utility models give the right of exclusivity, as well as authorship. The term of duration for such patents differ though. For inventions these patents are for 20 years, while for industrial designs and utility models they are valid for 5 years[508].

Lastly, unlike the EU Association Agreements, the EAEU also have provisions for plant variety and animal breeding protection (which is referred as selective achievements in the EAEU Treaty), which has a term of protection for 25 years[509]. The rights to be granted for the plant and animal breeding holders are left to be determined by the national authorities.

The EAEU is in the process of formation of single system of protection of intellectual property objects[510]. This means that the EAEU national authorities have to coordinate their action on violations of intellectual property rights (warning, investigation, prevention) and they have to harmonize and update their national intellectual property law. The EAEU Commission has the right to develop proposals to improve the functioning of the national authorities[511]. The EAEU is also in the process of formation of single appellation of origin. In other words, in the near future the goods produced within the EAEU will be marked as "Made in the EAEU".

One of the major advantages of the EAEU is that national treatment is provided within the EAEU for all the member states. The trademarks and service marks can be registered as EAEU trademarks and service marks, which would grant them protection within all the EAEU[512].

Moreover, the EAEU Commission has the single customs registry of intellectual property objects (trademarks, service marks, copyright and related rights, as well as appellations of origin). This registry contains intellectual property objects protected by all national authorities. The customs authorities then have to take

508 ibid, Art 27.

509 ibid, Art 33.

510 EAEU Treaty on Coordination of Action for Protection of Rights for the Intellectual Property Objects (8 September 2015) <docs.eaeunion.org> , accessed 15 August 2017.

511 ibid, Art 4.

512 Protocol on the protection and defense of the rights for the objects of intellectual property, Art 14, Annex 26 to the Treaty on the Establishment of the Eurasian Economic Union (29 May 2014) <docs.eaeunion.org> , accessed 15 August 2017.

necessary measures to prevent violations of intellectual property rights to such objects[513].

(b) Association Agreements of the EU with Moldova, Georgia and the Ukraine

Since Association Agreements are the first step in the direction of moving towards the membership of the EU, it is of no surprise that the intellectual property provisions of these agreements are shaped to move these countries closer to EU's policy on intellectual property, namely providing protection for its geographical indications, protecting EU pharmaceutical companies, ensuring that EU's copyright and patents are protected, making enforcement of the intellectual property rights more stringent[514]. Some of these provisions develop further WTO law and go beyond the TRIPS commitments in many instances.

There is a special chapter within the Association Agreements that is devoted to intellectual property issues. Indeed, they specify scope of the commitments contained in these provisions "as complementing and further specifying rights and obligations under the TRIPS and other international agreements on intellectual property"[515]. In other words, it means that that provisions in the Association Agreements go either further or deeper in their substance, as was pointed out above.

Several characteristic traits of the intellectual property provisions of the Association Agreements:

Copyright: The term of duration of the protection for copyright for authors of artistic and literary work is longer than the TRIPS and WIPO's treaties. It is the life of author plus seventy years[516]. However, the 50 year term applies to producers, performers and broadcasting organizations with some exceptions

---

513 EAEU Customs Code, Art 384 (26 December 2016) <docs.eaeunion.org> accessed 13 May 2017.

514 European Commission website, Trade, Intellectual Property <http://ec.europa.eu/trade/policy/accessing-markets/intellectual-property/> accessed 26 April 2019. European Commission Staff Working Document 'Report on the Protection and Enforcement of Intellectual Property Rights in the Third Countries' (21.02.2018) SWD (2018) 47 FINAL <http://trade.ec.europa.eu/doclib/docs/2018/march/tradoc_156634.pdf>.

515 EU – Moldova Association Agreement Article 278 (29 May 2014) <trade.ec.euorpa.eu/doclib/docs/2016/November/tradoc_155103.pdf> accessed 30 August 2017.

516 ibid, Art 286.

where 70 year term applies. In comparison, the TRIPS's term of duration of protection is life of author plus 50 years for artistic and literary work authors, 50 years for performers and producers of phonograms and 20 years for broadcasting organizations.

The Association Agreement also provides for artist's right of resale of arts[517]. This means that the artist gets a royalty from each resale of their work. Although, this right is enshrined in Berne Convention, it has a weak language there and is optional. France was the first country in the world recognizing this right on a mandatory basis, soon followed by the other EU members and adoption of the EU Directive on Resale Rights. However, the right is not universally recognized and has so far remained out of the universal application[518]. Thus, by inclusion in the RTAs, the EU is attempting to expand geographical application of this right, which so far had been difficult to adopt in the multilateral arena.

Trademarks: The provisions on trademarks are fairly few, yet they go deeper in the clarification of the existing TRIPS obligations. For instance, if the TRIPS provides an optional opportunity to oppose the registration of a trademark, the Association Agreements make it mandatory for the parties to provide such opportunities and require it to be adversarial in its procedure[519]. Or if the TRIPS requires the publication of each trademark before or upon its registration, the Association Agreements require them to be in electronic database available to the public[520]. The TRIPS leaves it to national authorities regarding the denial of the trademark, while Association Agreements require the negative decision on the trademark registration to be complemented with the argumentation in writing.

Geographical indications: It should be noted here that geographical indications as a whole were included in the TRIPS as a result of EU's targeted policy, as most of the geographical indications in the world are coming from the EU members. Therefore, geographical indications in the RTAs of EU mostly cover TRIPS+ issues.

The Association Agreements have separate lists annexed on protected geographical indications for agricultural goods, for wines, for spirits and for aromatized

517 ibid, Art 290.

518 Catherine Jewell 'The Artist's Resale Right: A Fair Deal for Visual Artists' (2017) WIPO Magazine <http://www.wipo.int/wipo_magazine/en/2017/03/article_0001.html> accessed 30 August 2017.

519 EU – Moldova Association Agreement Article 293 (29 May 2014) <trade.ec.euorpa.eu/doclib/docs/2016/November/tradoc_155103.pdf> accessed 30 August 2017.

520 ibid.

wines. Based on this list, Moldova, Ukraine and Georgia have to protect these geographical indications. Now, if the TRIPS allows for generic names exception to protect geographical indications, Association Agreements in practice do not allow this, as they have included some generic and semi-generic names such as champagne, madeira, marsala, port in the list of protected geographical indications.

Also, while the TRIPS allows for good faith exception for the protection of trademarks, the Association Agreements do not mention it and exclude this exception from application. Moreover, Association Agreements require that if a trademark is similar to a protected geographical indication, it is a ground for a refusal of registration of that trademark. As it can be seen, the EU has tried to narrow the exceptions for protection of geographical indication and intensify means to protect it. The Association Agreements also intensify the extend of protection by requiring more stringent administrative and customs protection for geographical indications.

Industrial designs: For industrial designs, the Association Agreements clarify criteria when design is considered to be new and original. It also allows for protection of designs that are not registered. The TRIPS allows for 10 years of protection for industrial designs. However term of duration of protection for designs in Association Agreements are different. Here, registered designs are eligible for 25 years of protection, while unregistered designs can be protected for 3 years[521]. Association Agreements also touch upon the relationship of copyright and design and allow for designs to be protected under copyrights[522].

Patents: In the field of patents, the main element of the Association Agreement provisions is prolonging the duration of the term of patent with regards to medicinal and plant protection products, where there is an administrative process for authorizing these products to enter the market. They add maximum of 5 years to the duration of the normal patent term[523]. The Association Agreements have strong data protection provisions for pharmaceutical products and plant protection products, where the administrative authorities cannot disclose the information submitted on such products for market authorization, nor rely on such test data for the approval of other products without the consent of the right holders[524].

521 ibid, Art 309.
522 ibid, Art 311.
523 ibid, Art 314.
524 ibid, Art 315.

The enforcement of intellectual rights chapter in these Association Agreements go really into detail where TRIPS just puts general rules. For instance, if TRIPS just requires that the judicial authorities need to have an authority to order the damages from the infringer of intellectual property rights, the Association Agreements go into detail on what should be included in the calculation of damages[525]. The other example is the legal costs. While the TRIPS mentions that, the parties may provide that the legal costs of the case to be borne by unsuccessful parties, the Association Agreements make it obligatory[526].

So overall, it can be observed throughout the Association Agreements that the scope of the protection of the intellectual property elements are quite high. This concerns especially areas such as enforcement, geographical indications, administration of trademarks. On the one hand, stronger intellectual property provisions might increase foreign direct investment and exports, as well as technology transfer from the EU towards these countries[527]. On the other hand, EU and its Association Agreement partners have different development level; therefore efficient implementation of intellectual property provisions within the Association Agreements might be a challenge for Moldova, Georgia and the Ukraine. If efficiently implemented, the costs of complying with intellectual property provisions can be high for the small and medium sized entrepreneurs of these countries.

(c) The CIS

The CIS has a number of treaties on several aspects of intellectual property, such as Treaty on the Cooperation in the Field of Copyright and Related Rights[528], Treaty on the Prevention of Use of False Trademarks and Geographical Indications[529] and so on. The treaties on intellectual property within the CIS refer to the main WIPO agreements and reiterate commitments arising from them. For instance, the CIS Treaty on the Cooperation in the Field of Copyright and

525 ibid, Art 326.

526 ibid, Art 327.

527 Emmanuel Hassan, Ohio Yaqub, Stephanie Diepeveen, *Intellectual Property and Developing Countries. A review of the literature* (2010, Rand, California), p. 8.

528 CIS Treaty on the Cooperation in the Field of Copyright and Related Rights (6 May 1995) <http://www.wipo.int/wipolex/en/other_treaties/details.jsp?group_id=21&treaty_id=377> accessed 03 September 2017.

529 CIS Treaty on the Prevention of Use of False Trademarks and Geographical Indications (4 June 1999) <http://www.wipo.int/wipolex/en/details.jsp?id=12428> accessed 03 September 2017.

Related Rights obliges member states to take necessary measures in their respective national systems for providing the same level of protection as the Berne Convention. Another example is the Eurasian Patent Convention which provides for supremacy of WIPO's Patent Cooperation Treaty in case of contradiction of the provisions[530].

In the area of patents, the CIS has established a special body – The Eurasian Patent Organization[531]. This is an independent international organization responsible for issuance of Eurasian patents for the inventions that are new, creative and industrially applicable in the territory of the CIS. The Eurasian patents are protected in the territory of the member states of the convention, which are the CIS countries plus Georgia.

One of the interesting treaties within the CIS is the Treaty on Mutual Protection of Interstate Secrets in the area of Legal Protection of Inventions[532]. This treaty makes it obligatory for the members to protect secret inventions of the former Soviet Union and not to disclose this kind of information. Secret inventions are defined in the treaty as the inventions containing state secrets. Any attempt to make these classified information as public should first go through the Temporary Working Group comprised of the members to the treaty.

The main importance of the CIS in the post-Soviet space has been its policy of encouragement of member states to adopt standards of protection of intellectual property objects as laid down in the WIPO's multilateral agreements. The CIS has streamlined this process and provided for exchange of information and practice within the member states. So, although the CIS has not brought anything innovative or progressive in the field of intellectual property, it has been crucial body within the post-Soviet space to encourage harmonization of national legislation with that of the WIPO.

v. Key Findings

This sub-chapter showed that many intellectual property provisions, especially those in Association Agreements further developed WTO law by going deeper,

530 The Eurasian Patent Convention (9 September 1994) <http://cis.minsk.by/reestr/ru/index.html#reestr/view/text?doc=3278> accessed 21 November 2018.

531 ibid.

532 Treaty on Mutual Protection of Interstate Secrets in the area of Legal Protection of Inventions (4 June 1999) <http://cis.minsk.by/reestr/ru/index.html#reestr/view/text?doc=924> accessed 21 November 2018.

adding more details and specificities. The following general points were observed regarding the RTAs in Eastern Europe, Central Asia and the Caucasus:

Firstly, coverage of the intellectual property elements are wider in these RTAs. For instance, while the TRIPS, as well as the many RTAs in the world only cover traditional intellectual property topics such as copyright and related rights, patents, geographical indications, industrial designs, trademarks, layout designs of integrated circuits and undisclosed information, the EAEU also provides protection of plant variety and animal breeding patents.

Secondly, these RTAs are more detailed. The TRIPS provide general contours for enforcement and protection of intellectual property, but RTAs go much deeper in details and thus ensure stronger protection and enforcement of intellectual property rights. These details can be seen in addition of specific time limits and extension of the minimum protection ensured by the TRIPS. Regarding the enforcement the same is true. For instance, the Association Agreements specify the details of calculation of damages which is not preset in the TRIPS or many other RTAs;

Thirdly, some of the provisions in the RTAs make mandatory those rights that were optional in the multilateral agreements. An example can be the right of resale of artists. This right was not included in the TRIPS and was merely optional in Berne Convention. But, Association Agreements require mandatory protection of it. Another example is legal costs. The Association Agreements make it mandatory for unsuccessful parties to bear the legal costs, which is merely optional in the TRIPS;

Fourthly, there are fewer exceptions and derogations from intellectual property protection within these RTAs. For instance, when it comes to geographical indicators, Association Agreements has limited exceptions and derogations from the protection of them compared to the global practice and relevant multilateral agreements;

It should be noted that, among the RTAs in the region, the highest standards for intellectual property protection and enforcement were included in the Association Agreements of the EU with Moldova, Georgia and the Ukraine. The most neutral language was observed in the CIS, leaving most of the protection and enforcement issues to the national authorities of the member states. The EAEU is in the process of further developing its single intellectual property market, so its relevant laws and regulations are constantly under the development.

While the link between intellectual property and increased trade has not been conclusive in the trade literature, the economists tend to agree that higher standards for protection and enforcement of intellectual property result in increased creativity and innovation[533]. When the companies know that their intellectual property products are going to be protected and enforced, they are more willing to export high technology products and invest in knowledge and creativity. From this perspective, it can be assumed that higher protection and enforcement standards for intellectual property enshrined in the Association Agreements create amicable environment for promotion of creativity and knowledge creation. Nonetheless, the implementation and enforcement level of intellectual property is not adequate. In 2018, the EU conducted a survey with regards the situation of intellectual property rights in the third countries[534]. This report only covered Russia and Ukraine from these region. This survey indicated serious problems such as copyright infringement and piracy (Ukraine and Russia), undue restrictions in the requirements of patentability and lack of opposition for trademarks (Russia), burdensome and bureaucratic procedures for protection of trade secrets (Russia), difficulty in obtaining preliminary objections for patents (Russia), efficiency of customs procedures (Ukraine), inefficient regulatory data protection (Ukraine), lack of infringement of copyright on the grounds of bad faith (Ukraine) and so on [535]. Furthermore, the report identified that Ukraine was not implementing its commitments arising from its Association Agreement[536]. As it can be seen, implementation and enforcement of intellectual property in Russia and Ukraine is not satisfactory. Even though the report did not cover other countries in the region, one might assume that the situation will be fairly similar. The reason for this is because the CIS and the EAEU laws are mainly drafted based on the Russian legal system.

It was mentioned earlier that the Association Agreements of the EU with Georgia, Moldova and Ukraine contain higher standards on issues such as geographical indications and enforcement provisions. As it can be seen, the reason why these provisions are reflected in the RTAs is because the WTO and other fora could not agree on further negotiations for liberalization. In this light, it can be said that these RTAs enshrine the intellectual property elements that failed to be

533 John M.Curtis 'Intellectual Property Rights and International Trade' 2012 CIGI Papers No 3, p. 9 <https://www.cigionline.org/sites/default/files/no.3.pdf> accessed 13 March 2018.

534 European Commission Staff Working Document 'Report on the Protection and Enforcement of Intellectual Property Rights in the Third Countries' (21.02.2018) SWD (2018) 47 FINAL <http://trade.ec.europa.eu/doclib/docs/2018/march/tradoc_156634.pdf>

535 ibid, p. 4.

536 ibid, pp. 19–20, pp. 23–24.

tackled within the multilateral fora. For instance, Association Agreements have higher protection standards for geographical indications of wines and spirits. These are the elements that the EU is including with all its trade partners. With the increase of trading partners and RTAs of the EU, these provisions are more widely accepted and included in the RTAs. Wide-spread use of these provisions can lead to easier adoption of them within the multilateral framework.

None of these RTAs have per se been innovative and progressive provisions on intellectual property, yet mandatory protection of resale rights of artists can be considered as such, because no other region in the world ensures mandatory protection of these rights, except those RTAs to which the EU is a party. This right ensures that artists get royalty from the subsequent resale of their art. Considering that EU has been promoting inclusion of this right in the RTAs that it has been concluding, one might assume that the universal application of this right will eventually grow stronger. So, mandatory protection of this right can be included in multilateralization of regionalism.

When it comes to the cost and gains of multilateralization of the intellectual property, there is one big gain for the countries. It would be easier for businesses, especially for small and medium sized entrepreneurs to enter new markets knowing that the intellectual property protection and enforcement rules are fairly similar to their own country vis-a-vis situations when they need to apply for patents in every country they enter or have different level of protection when it comes to their trade secrets.

However, the main problem with the intellectual property is enforcement. Without sound enforcement, multilateralization of intellectual property would not make a tangible impact. Instituting higher enforcement mechanisms require resources, including financial and human resources, which lesser developed countries do not easily have access to. So, multilateralization of intellectual property issues is possible, yet it would need transitional time and assistance for developing and least developed countries to adjust to this process.

5. Summary of the Chapter

This chapter analyzed rules of origin, SPS and TBT, trade facilitation and transparency and intellectual property provisions of the EAEU, CIS and Association Agreements of the EU with Moldova, Georgia and the Ukraine.

It was concluded that, RoO were the most pressing topic for the multilateralization of regionalism and that RoO softening mechanisms (allowance of diagonal/full cumulation, high share of de minimis) and more flexible documentary requirements (possibility of self-certification, electronic certification, operationalization of authorized economic operators concept) could form part of the multilateralization of regionalism. The main issue for the RoO provisions in this region was found to be their complexity. There is a necessity is to streamline and simplify the specific RoO for goods. This seems to be the most difficult task in order to reach a consensus among the various states. However, harmonization of RoO under the EU's Pan-Euro-Med Convention is a positive precedent in this regard which might which might lead to partial multilateralizaiton of RoO within the region. The chapter also concluded that the gains for simplification of the RoO within the region outweighed any possible costs that might occur.

Regarding SPS and TBT, the chapter concluded that by transposing Soviet GOST standards to internationally accepted standards, both Association Agreements and the EAEU make it possible for the companies from the former Soviet Union countries to reach further markets and thus further develop multilateral trade. RTAs also showed how certain RTA provisions on SPS and TBT worked in practice, which could be a working ground for further liberalization of multilateral trade agreements. The chapter suggested concept of regionalization and the minimization of labeling and marking requirements for multilateralization of regionalism. While the main gain of the multilateralization of TBT and SPS policy of the region is simplification of trade and business handling in the region, the main cost is that having the same SPS and TBT policy might not serve the countries. Yet the chapter suggested that multilateralization process should aim for achieving mutual recognition and equivalence system, where each country would recognize as equivalent the other country's SPS and TBT policy, even though it could be different. This will allow the countries to take into consideration their geographical and cultural characteristics when designing proper SPS and TBT policy, yet still be able to export to other countries in the region without hurdles.

When it comes to trade facilitation and transparency, it is one of the topics which are almost automatically multilateralized when they are adopted. The chapter concluded that since WTO Trade Facilitation Agreement was recently adopted, there was no urgent need for further development of the multilateral trade agreement on this matter. However, RTAs could provide a good example to show what worked well and what did not as a reference point for future development of the multilateral law. The chapter suggested that provision requiring the cost-effectiveness of appeal procedure, as well as provision on building connectivity between the customs check-points utilize in the RTAs of the region could also be utilized for any multilateralization process. It was also concluded that the theory and practice of the trade facilitation and transparency in the region were not adequate. While the region had quite progressive trade facilitation and transparency law, there were numerous incidents in which these laws and regulations were not observed. Thus, implementation of trade facilitation measures did not match the commitments enshrined in the RTA.

The chapter elaborated that intellectual property was also one of the areas which was almost always automatically multilateralized. The chapter concluded that the region had higher standards on issues such as geographical indications and enforcement provisions. Since both these areas are the topics where consensus have not been able to be forged within multilateral arena, the chapter hypothesized that with the increase and expansion of the RTAs, these provisions could be more widely accepted and included in the RTAs, which could lead to their eventual multilateralization. Inclusion of resale rights of artists was suggested as another area for multilateralization. The research elaborated that with the protection and enforcement of intellectual property, advancement of knowledge, innovation and investment, as well as increase of business is guaranteed. However, as was the case with trade facilitation and transparency, implementation of intellectual property provisions in the region was not adequate, which hindered the benefits of the RTAs.

Chapter 4 WTO Beyond Provisions of the Regional Trade Agreements in Eastern Europe, Central Asia and the Caucasus and Multilateralization of Regionalism[537]

The aim of this chapter is to introduce the WTO beyond elements of the RTAs in Eastern Europe, Central Asia and Caucasus and show if they can be used in the multilateralization of regionalism. The chapter assesses impact of these elements of the RTAs to the multilateral trade agreements. It analyzes whether these RTAs hinders and/or contributes to the development of multilateral trade negotiations.

This chapter consists of the following sub-sections: investment, competition, and energy. The chapter aims to see how these provisions in these RTAs affect the trade liberalization, if there are any innovative or progressive elements in these RTAs and if so, whether they can be taken as a basis of multilateral negotiations and if any element of the RTAs can be used in multilateralization of regionalism and possible the costs and gains of this.

1. Investment Provisions of the RTAs in Eastern Europe, Central Asia and the Caucasus

i. Investment in Multilateral Trade Agreements

Definition: Foreign direct investment (FDI) is a relationship of management between an investor in a country (home country) and an enterprise in a different country (host country)[538]. The key component of this relationship is that the investor manages the enterprise, which is seen as owning at least 10% share of

537 There is a difference between WTO plus and WTO beyond issues. WTO plus issues simply go deeper in areas covered already by the WTO. WTO beyond (it can also be referred as WTO extra) are the areas not covered by the WTO.

538 UNCTAD 'World Investment Report 2007' (2007): p. 245 <http://unctad.org/en/Docs/wir2007p4_en.pdf> accessed 18 January 2018.

the enterprise[539]. Management aspect is a key difference between foreign direct investment and portfolio investment, where the latter has no management interest. There are three main types of foreign direct investment: (i) equity capital: it is investing in shares of a foreign company, (ii) reinvesting capital: it is reinvesting the earnings from a capital, (iii) intra-company loans: it is lending and borrowing between direct investor and its affiliates[540].

Investment liberalization cover provisions that give better market access to investors, such as entry into market, employment of personnel, market access in services, transfer of funds[541]. Investment protection cover provisions that regulate rights of investors against expropriation, provision of fair and equitable treatment, non-discrimination after the establishment of investment, dispute-settlement, prohibition of performance and ownership requirements[542].

Investment and multilateral framework: Investment is an area closely associated with trade. Not surprisingly, Havana Charter which established International Trade Organization (ITO) contained provisions not only on trade, but also on investment[543]. However, Havana negotiations failed and ITO was never ratified. Subsequently, investment provisions were dropped from the multilateral trade agenda.

The next major step was taken in the Organization for Economic Cooperation and Development (OECD). 1961 OECD Code of Liberalization of Capital Movements and the Code of Liberalization of Current Invisible Operations became a main framework for liberalization of trade and investment[544]. The codes

---

539 OECD 'Benchmark definition of foreign direct investment' (2008) p. 17 <https://www.oecd.org/daf/inv/investmentstatisticsandanalysis/40193734.pdf> accessed 18 January 2018.

540 UNCTAD 'World Investment Report 2007' (2007, United Nations, Geneva and New York), p. 245 <https://unctad.org/en/Docs/wir2007_en.pdf> accessed 18 January 2018.

541 Molly Lesher, Sebastien Mirodout 'Analysis of the economic impact of investment provisions in Regional Trade Agreements' (2005) 36 OECD Trade Policy Paper, p. 61 <http://www.oecd-ilibrary.org/docserver/download/322248021805.pdf?expires=1516769068&id=id&accname=guest&checksum=0909AD65E913DF06FBDEC949206B80EE> accessed 24 January 2018.

542 ibid.

543 Richard Blackhurst, Adriaan Otten, 'Trade and foreign direct investment' (1996) WTO <https://www.wto.org/english/news_e/pres96_e/pr057_e.htm> accessed 18 January 2018.

544 UNCTAD. Investment Provisions in Economic Integration Agreements (2006, United Nations, Geneva and New York), p. 16. <https://unctad.org/en/docs/iteiit200510_en.pdf≥ accessed 17 January 2018.

complemented throughout the years with the decisions and protocols on the principles for liberalization of investment policies.

In 1994 Energy Charter Treaty was adopted which included investment provisions on energy. It provides protection for investment, tackles transit issues in detail and provides for dispute settlement for energy transit. Specifically, under the Energy Charter, there are obligations for the contracting parties to ensure the smooth and non-interrupted transit of energy flows and create non-discriminatory environment by providing national/most-favored nation treatment, as well as protection against non-commercial risks. Moreover, the Charter aims to create stability for investors and host governments by providing a forum for dispute resolution for investor-state and inter-state arbitration, as well as works for the energy efficiency and environmental protection in the member countries.

After the WTO was established, investment was included as one of the 'Singapore issues"[545]. Singapore Ministerial Decision recognized the increasing role of trade and investment on employment, economic growth and development, therefore it established a working group to analyze the relationship of trade and investment[546]. The main task of the Working Group was to provide definitions and scope of investment, relationship between host and home countries, transparency and non-discrimination in application of investment measures, and development associated with investment. However, since there was no consensus among the members, in 2004 investment was taken out of negotiations and the working group was canceled.

Currently, investment issues are partially covered within the following WTO agreements: GATS, TRIPS and Agreement on Trade Related Aspects of Investment Measures (TRIMS). GATS covers investment as a mode of supply of service (Mode 3 – commercial presence). TRIPS protects intellectual property associated with the investment. TRIMS protects investment from trade related measures that are inconsistent with GATT, such as local content or trade balance requirements. In substance, TRIMS only ensures the equality of treatment between imported and local product and does not per se regulate the entry and treatment of investment.

---

545 Singapore issues – trade facilitation, trade and investment, trade and competition, transparency in public procurement – were included in the WTO multilateral negotiations in 1996. However, only trade facilitation topic was preserved in the negotiations and all the other topics were dropped in 2004.

546 Singapore Ministerial Decision. WTO/MIN(96)/DEC, 18 December 1996.

As a result, investment is an area that is not fully regulated in the multilateral framework and thus it is tackled in bilateral and regional forums, such as bilateral investment treaties and the RTAs.

ii Investment in Regional Trade Agreements

Historically, investment issues were included in the friendship, navigation and commerce treaties. The first RTA containing rules on investment was the Rome Treaty on the Establishment of the European Community[547]. It had rules on the right of establishment and non-discrimination principle after the entry into the market. Soon, other RTAs started to emerge and many of them incorporated investment provisions as well. 1957 Agreement on Arab Economic Unity, 1964 Treaty Establishing Customs and Economic Union of Central Africa, 1969 Cartagena Agreement on Andean Community, 1973 Caribbean Common Market Treaty, 1987 ASEAN Agreement for Protection and Promotion of Investments were all among the pioneers in inclusion of different principles for liberalization and protection of investment.

The importance of the RTAs containing investment measures are increasing against a background of non-existence of multilateral agreement on investment. Currently, RTAs together with bilateral investment treaties comprise the main forum for development of practices on investment protection and liberalization. Although investment is mainly regulated through bilateral investment treaties, the scope of inclusion of this topic in the RTAs have also been increasing lately. The RTAs and the bilateral investment treaties differ in many aspects, such as the scope of liberalization and protection of investments, settlement of disputes, existence of action plan to achieve the liberalization and protection, existence of cooperation provisions and so on[548]. However, unlike the bilateral investment treaties, RTAs usually involve more than two parties which contributes to the development of a single framework for protection and liberalization of investment within certain countries[549]. While bilateral investment treaties would cover only investments, the RTAs are concluded with the aim of liberalization of the whole

547 UNCTAD. Investment Provisions in Economic Integration Agreements (2006, United Nations, Geneva and New York), p. 13. <https://unctad.org/en/docs/iteiit200510_en.pdf≥ accessed 17 January 2018.

548 UNCTAD. Investment Provisions in Economic Integration Agreements (2006, United Nations, Geneva and New York), p. 56. <https://unctad.org/en/docs/iteiit200510_en.pdf≥ accessed 17 January 2018.

549 ibid, p. 139.

area of trade and economy, therefore RTAs can be a better choice for countries wishing to integrate[550].

Usually there are 4 main issues with investments that are included in the RTAs. These are protection, cooperation, liberalization and promotion of investments[551]. These measures generally include provisions against expropriation, relevant compensation in case of such expropriation, ability of the investors to freely transfer funds between host and home economy, effective dispute settlement procedures including resort to international arbitration, various incentives for the promotion of investments, most-favored nation and national treatment principles applied to foreign investors, liberalization of barriers to enter the market and so on[552]. The OECD for instance classifies investment provisions of the RTAs in 6 broad categories: (i) pre-establishment phase rules, such as right to establishment, MFN and national treatment; (ii) non-discrimination in post-establishment phase; (iii) investment in services; (iv) investment protection rules; (v) dispute settlement; and (vi) investment promotion[553].

The scope of inclusion of investment provisions among the RTAs also differ from region to region. For instance, NAFTA contains more comprehensive provisions on investment, as this treaty includes similar provisions to bilateral investment treaties of the USA[554]. The OECD analysis shows that in comparison to the NAFTA, the EU RTAs have fewer rules on investment, since most of the investment provisions are usually included in the EU in the bilateral investment treaties[555]. Another considerable difference between NAFTA and the EU lies in

550 ibid, p. 140.

551 ibid.

552 Richard Blackhurst, Adriaan Otten, 'Trade and foreign direct investment' (1996) WTO <https://www.wto.org/english/news_e/pres96_e/pr057_e.htm> accessed 22 January 2018.

553 Molly Lesher, Sebastien Mirodout 'Analysis of the economic impact of investment provisions in Regional Trade Agreements' (2005) 36 OECD Trade Policy Paper, p. 9 <http://www.oecd-ilibrary.org/docserver/download/322248021805.pdf?expires=1516769068&id=id&accname=guest&checksum=0909AD65E913DF06FBDEC949206B80EE> accessed 24 January 2018.

554 UNCTAD. Investment Provisions in Economic Integration Agreements (2006, United Nations, Geneva and New York), p. 20. <https://unctad.org/en/docs/iteiit200510_en.pdf≥ accessed 17 January 2018.

555 Molly Lesher, Sebastien Mirodout 'Analysis of the economic impact of investment provisions in Regional Trade Agreements' (2005) 36 OECD Trade Policy Paper, p. 20 <http://www.oecd-ilibrary.org/docserver/

the substance of investment provisions. Many of the older EU RTAs cover mostly investment liberalization and leave investment protection to the member states. However, this trend is also being changed in more recent RTAs. NAFTA, on the other hand, has detailed provisions both on investment protection and liberalization[556]. Many older EU RTAs are silent on investor-state dispute settlement, while NAFTA and agreements designed after NAFTA contain detailed rules on this. Another example is protection against expropriation. While NAFTA and agreements modeled after NAFTA ensure clear-cut rules for protection from expropriation, the EU agreements are silent about it and leave it completely to national authorities.

iii. Investment and Multilateralization of Regionalism

When it comes to multilateralization of regionalism and investment, there are certain factors to take into account. Firstly, multilateralization of regionalism can be driven if there is a strong multilateral framework with an extensive membership. Unlike areas such as trade facilitation or intellectual property, in the field of investment there is no central framework with comprehensive membership. This makes the multilateralization process more difficult. Organizations like Energy Charter, UNCTAD, WTO, international and regional banks deal only with certain elements of investment. Even though the WTO tried to include investment as an area of negotiation, this attempt was not successful. So, the WTO regulates investment only from the aspect of services liberalization and relationship with trade.

Secondly, investment is an area which is almost in all cases instantly multilateralized. If a RTA includes investment liberalization measures, the implementing party will most probably apply this measure to all its trading partners. Of course, there can be instances where parties can arrange application of such liberalization measures towards each other, such as treating certain foreign investors better and withholding compensation from other parties. But, this is burdensome from administrative aspect and it requires additional resources.

Thirdly, in any multilateralization process, dispute settlement should be central. If there is no strong dispute settlement related to investment, investors will

download/322248021805.pdf?expires=1516769068&id=id&accname=guest&checksum=0909AD65E913DF06FBDEC949206B80EE> accessed 24 January 2018.

556 UNCTAD. Investment Provisions in Economic Integration Agreements (2006, United Nations, Geneva and New York), p. 26. <https://unctad.org/en/docs/iteiit200510_en.pdf≥ accessed 17 January 2018.

not feel protected. It should be noted that, certain frameworks for dispute settlement in the area of investment exist. For instance, arbitration is the most frequent dispute settlement mechanism referred in the investment treaties. International arbitration center of World Bank – International Center for Settlement of Investment Disputes exist to regulate investment disputes. However, arbitration has its own disadvantages. For example, arbitration has asymmetric nature and only investors can start the process, while states cannot initiate arbitration[557]. Many critics of arbitration argue that dispute settlement procedure should allow investor to investor and state to state dispute resolution. Furthermore, the ad hoc nature of arbitration leads to inconsistent decisions[558]. There are divergent arbitration decisions on comparable facts which augments the fragmentation of investment law[559] Not surprisingly, Transatlantic Trade and Investment Partnership envisaged creation of a separate investment court and an appellate body instead of referring cases to arbitration[560] .

iv. Investment Provisions within the RTAs in Eastern Europe, Central Asia and the Caucasus

(a) The EAEU

Attracting foreign investment is one of the main priorities of the foreign economic policies of the members[561] . Therefore, the EAEU tackles investment as a

557 Jonathan Ketcheson 'Investment Arbitration: Learning from Experience' in 'Shifting Paradigms in International Investment Law: More Balanced, Less Isolated, Increasingly Diversified' edited by S. Hindelang and M. Krajewski (2016, Oxford University Press, UK).

558 ibid.

559 Stephan Schill 'The Multilateralization of International Investment Law: Emergence of a Multilateral System of Investment Protection on Bilateral Grounds' (2010) 2 (1) Trade, Law and Development, p. 62 <http://www.tradelawdevelopment.com/index.php/tld/article/viewFile/2%281%29%20TL%26D%2059%20%282010%29/41> accessed 21 December 2018.

560 Jonathan Ketcheson 'Investment Arbitration: Learning from Experience' in 'Shifting Paradigms in International Investment Law: More Balanced, Less Isolated, Increasingly Diversified' edited by S. Hindelang and M. Krajewski (2016, Oxford University Press, UK).

561 Lira Shipovich 'Vliyania Inostrannix Investisiy na Finansoviy Krizis v Rossii' (Impact of foreign investment in financial crisis in Russia) (2013) 32 (323) Vestnik Chelyabinskoqo Qosudarstvennoqo Universiteta, p. 43 <https://cyberleninka.ru/

separate issue and gives considerable attention to it. The agreement uses asset-based definition when clarifying the scope of the investment. Thus, investment in the EAEU means material and non-material assets, invested by investor of one member-state in another member-state, which includes inter alia financial resources, stocks, right to do investment in extraction of natural resources, asset and other rights which have financial value[562].

Unlike the EU Association Agreements, the EAEU Treaty contains provisions both on protection and liberalization of the investments. Thus, in this aspect the EAEU is modeled after NAFTA. The EAEU covers both investment liberalization and services liberalization. The main principle regarding the investment liberalization is that EAEU countries commit not to adopt new discriminatory measures in trade in services and establishment and functioning of the juridical persons of members states in other member states[563]. They also commit to gradually liberalize the conditions of mutual trade in services, establishment, functioning and realization of investments[564]. In regulation of these matters, member-states agree to provide administrative cooperation to each other, which includes exchange of information, establishment of a mechanism for prevention of violations of rights of consumers by service suppliers. However, apart from services sectors liberalization plans, the Treaty does not specify what types of liberalization steps should be taken towards investors. It leaves it to the national authorities.

The only notable investment liberalization measure is when member states cancel any restriction in payments and money transfers related to trade in services, establishment and functioning of investments[565]. The exception is balance of payment difficulties, when member can restrict such transfers and payments for a limited period[566].

---

article/v/vliyanie-inostrannyh-investitsiy-na-finansovyy-krizis-v-rossii> accessed 21 December 2018.

562 EAEU Treaty, Protocol No16 On trade in services, establishment, functioning and realization of investments, Article 6 <https://docs.eaeunion.org/docs/ru-ru/0043610/itia_05062014> accessed 02 February 2018.

563 EAEU Treaty, Article 66, <https://docs.eaeunion.org/docs/ru-ru/0043610/itia_05062014> accessed 02 February 2018.

564 ibid.

565 EAEU Treaty, Protocol No16 On trade in services, establishment, functioning and realization of investments, Article 8 <https://docs.eaeunion.org/docs/ru-ru/0043610/itia_05062014> accessed 02 February 2018.

566 ibid, Article 11–14.

When it comes to investment protection, dispute settlement provisions are central. Disputes between investor of a state party and a state party to the EAEU is settled mainly through negotiations. But if there is no solution, then parties may apply to local court of choice, international arbitration court within the trade chambers of the parties, ad hoc court and International Center for Settlement of Investment Disputes. The other investment protection measures are ensuring national treatment, guarantees against expropriation and nationalization, as well as payment of compensation in such cases and ability to transfer rights[567].

National treatment is offered towards the investments and trade in services. Each member state has its own list of specific restrictions towards national treatment, which is reflected in a special annex. Most-favored nation treatment is offered to trade in services[568]. Quantitative restrictions and measures that limit investments are banned among EAEU members. These measures are related to number of permitted service suppliers, number of permitted companies to establish or control, limitations towards operations of service supply, operations of investor, form of the establishment of legal person, percentage of participation in establishment capital of a legal person and number of natural persons permitted to be employed in a certain service sector, apart when such limitations are listed in the specific annex by members[569]. Member cannot pre-condition establishment and functioning of investment by requiring import/export, purchase of goods and services of that member, limitations towards purchase and sale of goods/services and requiring transfer of know-how[570]. However, these limitations are permitted if they are already in the specific annex to the protocol.

As it can be seen, EAEU members tried to limit any restrictions towards establishment and functioning of investments. However, members have been permitted to list restrictions that they were unwilling to remove and the EAEU is silent on whether there is liberalization of such measures in the future. Restrictions towards movement of natural persons are also eliminated[571]. Also, current practices show that although members have been adopting measures to liberalize investment, there have also been numerous cases where additional impediments for investment are adopted. For instance, Russian Federation law on

567 ibid, Articles 74–84.
568 ibid, Article 27.
569 ibid, Article 30.
570 ibid, Article 32.
571 ibid, Article 35.

investment in strategic fields excludes almost half of the economic sectors from its application[572].

(b) Association Agreements of the EU with Moldova, Ukraine and Georgia

In contrast with the EAEU, the Association Agreements do not define investment. These agreements also do not contain provisions on investor-state dispute settlement, investment promotion, investment guarantees, in other words investment protection measures. This is a characteristic trait of the EU FTAs. The treaty itself specifies that investment protection measures, except for national treatment are not covered by Association Agreement[573]. Nonetheless, the agreement states that future negotiations can lead to inclusion of investor protection measures, as well as investor-to-state dispute settlement procedures into the treaty[574].

The substance of the provisions are merely on liberalization. For investment liberalization, a top-down approach is used[575]. In this approach, the commitments of the treaty applies to all sectors with the exception of some. Association Agreements contain detailed rules on the free movement of capital, rules on the establishment of juridical persons, carve-outs by the members which allow them to maintain restrictions in investment on their respective national legislation.

Association Agreements, unlike the EAEU and the CIS, dedicate considerable part of the treaty to services liberalization. Trade in Services chapter is very much designed after the GATS. Entry of natural persons, employment in

---

572 Irina Kvashnina 'Inostrannie investisiyii v Rossii: vozmojnosti I oqranichenii' (Foreign investments in Russia: possibilities and limitations) (2014) 12 Rossiyskiy vneshnoekonomicheskiy vestnikm p. 91 <https://cyberleninka.ru/article/v/inostrannye-investitsii-v-rossiyu-vozmozhnosti-i-ogranicheniya> accessed 21 December 2018.

573 EU – Ukraine Association Agreement, EU – Georgia Association Agreement, EU – Moldova Association Agreement Article 87, footnote 1 (29 May 2014) <trade.ec.euorpa.eu/doclib/docs/2016/November/tradoc_155103.pdf> accessed 07 February 2018.

574 EU – Ukraine Association Agreement, EU – Georgia Association Agreement, EU – Moldova Association Agreement Article 89 (29 May 2014) <trade.ec.euorpa.eu/doclib/docs/2016/November/tradoc_155103.pdf> accessed 07 February 2018.

575 Top-down approach is when all the sectors for liberalization is listed unless specifically excluded. See: Howard Mann 'Investment Liberalization: Some Key Elements and Issues in Today's Negotiating Context' (2007) in Issues in International Investment Law: Background Papers for the Developing Country Investment Negotiator's Forum, p. 3. <https://www.iisd.org/pdf/2007/inv_liberalization.pdf> accessed 26 April 2018.

member countries and visa issues are left outside the scope of the Association Agreements. They provide for progressive liberalization of the investment and trade in services and maintaining consultations for further liberalization in the future. Several sectors are excluded from the measures on liberalization of establishment. These are audiovisual services, services related to nuclear arms, as well as trade in arms, munitions and other warfare, national maritime sabotage and air transport services[576]. National treatment and most favored nation principles are ensured to the establishment of juridical persons[577]. Parties agree to review these terms periodically, to assess any obstacles and to start negotiations on removing them, including negotiations on investment protection and investor-state disputes if necessary[578].

(c) The CIS

The CIS countries -Armenia, Belarus, Tajikistan, Moldova, Kazakhstan and Kyrgyz Republic in 1997 signed CIS Investor Rights Convention[579]. The Convention gives the definition of investment as material and financial resources in different activity fields, as well as rights to physical and intellectual property[580]. This Convention mainly provides for investment protection, rather than investment liberalization. It ensures the most-favored treatment for investments and notes that if any of the parties adopts legislation which at the opinion of the other party deteriorates the investment environment, the latter can take this matter to Economic Court of the CIS or any other international court and arbitration[581]. The Convention goes further and adds that in case the aforementioned courts rule in favor of the applicant, then the country should stop the force of the legislation for five year period. In general, the dispute settlement provisions of the Convention is quite strong, because the parties can take matters not only to their own court and CIS Economic Court, but also to any international court and arbitration of their choosing. Of course, the agreement does not provide unconditional

576 EU – Ukraine Association Agreement, EU – Georgia Association Agreement, EU – Moldova Association Agreement Article 78 (29 May 2014) <trade.ec.euorpa.eu/doclib/docs/2016/November/tradoc_155103.pdf> accessed 07 February 2018.

577 ibid, Article 79.

578 ibid, Article 80.

579 CIS Investor Rights Convention (28 March 1997) <http://investmentpolicyhub.unctad.org/Download/TreatyFile/3127> accessed 18 April 2018.

580 ibid, Article 1.

581 ibid, Article 5.

access to such a right, as there is a list of exceptions, such as national security, defense, protection of environment, morals and health of the population, taxing, and other exceptions listed previously by the parties. The CIS Convention also guarantees the investor's right against expropriation, compensation right, guarantees for the use of income.

Another treaty among the CIS countries regarding investment is the Treaty on Promotion and Mutual Protection of investment in the Eurasian Economic Community member states[582]. Again this treaty focuses entirely on investment protection. It provides rights of investors against expropriation, access to compensation, use of the incomes, openness and accessibility of legislation and dispute settlement rights. Investors can choose to use either courts of the parties of the convention, international commercial arbitration court of the trade chamber of the parties, ad hoc arbitration court, as well as International Center for Settlement of Investment Disputes.

It should be noted here that both of the above-mentioned treaties contain almost the same provisions as the bilateral investment treaties in the CIS region.

v. Key Findings

This sub-chapter examined the investment provisions of the RTAs in Eastern Europe, Central Asia and the Caucasus and their relationship with multilateral trade agreements. The following general trends were observed regarding the investment provisions in the RTAs of the region: First of all, investments are not entirely tackled through the RTAs. Some of the issues related to investments are regulated by the RTAs, while many issues are left to the national authorities. For instance, none of the agreements in the region contained incentives for foreign investors, such as alleviation of tax burdens, financial stimulus or subsidization. This matter was left entirely to the national authorities.

Secondly, in the EAEU and Association Agreements investments and services provisions are regulated together. This is because Mode 3 of the services represent the foreign establishment. However, the services liberalization provisions in the EAEU and Association Agreements go deeper than the WTO services

582 This Treaty is in force between Russia, Belarus, Kazakhstan, Tajikistan, Kyrygz Republic and came into force on 11 January 2016. See more: Treaty on Promotion and Mutual Protection of investment in the Eurasian Economic Community member states (12 December 2008) <http://investmentpolicyhub.unctad.org/Download/TreatyFile/2997>

schedules, thus making it possible for the parties to have better market access to each others' services sectors.

Thirdly, dispute settlement represent an important aspect of the investment protection. Dispute settlement provisions of the investment parts are strong in the EAEU and the CIS treaties and they are quite similar. However, Association Agreements have not included investor-to-state dispute settlement options. It should be noted here that there are some important elements of dispute settlement procedure related to investment in the EAEU and the CIS: (i) investor-to-state dispute settlement provisions in the EAEU and the CIS prohibit parallel trials and ensure that arbitration decisions are final. This is the traditional approach used in such RTAs and it ensures clarity, transparency and efficiency for investors; (ii) Neither the EAEU, nor the CIS, state what kind of investment provisions can be brought under this dispute settlement mechanism. This is a broad approach for dispute settlement. In contrast, for instance, EU-Canada FTA clarifies that investor-to-state dispute settlement is applying only to the few important breaches of investment protection, so the dispute settlement cannot be used for investment liberalization, such as obtaining better terms in the market. Thus, the scope of dispute settlement for investment cases are broad under the EAEU and the CIS; (iii) The EAEU and the CIS have not created a special tribunal for investment dispute settlement, but rather refer the parties to choose one of the four court options indicated in the previous section; (iv) The states are obligated to implement decisions of arbitration courts in accordance with their legislation; (v) There are no provisions indicating that the losing party pay the costs for dispute settlement. Thus, every party pays for their own costs, which makes the dispute settlement an expensive tool for small investors.

Fourthly, bilateral investment treaties are complementary to the RTAs in the region. Investment protection is either left to the bilateral investment treaties or merely repeats provisions of such treaties. Association Agreements do not contain any investment protection measures, except for national treatment. In the case of the EAEU and the CIS, investment protection measures are solely repetitions of what is included in the bilateral investment treaties. The main difference between the investment chapters of these RTAs and bilateral investment treaties is that, the latter only contains investment protection, while the RTAs in the region combine investment liberalization and protection.

Lastly, none of the RTAs in the region calls for cooperation on investment policies. However, there are general provisions calling for cooperation for general issues, so it can be assumed that investment policies would also be covered as such.

When it comes to the relationship of investment and trade, currently, there is no single and comprehensive multilateral framework for liberalization or protection of investment. For many years bilateral investment treaties have been tackling investment protection issues. However, the RTAs have gone a step further by inclusion of the investment liberalization, as well as detailed clauses on the liberalization of services, and therefore establishment. So, by combining protection and liberalization, RTAs have provided common investment policy framework in the region and thus have united defragmented rules. As such, these RTAs made the provisions on investment more accessible, transparent and predictable for the business world. If FDI statistics is examined, in 2016 the EAEU witnessed increase in mutual FDI by 15.9%[583]. However, with the Association Agreement countries situation is a bit different. In 2016, all 3 agreements of the EU with Ukraine, Georgia and Moldova came into force. However, the same year FDI flows between EU – Georgia and EU – Ukraine witnessed a decline[584]. Despite this, the FDI between EU and Moldova increased[585]. So, FDI statistics show different results for different countries. Although, increase in investment can not solely be accounted on the RTAs, it can be assumed that though in theory better terms in investment liberalization and investment protection positively impact the trade in the region, however there are other factors to take into account in practice, which can lead to deterioration of investment relations, even when the legislative norms are in place.

The analysis showed that there was no innovative or progressive element in the RTAs on investment per se, but it also showed that these RTAs developed trade and investment across the region. Therefore, it can be assumed that RTAs can develop the global trade law even when they do not possess such elements.

583 Eurasian Development Bank 'Monitoring of Mutual Investments in CIS Countries in 2017' (2017) Report 45, p. 6<https://eabr.org/upload/iblock/3fe/EDB-Centre_2017_Report-45_MIM-CIS_ENG_2.pdf> accused 27 April 2018.

584 European Commission Directorate-General for Trade 'Georgia' (2017) <http://trade.ec.europa.eu/doclib/docs/2006/september/tradoc_111507.pdf> accessed 27 April 2018.
European Commission Directorate-General for Trade 'Ukraine' (2017) <http://trade.ec.europa.eu/doclib/docs/2006/september/tradoc_111613.pdf> accessed 27 April 2018.

585 European Commission Directorate-General for Trade 'Moldova' (2017) <http://trade.ec.europa.eu/doclib/docs/2006/september/tradoc_111540.pdf> accessed 27 April 2018.

Investment provisions of the RTAs can be used for further development of multilateral trade agreements, because they go further than WTO agreements, as well as bilateral investment treaties. Predecessor of WTO – International Trade Organization – contained an article on international investment for economic development and reconstruction where members recognized importance of investment, elaborated rights of members with regards to investments, commitment to provide reasonable opportunities for investment and which called on the members to enter into bilateral and multilateral agreements with regards to investment liberalization and protection[586]. However, this organization failed and WTO did not include investment. Singapore issues also contained investment, but this was not successful as well and investment was dropped from the negotiations. The current multilateral treaties that are dealing with investment are OECD and Energy Charter, but again these organizations have limited membership. Therefore, having one multilateral agreement on investment within the WTO or independently, but covering substantial amount of world countries, could contribute to the development of trade and investment globally. This has been lobbied by some transnational companies worldwide, but so far, it has not been successful. But if this initiative is successful, the role model for the treaty could be the elements of the RTAs on investment, because they show in practice how they impact the economies of certain countries.

The gain from multilateralization of investment policies is high. Any such framework will harmonize the diverse national rules and regulations of investment and make the trade rules for investors easier and more accessible. However, the main barrier seems to be the political will of the countries. Issues central to investment liberalization, such as entry and stay of physical persons, visas, quotas, establishment of juridical persons can be quite sensitive for a number of countries which will resist to multilateralization process. So, multilateralization process can focus on investment protection, dispute settlement procedures, definitions of investments, while investment liberalization could be left to national authorities.

586 United Nations Conference on Trade and Employment: Final Act and Related Documents: Article 12 (1947) <https://www.wto.org/english/docs_e/legal_e/havana_e.pdf> accessed 30 April 2019.

2. Competition Provisions of the RTAs in Eastern Europe, Central Asia and the Caucasus

i. Competition in the Multilateral Trade

Competition law is a set of governmental rules that counteract attempts to monopolize the market either unilaterally or through agreements between the companies[587]. This law is also often called antitrust law. Tackling competition law multilaterally is important because even when the markets are liberalized, measures such as mergers between cartels, market sharing and price-fixing agreements could hamper market access in a given country[588].

Initially, competition policy was a part of the Havana Charter of International Trade Organization, which contained a whole chapter on restrictive business practices[589]. However, when the International Trade Organization failed, competition was also dropped from multilateral negotiations. Competition was re-included again among the Singapore issues, but it was dropped again in 2004[590]. Currently there is no discussion on the topic within the WTO. The Working Group on Competition and Trade, which was established during the Singapore negotiations, became inactive.

The WTO does not address competition policy as a whole, however there are certain references to government's response to anticompetitive practices, principles for monopolies and exclusive service suppliers in the GATT, GATS or TRIPS. For instance, the GATS gives definition for monopoly service providers and lists main principles and rights applicable to competition law. It defines monopoly

---

587 Bernard Hoekman, Petros Mavroidis 'Economic Development, Competition Policy and the World Trade Organization' (2002) World Bank Policy Research Working Paper 2917, p. 4 <https://openknowledge.worldbank.org/bitstream/handle/10986/19221/multi0page.pdf?sequence=1&isAllowed=y> accessed 3 May 2019.

588 UNCTAD 'Consumers, Multilateral Competition Policy and the WTO: Technical Report' (2003) p. 14 <https://www.wto.org/english/tratop_e/dda_e/symp03_ci_tech_report_e.pdf> accessed 9 May 2018.

589 United Nations Conference on Trade and Employment: Final Act and Related Documents: Chapter V (1947) <https://www.wto.org/english/docs_e/legal_e/havana_e.pdf> accessed 30 April 2019.

590 See: Singapore MInisterial Declaration (13 December 1996) WT/MIN(96)/DEC <https://www.wto.org/english/thewto_e/minist_e/min96_e/wtodec_e.htm> accessed 30 April 2019.
WTO General Council Decision (1 August 2004) WT/L/579 <https://www.wto.org/english/tratop_e/dda_e/draft_text_gc_dg_31july04_e.htm> accessed 30 April 2019.

service provider as any person who is authorized as a sole service provider in the market of the country[591]. The core principle of the WTO – non-discrimination is applied to the competition law and therefore, national authorities cannot discriminate between their international partners when they are applying their domestic competition law. This is provided in the GATS Article VIII which makes clear that, monopolies and exclusive service suppliers of a member country has to ensure that monopolies act in accordance with MFN principle and specific commitments of the given member. Article IX of the GATS gives a right to members to enter into consultations with other members, whose business practices of service providers they deem to be restrictive. |A specific annex of the GATS on Telecommunications ensures equal rights and market access to telecommunication sector for service providers. The annex on Financial Services requires a listing of the monopoly rights and their reduction.

The GATT Article II indicates that if a country has a monopoly on the importation of a good, it shall not provide protection in excess of the protection already covered in that member's schedule of commitments[592]. Certain types of monopolies, for instance, export cartels which restrict exports, as well as cartels limiting competition by imposing quantitative restrictions such as quotas can be interpreted under the GATT Article XI[593]. Article XVII of the GATT (state-trading enterprises) also partly covers competition provisions. It states that if a country has a state-trading enterprise, the latter has to act non-discriminatorily in the sale and purchase of a product[594].

The TRIPS recognizes that certain licensing practices and conditions related to intellectual property can restrain the competition and in such cases members

591 WTO General Agreement on Trade in Services, Article XVIII (h) (April 15, 1994) Marrakech Agreement Establishing the WTO <https://www.wto.org/english/docs_e/legal_e/26-gats.pdf> accessed 7 May 2018.

592 WTO General Agreement on Trade and Tariffs, Marrakech Agreement on the the Establishment of the WTO, Annex 1A (April 15, 1994), Article II <https://www.wto.org/english/docs_e/legal_e/gatt47.pdf> accessed 17 May 2018.

593 Bernard Hoekman, Petros Mavroidis 'Economic Development, Competition Policy and the World Trade Organization' (2002) World Bank Policy Research Working Paper 2917, p. 15 <https://openknowledge.worldbank.org/bitstream/handle/10986/19221/multi0page.pdf?sequence=1&isAllowed=y> accessed 7 May 2018.

594 WTO General Agreement on Trade and Tariffs, Marrakech Agreement on the the Establishment of the WTO, Annex 1A (April 15, 1994), Article XVII <https://www.wto.org/english/docs_e/legal_e/gatt47.pdf> accessed 17 May 2018.

may adopt appropriate measures to prevent such practices[595]. Moreover, a member may use compulsory licensing to remedy anti-competitive practices[596].

The main discussions during the Singapore negotiations, which was initiated by the EU, was to eliminate hard-core cartels and to provide principles of cooperation between the countries which have competition laws[597]. Some core principles associated with the competition were identified during this period: transparency, non-discrimination and procedural fairness[598].

In general, major part of any multilateral competition policy discussion is about hard-core cartels. Hard-core cartels has been defined by the OECD as "anticompetitive agreements by competitors to fix prices, restrict output, submit collusive tenders or divide or share markets"[599]. The OECD adopted in 1998 some principles which highlighted the negative affect of the hard-core cartels for consumers and trade, which prompted many developed countries in the world to restrict activities of cartels and to adopt necessary legislative changes[600].

Other than hard-core cartels, multilateral competition policy negotiations usually cover provisions on cooperation for preventing the abuse of dominance and monopolization, competition enforcement practices, as well as provisions on liberalization and intervention in regulated sectors, as well as mergers.

The OECD is the main organization which looks into competition policies. It has a Regional Center for Competition established in 2005 which joins together competition authorities and provides training and expertise for the developing countries and countries in transition for this region – Eastern Europe, South East and Central Europe.

Besides the OECD, the second international organization which has tackled competition policy is the UNCTAD. The UNCTAD drafted a Code on

---

595 WTO Agreement on Trade Related Aspects of Intellectual Property, Marrakech Agreement on the Establishment of the WTO, Annex 1C (April 15, 1994), Article 40 <https://www.wto.org/english/docs_e/legal_e/gatt47.pdf> accessed 21 May 2018.

596 ibid, Article 31.

597 ibid.

598 Paul Kuruk 'Negotiating Competition Policy in Multilateral Trade Agreements: European Union Overtures to West Africa and the WTO' (2015) 36 (3) University of Pennsylvania Journal of International Law 3, p. 652.

599 OECD 'Hard Core Cartels' (2000) p. 6 <http://www.oecd.org/competition/cartels/2752129.pdf> accessed 9 May 2018.

600 OECD ' Recommendation Concerning Effective Action Against Hard Core Cartels' (25 March 1998) (98)35/FINAL <http://www.oecd.org/daf/competition/2350130.pdf> accessed 9 May 2018.

Transnational Companies in 1980 which had a number of provisions on competition policies, however this code was not adopted as there was major differences between the developing and developed countries on the issue[601]. Nonetheless, the UNCTAD adopted a set of rules on restrictive business practices in 1980[602]. Though not mandatory, this set of rules creates conducive environment for further adoption of multilateral tools on this topic.

International Competition Network is a voluntary union of competition authorities of world countries and it disseminates information on best practices in the field of competition[603]. It holds regular meetings where the competition authorities exchange information. Other multilateral platforms include regional development banks conducting competition law and policy assistance to national authorities.

ii. Competition in Regional Trade Agreements

Competition or antitrust policy is one of the novel features of the RTAs. More and more countries feel that competition policies should be included in the RTAs so as to ensure that liberalization achieved from RTAs would not be hampered by national competition policies. Moreover, customs union and economic unions have to include competition provisions for an effective integration region-wide. Furthermore, small developing countries lacking relevant expertise and resources on competition, are more susceptible to the activities of international cartels seeking market dominance. Therefore, RTA provisions on competition assist such countries to curb abuse of dominant position by cartels.

Usually RTAs differ on the scope of the competition provisions. While some RTAs use non-binding language, other RTAs can be more binding. Certain common competition policies found in the RTAs are provisions on cooperation, consultation and coordination of activities between competition agencies; principles applicable in the competition policies, such as non-discrimination, procedural fairness, due process and transparency; negative and positive comity

601 Paul Kuruk 'Negotiating Competition Policy in Multilateral Trade Agreements: European Union Overtures to West Africa and the WTO' (2015) 36 (3) University of Pennsylvania Journal of International Law, pp. 657–8.

602 U.N. Conference on Trade and Development (UNCTAD), The United Nations Set of Principles and Rules on Competition, U.N. Doc.TD/RBP/CONF/10/Rev.2 (2000), p. 1 <https://unctad.org/en/docs/tdrbpconf10r2.en.pdf> accessed 17 May 2018.

603 Umut Aydin 'International Competition Network: Cooperation and Convergence in Competition Laws' (2010) 11(3) Rekabet, p. 53.

provisions where competition authority of one RTA partner can request proceedings against national of the other party or advise the party in the proceedings against national of that party; provision on creation of supranational competition body; provisions calling for adoption or maintenance of national competition policies, including legal and institutional framework, as well as enforcement mechanism; provisions on harmonization of regional competition policies; provisions on specific anti-competitive provisions, such as calls to curb abuse of dominant positions in the market, monopolization or hard-core cartels; provisions on special and differential treatment on competition polices toward developing partners; dispute settlement provisions regarding the competition related provisions; sectoral exemptions, such as energy and agriculture, which are usually more resilient to liberalization under the RTA competition policies, as the members may want extra protection than anti-competitive practices may grant[604] ; provisions excluding anti-dumping provisions for the RTA partners; provisions related to the conditions of trade remedy measures, such as countervailing measures, safeguard measures or anti-dumping measures[605].

It should be noted that, the NAFTA and RTAs built around the NAFTA model contain more provisions on consultation and cooperation regarding competition issues, while the EU tends to include more provisions for harmonization of competition law, as well as substantive provisions on competition, such as abuse of dominant position, hard-core cartels and etc.[606]. Also, competition provisions are more likely to be included in the RTAs when one party is a developed country, while developing countries tend not to cover competition in the RTAs between them[607].

iii. Competition and Multilateralization of Regionalism

There are certain factors to take into consideration when multilateralizing competition provisions. Firstly, harmonization of competition law might not be feasible. Every country's economy is different, therefore every country's competition environment is different. Requiring the same set of rules to govern competition in all economies therefore might not be feasible. Yet, multilateralization of

604 Philippe Brusick, Ana Maria Alvarez, Lucian Cernat 'Competition Provisions in Regional Trade Agreements: How to Assure Development Gains', px (2005) UNCTAD Publication <http://unctad.org/en/docs/ditcclp20051_en.pdf> accessed 21 May 2018.
605 ibid, p. 451.
606 ibid, px.
607 ibid, pxii.

competition could work as an umbrella agreement. In other words, any multilateral framework for competition needs to focus on the common ground, which could be core principles affecting the competition, common definitions, dispute settlement, call for cooperation, minimum standards of competition and so on. Another approach could be as WTO Trade Facilitation Agreement, where the parties could choose their own commitment level based on their national competition policies.

Second, competition in almost all cases is instantly multilateralized. If a RTA includes favorable conditions for competition provisions and RTA party therefore adopts more flexible competition policy, it will automatically be applied to all the trade partners. Of course, RTA party can condition the favorable conditions to be applied only to a specific RTA party, but this is an administratively burdensome and complicated process, therefore it is logical that competition would be instantly multilateralized.

Thirdly, multilateralization of competition requires a sound mechanism to ensure enforcement of competition provisions. Many RTAs either exclude competition from dispute settlement or have weak enforcement language for it[608]. In the region analyzed this is not the case however, which creates favorable conditions for multilateralization. EU agreements usually refer RTAs to Association Councils or arbitration, in the case of the CIS and the EAEU the EAEU Court or CIS Economic Court handle the disputes in the case of the CIS and the EAEU.

iv. Competition Provisions within the RTAs in Eastern Europe, Central Asia and the Caucasus

(a) Association Agreements of the EU with Georgia, Moldova and the Ukraine

Association Agreements of the EU with Georgia, Moldova and the Ukraine contain limited provisions on competition. First of all, the agreements ensure that parties have competition legislation and relevant competition authority in place to ensure effective implementation of the competition law[609]. So, the parties do not undertake to establish supranational competition authority between them, nor do they call for harmonization of their competition legislation.

608 ibid, p. 78.

609 EU – Georgia Association Agreement Article 204 (29 May 2014) <http://eur-lex.europa.eu/legal-content/en/TXT/PDF/?uri=CELEX:22014A0830(02)> accessed 24 May 2018.

The main important element is to ensure that competition law and policy are applied based on the principles of transparency, procedural fairness, non-discrimination and due process. Substance of competition law should cover anti-competitive agreements, concerted practices and anti-competitive unilateral conduct of firms with dominant market power, as well as effective control of concentrations[610]. This means that competition law and policy have effective provisions against hard-core cartels – firms which abuse dominant market power.

Cooperation among the competition authorities are purely limited to non-confidential issues[611]. Cooperation regarding confidential issues are left to the discretion of the national authorities. While the Association Agreements provide that state monopolies and state enterprises with special and exclusive rights are permitted, it states that when these enterprises are of commercial character, they should fall under the competition laws[612].

Dispute settlement is not applied to competition provisions, except for subsidies and confidentiality provisions[613]. The agreements recognize that subsidies fall under the competition policies and require transparency in this field. In effect it means that parties notify each other every two years regarding their subsidy policies.

Here trade remedy measures should also be touched, because trade remedy curbs unfair competition practices. Unlike other RTAs, Association Agreements do not exclude application of trade remedy measures to its parties. Articles 37–43 of the Association Agreements lay details of how safeguard, anti-dumping and countervailing measures can be applied. The only exception is that trade remedy measures do not fall under the dispute settlement. Trade remedy measures in the Association Agreements mainly repeat the WTO Agreements on Anti-Dumping, as well as Safeguards and Countervailing Measures[614] . But unlike the WTO provisions, it also provides for lesser duties of anti-dumping and countervailing measures compared to dumping or countervailing subsidy margin, if lesser duty remedies the injury to the domestic market, as well as non-applicability of anti-dumping and countervailing measures if the public interests

---

610 ibid.

611 ibid, Article 209.

612 ibid, Article 205.

613 ibid, Article 207.

614 Trade remedy measures are important from competition point, because dumping, subsidies can lead hampering of fair and equitable competition and lead to restrictive business practices.

demand so[615]. Safeguard measures also need to be imposed in a way affecting bilateral trade the least[616].

(b) The EAEU

Article 74 of the EAEU Treaty delineates general measures for anti-competitive practices in the markets of the members, as well as practices that have negative affect on competition of the trans-border markets of two or more states[617]. Members are free to impose more bans and restrictions than what have been put forward in the EAEU Treaty. Nonetheless, competition policy towards third countries are coordinated by the EAEU Commission[618]. Also, based on Annex 19 to the EAEU Treaty, which is the Protocol on General Principles and Rules of Competition, while tackling anti-competitive measures within their borders fall with national authorities, the EAEU Commission comes into play when such measures affect competition of trans-border markets, except for trans-border financial markets[619]. The EAEU Commission can request information or material from any national authority, which the latter has to present.

Competition principles enshrined in the Article 75 of the EAEU Treaty is non-discrimination, transparency and cooperation of competition authorities. It states that anti-competition fines should be adequate, efficient, irreversible and transparent[620]. Though it is not obligatory in the treaty, but parties recognize that highest anti-competition fines are imposed to the highest violation of competition rules and the fines are preferably deducted from the product profits of the competition violator[621].

The parties undertake to create competition authority responsible for determination and control of anti-competitive practices. Among other anti-competitive

615 EU – Georgia Association Agreement Article 42–43 (29 May 2014) <http://eur-lex.europa.eu/legal-content/en/TXT/PDF/?uri=CELEX:22014A0830(02)> accessed 24 May 2018.

616 ibid, Article 39.

617 EAEU Treaty, Article 74, <https://docs.eaeunion.org/docs/ru-ru/0043610/itia_05062014> accessed 28 May 2018.

618 ibid.

619 Annex 19 to the EAEU Treaty, Protocol on General Principles and Rules of Competition, Article 8 and 9 <https://docs.eaeunion.org/docs/ru-ru/0043610/itia_05062014> accessed 30 May 2018.

620 EAEU Treaty, Article 75, <https://docs.eaeunion.org/docs/ru-ru/0043610/itia_05062014> accessed 28 May 2018.

621 ibid.

practices, the EAEU Treaty forbids the agreements between government agencies, municipal bodies and other parties undertaking government functions, if these agreements lead to limitation, ban or elimination of competition except for the cases determined in advance[622]. Moreover, except for the cases predetermined, government and municipal preferences are also ruled out in the EAEU Treaty.

What is considered anti-competitive practices are clearly stated in the Article 76 of the EAEU Treaty. For instance, abuse of dominant power, leading among other things, to limitation, elimination of competition, violation of interests of other parties is prohibited. Result of abuse of dominant power could be in this case: determination of monopoly high or monopoly low prices of a good, extraction of a good from market as a result of which the price of the good is increased, imposing unprofitable and economically and technologically unfounded conditions of agreement on the counterparts, reduction or halt of the production of a good to which there is a demand in the market and no grounded reason for the halt of the production, rejection of agreements with buyers without any economic or technologically founded reasons, creation of different prices for the same product without justification, creation of hurdles for the market entry and exit for the other parties[623]. Another example is unscrupulous competition, including dissemination of false information damaging reputation of a trading partner, deceiving customers regarding the product, its production and its producers, incorrect comparison of products and producers with other product and producers, which is banned[624]. Another case is agreements between competitors, which can lead to determination of prices for products, determination of prices in auctions, reduction or elimination of production, division of the market, rejection of certain purchasers, which are prohibited[625].

The EAEU Treaty dedicates a specific section to natural monopolies. The list of natural monopolies of the members are listed to the annex of the treaty. The parties undertake to harmonize spheres of natural monopolies. The enlargement of spheres of natural monopolies are permitted only if such sphere is listed by another member or by the decision of the EAEU Commission. As it is seen, the EAEU Commission has more power regarding the enlargement of spheres of natural monopolies.

622 ibid.
623 ibid, Article 76.
624 ibid.
625 ibid .

Anti-competition rules are also enshrined in specific sectors, for instance energy. Specifically, in energy sector and railroad transport sector, member states have natural monopolies. Here, the EAEU states that other state parties have equal access to the services of natural monopolies on energy. However, the provision of local needs comes as a priority when answering such demands for access[626].

The EAEU Treaty dedicate special provisions to cooperation between national authorities. Apart from exchange of information and documents, one state party can initiate competition investigation at the request of the another state party[627]. Also, one state party can request performance of proceedings at the other state party[628].

(c) The CIS

The main characteristic trait of the CIS countries is that they are successors of the Soviet Union and as such, competition policy was absent in these countries. Relevant laws and regulations on competition date back to their independence. However, as no free trade agreement would be viable without a sound competition policy in place, the CIS countries also realized this and signed Treaty on the Implementation of Coordinated Competition Policy in 1993 in Ashgabat[629]. In 2000, this agreement was renewed in Moscow.

This treaty provides for cooperation between competition authorities of the parties, harmonization of the legislation, as well as delineates main issues that the treaty tackles, which are – abuse of dominant position, anti-competitive agreements between economic subjects and unfair competition. The treaty aims to coordinate the anti-competition policies of the members, create conditions for the development of competition, approximation of competition legislation, coordination of review of monopolistic activities. The treaty created regional competition body – Interstate Council on Anti-monopoly Policy. The Council's main task is to develop cooperation between the parties, improvement of national competition laws, development of human resources of national competition

626 ibid, Article 82.

627 Annex 19 to the EAEU Treaty, Protocol on General Principles and Rules of Competition, Article 22 <https://docs.eaeunion.org/docs/ru-ru/0043610/itia_05062014> accessed 30 May 2018.

628 ibid, Article 30.

629 CIS Intergovernmental Treaty on the Implementation of a Coordinated Competition Policy (24 December 1993) Ashgabat.

authorities, developing of common approaches for competition law violations, implementing reforms in public procurement systems, as well as raising awareness of the stakeholders with the need to comply with competition laws and regulations[630].

In 1999, CIS countries signed Regulations on the Mechanism of Cooperation for Elimination of Monopolistic Activity and Unfair Competition which provided for the use of one of the following cooperation mechanisms: notification, request for information, consultation, application for investigation of a case[631] . CIS countries also exclude confidential information from the scope of information exchange on competition policy.

It is also worth to note that most of the national laws on competition are based on the CIS Model Law on Protection of Economic Competition.

Regarding the trade remedy measures, such as anti-dumping, subsidies and countervailing measures, these are dealt at CIS Free Trade Agreement of 2011. In general, the parties do not exclude the possibility of application of such measures towards each other. However, necessary notifications should be given, as well as due process should be observed[632].

v. Key Findings

This sub-chapter examined the competition provisions of the RTAs in Eastern Europe, Central Asia and the Caucasus and their relationship with multilateral trade agreements.

Based on the analysis, the following general traits of the region were observed: Firstly, cooperation, consultation, coordination and exchange of information is the cornerstone of all the agreements. The scope of competition policies tackled in the RTAs differ, but all of them have at least provisions on the above-mentioned measures. The CIS provisions on competition are purely limited to

---

630 ibid.

631 Agreement for Implementation of the Harmonized Antimonopoly Policy (25 January 2000).
Annex 1. Regulations on the Prevention of Monopolistic Activity and Unfair Competition dated 25 January 2000 Annex 2. Regulations on the Interstate Council for Antimonopoly Policy dated 25 January 2000
<http://cis.minsk.by/reestr/ru/index.html#reestr/view/text?doc=1000> accessed 6 June 2018.

632 CIS Free Trade Agreement, Articles 8–10, (18 October 2011) <http://cis.minsk.by/reestr/ru/printPreview/text?id=3183> accessed 6 June 2018.

these issues, while EAEU for instance goes further. However, in all agreements extent of cooperation is limited to non-confidential issues;

Secondly, two of these RTAs have established specific mechanisms for competition policies. For instance, the CIS created an independent competition policy agency – the CIS Interstate Council on Anti-Monopoly Policy. However, this agency has no authority to conduct competition policy within the CIS market itself. It is purely limited to join together national authorities, to build their potential, to be a platform for adoption and improvement of national competition policies. The main mechanism for competition within the EAEU is the EAEU Commission. This Commission has broad powers. It has authority to rule on competition issues affecting trans-border markets. In the case of Association Agreements, there is no separate mechanism created for competition issues, however the regular meetings held for consultation between the parties tackle competition policies as well;

Thirdly, transparency and non-discrimination are defined as the main common principles. While most of the RTAs have these two main principles, the other principles differ. For instance, the EAEU focuses on cooperation as the principle, as well as adequacy, irreversibility and size versus gravity of the anti-competition fines. For the Association Agreements however, due process and procedural fairness are important principles that have been included in the RTAs. The CIS on the other hand has only focused on the sovereignty and non-discrimination of the parties to the agreement, rather than competition.

Fourthly, dispute settlement is provided for competition policies. The scope of the dispute settlement in this regard is different for each RTA. In terms of dispute settlement regarding competition policies, the broadest power lies in the EAEU, because all the competition issues can be disputed in the EAEU Court. Association Agreements exclude the bulk of the competition provisions from the dispute settlement procedures. The CIS's dispute settlement procedure is limited to purely negotiations and consultation of the members;

Fifthly, trade remedy measures are included in the RTAs. Trade remedies are essential for the competition policies, as they curb uncompetitive practices that hinder free trade. As such, none of the RTAs exclude anti-dumping or countervailing measures provisions from application to each other;

Lastly, sectoral exemptions are present in most RTAs for energy and transport. The EAEU has sectoral exemptions from competition. Natural monopolies exist in energy and railroad transport. The same is true for CIS. However, the Association Agreements do not have any sectoral exemptions.

The analysis showed that competition provisions of the RTAs complement the free trade agreements in the region, because without sound national competition provisions, any free trade privileges would have little real effect. Trade liberalization is therefore somewhat dependent on sound national legislation on competition. When there is a strong competition framework in place, trade would flourish, because there will be conditions for the traders to participate in the market on an equal footing. However, theory and practice is different regarding competition in this region. The region is characterized by high monopolization, ineffective market regulation[633]. This shows that for real changes in competition sector, there should be a willingness from the countries to implement the competition laws.

As it was the case with investment, competition issues are also not handled in the multilateral agreements. Currently there are no talks within the WTO to liberalize global competition provisions. Since WTO has no provisions on competition law and policy, all the provisions of the RTAs on competition develop new standards in the multilateral trade. Of course, there are some international organizations, such as OECD, UNCTAD which are dealing with competition policy and law issues. But their agreements are more of a model law, rather than binding agreement. As such, RTAs are the real platform for liberalization and harmonization of competition policy across the region. In the analysis subject of this research, RTAs in Eastern Europe, Central Asia and the Caucasus managed to harmonize the otherwise scattered competition issues among the former Soviet Union countries.

Competition was dropped from Singapore issues because the WTO members could not reach a consensus over these issues. But when competition issues come back to the negotiation table, RTAs could be a platform to look for the elements of such multilateral trade agreement.

The analysis showed that there was no innovative or progressive element in the RTAs on competition per se, but it also showed that these RTAs developed trade and investment across the region. Even though, there is no innovative or progressive provision among them, but they are important for harmonization of the scattered competition policies. Therefore, all the elements of these RTAs on competition policy can be used in multilateralization of regionalism. Multilateralization of competition provisions in the RTAs can lead to the global

633 Irina Ruyqa, Olqa Ruskix 'Sovremennie tendenchii rinka pryamix inostrannix investisiy' (The modern tendencies of the direct investment market) (2015) 3 Konsept, p. 6 <https://cyberleninka.ru/article/v/sovremennye-tendentsii-rynka-pryamyh-inostrannyh-investitsiy>accessed 21 December 2018.

competition policy treaty which would ensure global framework for liberalization and harmonization of the competition policy.

The main resistance towards the multilateralization of competition stems from the lack of the adequate willingness from the countries. Competition is viewed as internal affair by many and not surprisingly many states are not willing to concede their authority on this issue to any multilateral framework. This is the reason why multilateral negotiations within the WTO on competition has failed. Many developing countries do not also have the same level of competition law as the developed countries. The market conditions also differ. While developed countries are more open and resilient towards external competition, small and medium entrepreneurship in lesser developed countries cannot compete against transnational companies. This is another reason for resisting the multilateralization of competition provisions by the developing countries. A solution for this could be the model used for Trade Facilitation Agreement, where countries can choose their relevant commitment level, whether they would undertake to implement commitments straightaway, or after transitional time or after transitional time and assistance. Another possibility could be focusing on non-substantive competition rules, such as main principles, cooperation, information exchange and etc.

The gains from such a multilateralization process is huge. Having a sound anti-trust law, regulating mergers and acquisitions, making the competition law and practice predictable, transparent and efficient will boost world trade, make it easier for the companies to enter foreign markets and will facilitate exchange of know-how and technology. As the world continues to globalize, the need for multilateralization of competition will also grow and resilience towards it weaken. So, even if the International Trade Organization and early years of the World Trade Organization might not have been good timing for this process, in due course competition issues could return to the negotiations table, because there is a high demand for this process from business worldwide.

3. Energy Provisions of the RTAs in Eastern Europe, Central Asia and the Caucasus

i. Energy and Multilateralism

Definition: This sub-chapter looks into the energy liberalization provisions across the RTAs of the region. The term "energy" can refer to refer both to goods and services. Energy goods are the physical goods that are used for extracting energy. They can be in traditional or renewable form. Renewable forms are solar, wind, biofuels, hydro energy and atomic energy. Traditional forms are coal, petroleum, gas and etc. Energy service is the process of delivering energy from its extraction to the consumption, which can include various stages such as transportation, transmission, management and other important elements necessary for this delivery[634].

WTO and energy: The WTO does not possess any rules on energy specifically. When the International Trade Organization and later the WTO was formed, there was no need felt among the members to include energy as a separate issue. The rationale for this stemmed from the fact that many energy producing and exporting countries were not signatories of the GATT, in addition energy was considered a special product in the international trade which demanded a different approach and many key energy companies wanted energy outside the scope of global trading rules[635].

The general understanding was that multilateral agreements of the WTO would cover energy as well[636]. Therefore in the WTO, the only rules concerning specifically the energy are on transit and transportation, which was included in the GATT and further developed in Trade Facilitation Agreement. In addition, GATT Articles such as Article XX (general exceptions) and Article XXI (national security exception) could directly be applied to the energy issues[637].

The services sectoral classification list W20 – the main document which lists all services sectors for liberalization purposes did not contain specific services sectors for energy[638]. On the contrary, energy services were included within transportation services or business services, under classification of "transportation of fuels", "services incidental to mining", "geological, geophysical and other scientific prospecting services" and "services incidental to energy distribution"[639].

---

634 WTO Council for Trade Special Session, USA proposal on energy services S/CSS/W/24, 18 December 2000.

635 Anna Marhold 'The World Trade Organization and Energy: Fuel for Debate' (2013) 2 (8) ESIL Reflections, p. 2.

636 Thomas Cottier, Garba Malumfashi, Sofya Matteotti-Berkutova, Olga Nartova, Joelle de Sepibus, Sadeq Z. Bigdeli 'Energy in WTO Law and Policy' (2010) p. 1 <https://www.wto.org/english/res_e/publications_e/wtr10_7may10_e.pdf> accessed 15 September 2017.

637 See: United National Conference on Trade and Development 'Trade Agreement, Petroleum and Energy Policies' UNCTAD/ITCD/ (2000, United Nations, New York and Geneva), p. 26.

638 WTO Services Sectoral Classification List MTN.GNS/W/120, 10 July 1991.

639 ibid.

Furthermore, the original members of the WTO mostly did not commit for energy services at all. Nor were energy goods included in the schedules of commitments for most of the original members.

Despite all of this, the role of energy has been increasing over the years. As such, more and more acceding countries are requested to commit to liberalizing market access for energy[640]. There is a growing need to streamline energy in the multilateral trade. Increase of accession of energy producing countries to the WTO, correlation of energy and environment, concern over non-tariff barriers existent in the energy sector, lack of coherent disciplines in energy and proliferation of energy subsidies worldwide brought this topic into the table of negotiations in the WTO Doha Round[641]. Some of the members even suggested to draft a multilateral WTO agreement on energy, however this suggestion has not been successful yet[642]. Instead, Doha Round of negotiations have been focusing on defining energy as a services sector and putting more precise and clear disciplines on problems associated with the energy[643].

There are a number of issues correlated with energy liberalization. First of all, WTO agreements do not define whether an energy is a good or service[644]. This is an important distinction, because based on this classification different trade rules are applicable. Initially, the common understanding was that the GATT defined rules on energy commodities, while the GATS regulated services connected with energy. However as time passed, it became unclear whether certain energy forms such as electricity, which cannot be physically touched or felt, would fall under the category of goods of services. This issue was somewhat solved in another forum, namely the European Court of Justice which considered Almelo case in 1994 and ruled that electricity would fall under the category of goods[645]. However, this issue still remains disputed by many, as electricity seems a mixture of both goods and services. Therefore, there is a necessity for a

640 Craig Van Grasstek *The history and future of World Trade Organization* (2013, World Trade Organization Publications, Geneva), p. 137.

641 Thomas Cottier, Garba Malumfashi, Sofya Matteotti-Berkutova, Olga Nartova, Joelle de Sepibus, Sadeq Z.Bigdeli 'Energy in WTO Law and Policy' (2010) <https://www.wto.org/english/res_e/publications_e/wtr10_7may10_e.pdf> accessed 15 September 2017.

642 ibid.

643 ibid.

644 Anna Marhold 'The World Trade Organization and Energy: Fuel for Debate' (2013) 2 (8) ESIL Reflections, p. 3.

645 Case C-393/92 Gemeente Almelo and Others v.Energiebedrijf IJsselmij NV, European Court of Justice, 27 April 1994.

multilateral forum which could clarify the emerging issues linked to energy, such as classification of energy goods and services, applicable rules to trade in energy, market access and so on.

Secondly, liberalization of trade in energy is very closely related to liberalization of investment and competition. In many countries, foreign investment is restricted or limited in the energy field. Even when there is no restriction, investing in this sector requires assurances and guarantees from acts such as expropriation and requisition by the state. Therefore, liberalization of energy also requires liberalization, as well as protection of investment.

With regards to relationship of competition and energy, energy rules can affect the competition when there is a dual pricing. Dual pricing happens when a country applies different pricing policies for energy for domestic consumption and exports. Usually in such cases, domestic prices are lower than the cost of production of energy, which gives unfair advantages to the local businesses and makes it hard for foreign companies to compete with them[646]. Moreover, local companies use the reduced prices of energy to gain advantage in the export markets, thus distorting the fair competition rules in the world trade. In the WTO, dual pricing is specifically raised by EU. Acceding countries are requested to commit in this area by the EU, which cites dual pricing being contrary to the WTO Subsidies and Countervailing Measures Agreement[647]. For instance this was a major concern in the accession negotiations of the EU and Russia. However, energy producing countries have been reluctant to commit on this. So far, none of the major energy producing WTO members, including Russia and Kazakhstan have committed to removing dual pricing.

Thirdly, liberalization of energy necessitates a close look at a country's policy on subsidies, quantitative restrictions, procurement. For instance, when a country grants subsidies for the use of renewable energy in order to promote their use, such subsidies may fall under the actionable subsidies in the WTO agreements. Similar issue arise with the green procurement which is a grey area within the WTO. The latter does not regulate how to incorporate green procurement in

646 Anna Marhold, *Fossil Fuel Subsidy Reform in the WTO: Options for Constraining Dual Pricing in the Multilateral Trading System* (2017, International Center for Trade and Sustainable Development, Geneva) p. vi <https://www.researchgate.net/publication/321722933_Fossil_Fuel_Subsidy_Reform_in_the_WTO_Options_for_Constraining_Dual_Pricing_in_the_Multilateral_Trading_System> accessed 26 December 2018.

647 '*Europe's Global Role: External Policies of the European Union*' edited by Jan Orbie (Routledge, 2008).

WTO rules. Whether it is ok for a state to give preference to procurement solely because that procurement is environmentally friendly is unclear, as WTO rules do not touch upon such issues.

Although there are many energy organizations dealing with different aspects of energy regulations, none of them tackles liberalization of energy at the global level. Some of them are with limited membership, while the others have limited scope. For instance, International Energy Agency deals with four main issues: energy security, economic growth and elimination of energy poverty, reduction of negative impact of energy on environment and cooperation with other countries in the accomplishment of shared objectives[648]. The main mission of Organization of Petroleum Exporting Countries is to coordinate and unify the policies of petroleum exporting countries and stabilize the global oil market[649]. International Renewable Energy Agency is a multilateral platform for the promotion of sustainable use of renewable energy.

Among all the energy organizations, special mention should be made of Energy Charter. It provides protection for investment, regulates transit in detail and provides rules for dispute settlement in energy transit[650]. There are obligations for members to ensure smooth and non-interrupted transit of energy flows, national and MFN treatment, as well as protection against non-commercial risks. Energy Charter creates stability for investors and host governments by providing a forum for dispute resolution for investor-state and inter-state arbitration, as well as works for the energy efficiency and environmental protection in the member countries. Energy Charter has 52 member countries. Armenia, Azerbaijan, Georgia, Kazakhstan, Kyrgyz Republic, Moldova, Tajikistan, Turkmenistan, Ukraine and Uzbekistan are the members of the Energy Charter. Russia and Belarus are signatories, but not ratifiers of the Charter Treaty. The relationship of Russia with the Energy Charter Treaty is largely peculiar[651]. When the country signed the Treaty, it accepted provisional application of it until the ratification.

---

648 Daniel Linott, Filip Reyxlin 'Enerqetika i Bezopasnost: Qlobalnie Vizovi' (Energy and security: Global challenges) (2005) 3 (39) Centralnaya Aziya I Kafkaz, p. 125 <https://cyberleninka.ru/article/v/energetika-i-bezopasnost-globalnye-vyzovy> accessed 26 December 2018.

649 ibid.

650 ibid.

651 Irina Pominova 'Risks and Benefits for the Russian Federation to Participate in the Energy Charter: Comprehensive Analysis' (2014) Energy Charter Secretariat Knowledge Center, p. 1 <https://energycharter.org/fileadmin/DocumentsMedia/Occasional/Russia_and_the_ECT_en.pdf> accessed 09 September 2017.

However, in 2009 Russia refused to ratify it and formally gave a notice of it to the Secretariat and stopped the ratification process as a whole. The reason for this move is cited by experts as Russia's unwillingness to lose its sovereignty over energy policy and prevention of loss by its energy companies[652]. A close ally of Russia – Belarus – is applying the Treaty provisionally pending ratification.

Usually, energy and environmental protection are the issues that are intertwined. The main multilateral agreement on environmental protection is Kyoto Protocol of 1997 and Paris Agreement under the United Nations Framework Convention on Climate Change which entered into force in 2016. Kyoto Protocol was adopted by all the EAEU members. All the countries in the region except for Moldova have signed Paris agreement, yet Kyrgyz Republic and Russia still need to ratify it.

It should also be noted that currently 18 WTO members are negotiating a plurilateral agreement – Environmental Goods Agreement which, once adopted and entered into force, would offer tariff-free treatment to environmentally friendly goods and thus promote the use of renewables and clean technology. This agreement would be applied on a MFN principle and thus will be applied to not only the imports from agreement parties, but also to the whole WTO membership. None of the countries from the Middle East, CIS or Latin America are taking part in these negotiations, but main energy importing countries such as EU, USA, Canada, Japan, South Korea are the negotiating parties in this agreement. The draft agreement is aimed also to remove the non-tariff barriers and regulations in this area.

One of the key challenges associated with energy is economic security. Dependence of energy routes and supplies/demands on other international players can create a challenge for economic security of the importing, as well as exporting countries[653]. This is one of the factors that shape the foreign economic policy of energy importing and exporting countries.

---

652 Yuliya Kukushkina 'Znacenie Requlirovanie Torqovli v Ramkax VTO dlya Enerqidialoqa Rossii s Evropeyskim Soyuzom' (Important of trade regulation in the framework of WTO for energy dialogue of Russia with European Union) (2014) 4 Finansi: Teoriya I Praktika, p. 106 <https://cyberleninka.ru/article/v/znachenie-regulirovaniya-torgovli-v-ramkah-vto-dlya-energodialoga-rossii-s-evropeyskim-soyuzom> accessed 25 December 2018.

653 Daniel Linott, Filip Reyxlin 'Enerqetika i Bezopasnost: Qlobalnie Vizovi' (Energy and security: Global challenges) (2005) 3 (39) Centralnaya Aziya I Kafkaz, p. 106 <https://cyberleninka.ru/article/v/energetika-i-bezopasnost-globalnye-vyzovy> accessed 26 December 2018.

ii. Energy in Regional Trade Agreements

Regional Trade Agreements have been a more popular platform for covering energy issues over the last decades[654]. They are also a forum for harmonizing diverse rules and regulations across the RTA partners on energy[655]. However, it is also notable that there are only a handful of RTAs which have provisions solely on liberalization of energy. This is due to the fact that not every RTA partner has energy resources. As such, liberalization of energy in such circumstances benefit not all the parties. Therefore, in most cases, RTAs cover other energy related topics such as renewables, relationship of energy and environment, climate change mitigation, energy transit and security and energy efficiency.

The NAFTA in its "Energy and basic petrochemicals" chapter has laid the foundation for liberalization of energy trade in both energy goods and services. There is a commitment not to maintain quantitative or minimal/maximal price restrictions and export taxes for energy goods[656]. But notwithstanding this, liberalization in NAFTA is quite limited as well. This can be seen with regard to Mexico, where foreign ownership in the energy sector is prohibited and this provision is incorporated in the NAFTA[657]. It is a clear example how scattered energy resources among the RTA partners can result in the diminished effect of energy liberalization covered in the RTA.

The ASEAN (Association of South-East Asian Nations) and Mercosur also have policies on energy integration. However, among all the RTAs special attention should be applied to the EU. The EU formed the European Coal and Steel Community and European Atomic Energy Community early in its formation in

654 Rafael Leal-Arcas, Constantino Grasso. and Juan Alemany Rios, *Energy security, trade and the EU: regional and international perspectives.* (2016, Edward Elgar Publishing Limited, Cheltenham), p. 85.

655 Evqeni Vinokurov 'Obshiy Elektroenerqeticeskiy Rinok SNQ kak Instrument Ekonomiceskoqo Razvitiya i Reqionalnooy Inteqracii' (Common electricity energy market of CIS as a tool of economic development and regional integration) (2008) 1 (1) Evraziyskoe Ekonomiceskoe Inteqrasiya, p. 62 <https://cyberleninka.ru/article/v/obschiy-elektroenergeticheskiy-rynok-sng-kak-instrument-ekonomicheskogo-razvitiya-i-regionalnoy-integratsii> accessed 26 December 2018.

656 NAFTA, the North American Free Trade Agreement: a guide to customs procedures. (1994). Washington, DC: Dept. of the Treasury, U.S. Customs Service: Supt. of Docs., U.S. G.P.O.

657 Rafael Leal-Arcas, Constantino Grasso and Juan Alemany Rios 'Multilateral, regional and bilateral energy governance'(2014) Queen Mary University of London Legal Studies Research Paper N 188/2014, p. 53.

the 1950s. Presently, the EU has an integrated internal energy market as a result of reforms of the energy market through adoption of energy packages. The EU has taken energy integration into a further level by developing rules for energy union, promoting use of renewables and ensuring security of supply, which is a challenge for the EU[658].

iii. Energy Provisions within the RTAs in Eastern Europe, Central Asia and the Caucasus

(a) The EAEU

General trends: Energy resources within the EAEU are concentrated mainly in Russia and Kazakhstan. Russia is the world's top crude oil and electric power producer, as well as second largest natural gas producer[659]. Within the former Soviet Union block, Kazakhstan is considered to be the second largest producer of energy resources, after Russia[660]. Though Armenia possesses some nuclear energy and Kyrgyz Republic has hydropower, nonetheless, all the other EAEU members, except for Kazakhstan, are dependent on energy imports from Russia. For instance, Russian subsidiary company "Gazprom Armenia" controls 100% of the gas supply and sale to Armenia. 97% of energy imports to Belarus come from Russia and more than 80% of the Belarusian energy use is dependent on Russia[661].

---

658 Aleksandr Poluektov 'Transatlanticeskoe Torqovoe I Investicionnoe Partnerstvo Mejdu ES I SShA: Proobraz Obnovlennoy VTO?' (Transatlantic Trade and Investment Partnership Between EU and USA: model of renewed WTO?) (2016) 2 (6) Torqovoaya Politika, p. 36 <https://cyberleninka.ru/article/v/transatlanticheskoe-torgovoe-i-investitsionnoe-partnerstvo-mezhdu-es-i-ssha-proobraz-obnovlennoy-vto> accessed 26 December 2018.

659 Andrey Dryakin 'Enerqeticeskaya Diplomatiya Rossii v Aziatsko-Tixookeanskom Reqione: Osnovnie Aspekti i Napravleniya' (Energy diplomacy of Russia in Asian-Paific region: main aspects and directions) (2014) 4 (32) Izvestie Vuzov: Povoljskiy reqion. Qumanitarnie nauki, p. 107 <https://cyberleninka.ru/article/v/energeticheskaya-diplomatiya-rossii-v-aziatsko-tihookeanskom-regione-osnovnye-aspekty-i-napravleniya> accessed 35 December 2018.

660 Ardak Yesdauletova 'Kazakhstan's energy policy: its evolution and tendencies' (2009) 6 (4) Journal of US-China Public Administration, p. 31.

661 Margarita Balmaceda 'Belarus: oil, gas, transit pipelines and Russian foreign energy policy' (2006) Institute for the Analysis of Global Security, Global Market Briefings, p. 6.

Having two big energy producing countries as RTA partners has resulted in energy being one of the key factors for the integration in the eyes of energy importing RTA partners. Common energy market means that all RTA partners have equal rights to access the energy resources of their other RTA partners. In this case, it meant that Armenia, Belarus and the Kyrgyz Republic would be able to access the Russian energy resources on the same terms as Russian companies. This is considered to be a key motivation for deeper integration within the EAEU.

The EAEU Treaty has a chapter on energy integration, which is further developed in 3 Annexes – Annex No 21, 22 and 23. Based on the EAEU Treaty, the energy market is formed in 3 forms: oil and petroleum products market, common gas and common electricity energy market[662]. There are deadlines for the establishment of this market. Those are: 1 July 2019 for the common electricity market and 1 January 2025 for the other energy markets[663]. For these markets to be operational, a special international agreement of the EAEU partners should be concluded, as well as action plans and concept papers should be developed in advance.

Common gas market: Annex No22 is about the common gas market. It regulates cooperation, entry to market, natural monopolies and pricing policies. The main principle is that import and export duties are eliminated within the EAEU[664]. This was a concession sought by Belarus, and later by Armenia and the Kyrgyz Republic. Besides that, the annex has provisions on harmonization and approximation of the legislation, as well as on environmental safety[665]. The main pre-condition for the formation of the common gas market is the economic profitability. In other words, the EAEU members should have such market prices that it should be economically beneficial to sell gas to the EAEU members[666]. The EAEU itself does not regulate volume, price and tariff, leaving this to the authority of national governments[667]. Thus, energy producing countries – Russia

---

662 Treaty on the Establishment of the Eurasian Economic Union: Article 81, 83 and 84 (29 May 2014) <docs.eaeunion.org> , accessed 2 November 2017.

663 ibid, Article 104.

664 Annex 22 to the EAEU Treaty, Protocol on Rules for the access to the services of natural monopolies in the sphere of transportation of gas through gas transporting systems, as well as price formation and tariff policy, Article: 3.1 (29 May 2014) <docs.eaeunion.org> accessed 2 November 2016.

665 ibid,, Article 3.4–3.5.

666 ibid, Article 5.

667 ibid, Article 7.

and Kazakhstan – still maintain their sovereignty over these issues. The economic benefit pre-condition also gives a chance for these countries to move away from the common market commitment if they find it non-profitable.

On 31 May 2016, the concept of the formation of the common gas market was adopted[668]. According to this concept, formation of the common gas market is conditioned upon the development of the internal gas markets of the members. The concept ensures that internal gas needs of the members are answered with the resources of the given member or other members and in some cases even third party countries[669]. However, the price formation and other commercial/technical conditions of the transportation of the gas are determined through the bilateral agreements. Also, in case of threats to economic and energy security of a member, countries have a right to adopt relevant regulative steps, which means that they can limit application of common energy market in such cases[670].

The common gas market is envisaged to be formed in several stages. The first stage covers the period until 2020, when the legislation is to be harmonized, access to information is to be provided, norms and standards for gas are to be unified, formation of indicative balance of gas of the union and adoption of the rules for the auctions on the gas are to be completed. The second stage covers period up to 2021 when one or more auctions on gas are operational in the EAEU territory, members have access without barriers to the auctions located in the territory of other members and they have access to the gas transportation systems of each other. The third and final stage covers the period up to 2025 when the agreement on common market for gas enters into force, the supply of gas through bilateral agreements or auctions are ensured freely and the members adopt the price for gas which is equally beneficial to all the members.

Common oil and petroleum products market: Annex 23 of the EAEU Treaty regulates common oil and petroleum products market[671]. Again, tariffs for the transportation services of oil and petroleum products are in the hands of national authorities[672] . The concept of formation of common oil and petroleum

668 Decision N7, dated 31 May 2016 of the Eurasian Economic Council on the concept of the formation of common gas market of the EAEU.

669 ibid, Article 3.

670 ibid.

671 Annex 23 to the EAEU Treaty, Protocol on Rules for organization, governance, functioning and development of common oil and petroleum products market (29 May 2014) <docs.eaeunion.org> accessed 2 November 2016.

672 ibid, Article 7.

products market was adopted on May 31, 2016[673] . Major principles reflected in the document are ensuring competition in the energy market with the exclusion of the services of natural monopolies for the transportation of oil and petroleum products; removing administrative, technical and other principles in the common market; non-discriminatory access of the members to common oil and petroleum products market; ensuring commercial and transport infrastructure of common oil and petroleum products market; prioritizing supply of needs of EAEU members in oil and petroleum products; non-application of quantitative restrictions in mutual trade; harmonization of legislation for technical and commercial infrastructure of common market; unification of norms and standards for oil and petroleum products; ensuring favorable conditions for attraction of investments and ensuring ecological safety[674].

Again, as the case was with the common market of gas, mutual trade of the members in the common market can be realized through either bilateral agreements, or through auctions. The oil and petroleum products price formation is realized through market prices, excluding services of the natural monopolies for transportation of oil and petroleum products, where prices are formed by national authorities[675]. Thus, profitability of selling gas to the member states are ensured. The following principles are further applied: (I) tariffs are formed based on national legislation; (II) tariffs for legal persons cannot be higher than the tariffs determined for the legal persons through the territory of which oil and petroleum products are transported; (III) members are not obliged to offer lower tariffs than the tariffs determined for legal persons through territory of which oil and petroleum products are transported[676].

Similarly to the common gas market, the common oil and petroleum products market is also formed in 3 stages. The first stage covering 2016–2017 envisaged adoption of the program of formation of such market, the second stage covering 2018–2023 envisages realization of actions included in the program and the last stage covering 2024 envisages conclusion and adoption of international agreement on common oil and petroleum products between the members[677].

---

673 Decision N8, dated 31 May 2016 of the Supreme Eurasian Economic Council on the adoption of the Concept of common EAEU oil and petroleum products market.

674 ibid, Article 4.

675 ibid, Article 4.

676 ibid, Article 9.

677 ibid Article 10.

Common electricity market: In 2015, the EAEU adopted the concept for the formation of the common electricity market[678] . Belarus agreed to the concept with a special opinion stating that common electricity market will not be fully operational until the common gas market is formed. The concept determines several main tasks for the common electricity market, such as development and increase of the efficiency of the market mechanisms for mutual trade in electricity energy, increasing transparency of the price formation, creating conditions for the access without barriers to the services of natural monopolies on electricity energy (as long as technical conditions technical capabilities make it possible and with the condition that these services will be as a priority used for the internal needs in the transmission of interstate energy), creating conditions for the access of the producers and consumers of the electricity energy to the electricity energy market of the members (with pre-condition of taking into account the national interests), increasing opportunities for the mutual trade in electricity energy, decreasing the increase rate of the prices of electricity energy for final consumers and creating favorable conditions for the investment in electricity energy objects[679].

According to the concept, common electricity market is to be created based on the parallel functioning electricity systems of the members. Thus mutual trade is to be handled both through the bilateral agreements, as well as through the centralized auctions. The price formation for the bilateral agreements and the centralized auctions will be different. While prices for electricity energy will be determined within the bilateral agreements, in auctions the prices will be formed based on the algorithms of the common electricity market regulations[680]. A special program for the formation of common electricity market was developed by the EAEU Commission, but the document is still pending for adoption by the Supreme Eurasian Economic Council.

(b) The Association Agreements of the EU with Moldova, Georgia and the Ukraine

Throughout the Association Agreements, special emphasis is allocated to energy transit issues. This is because neither Moldova, nor Georgia, nor Ukraine are energy producing countries. They are, especially Georgia and Ukraine are transit

---

678 Decision N12, dated 8 May 2015 of the Supreme Eurasian Economic Council on the adoption of the Concept of common EAEU electricity market.

679 ibid, Article 2.

680 ibid, Article 9.

for energy resources. Ukraine serves as a transit point for Russian energy, while Georgia serves as a transit point for energy resources coming from Azerbaijan, as well as Central Asia. Considering that there were several past cases when supply of energy transit was interrupted from Russia to the EU and it resulted in shortage and energy crisis in some EU countries, it is not surprising that the EU has put an emphasis on energy transit issues in the Association Agreements.

Association Agreements cover the following main provisions with regard to energy transit[681]: Firstly, the agreements ensure security of transit and in this context refers to the provisions of the Energy Charter Treaty[682]. Secondly, they prohibit unauthorized seizure of energy goods in transit[683]. This concerns only the seizure by entities which are under the control of the contracting parties or under its jurisdiction. Thirdly, they ensure uninterrupted flow of transit of energy goods[684]. Moreover, it is explicit that in case of energy disputes, it is not permissible to reduce or stop energy transit prior to the conclusion of the dispute settlement. Fourthly, they provide for transit obligation for operators[685]. Basically it commits the operators to take necessary measures against accidental interruption of energy transit and, in case this happens, to take a prompt action. Fifthly, they oblige the members to establish independent regulatory authorities for gas and electricity market[686]. This regulatory authority has to be impartial towards all market participants and shall ensure appeal from its decisions. Sixthly, they reiterate the following principles for energy markets: non-discrimination of market participants, transparency, competition, security and environmental sustainability[687]. In cases when market prices of energy are regulated by the government, the agreements obligate the government to publish methodology for calculation of the price prior to imposition of this price. Association Agreements grant access to energy transport facilities and liquefied natural gas and storage facilities of members to third parties[688]. Lastly, Association Agreements provide

681 EU – Ukraine Association Agreement, EU – Georgia Association Agreement, EU – Moldova Association Agreement Chapter 11 (29 May 2014) <trade.ec.euorpa.eu/doclib/docs/2016/November/tradoc_155103.pdf> accessed 25 June 2018.

682 ibid, Article 211.

683 ibid, Article 212.

684 ibi, Article 213.

685 ibid, Article 214.

686 ibid, Article 215.

687 ibid, Article 216.

688 ibid, Article 217.

prevalence of Energy Community Treaty over the Association Agreements[689]. However, this provision applies only when Moldova, Ukraine and Georgia become parties to the Energy Community Treaty.

Beyond energy transit, parties pay special attention to energy cooperation. They agree that Ukraine, Georgia and Moldova will approximate its legislation on energy to that of EU[690]. They also agree to hold a regular energy dialogue on a range of energy policy issues, including energy security, regional energy issues, energy and investment, energy and environment, development of competitive energy markets etc.

Another area of interest regarding energy in the Association Agreement is energy efficiency and relationship of energy with the environment. The parties acknowledge the need to promote energy efficiency, as well as importance of removing obstacles to trade of renewable energy and energy efficiency products and services[691].

Finally, the last issue concerning energy within the Association Agreements are related to dispute settlement. Dispute resolution towards the urgent energy matters covers conciliation, arbitration, shorter dispute periods, as well as availability of remedies such as cancellation of other trade in goods preferences.

In respect of energy services, the EU has put a limitation on national and MFN treatment if the juridical person of Georgia, Ukraine or Moldova is controlled by a juridical or natural person of other country which has more than 5% share of energy market in the EU[692]. This restriction in fact secures the energy supply within the EU and is a testament of EU's unwillingness to become dependent on energy supply from third countries and in this example this third country is most probably Russia.

(c) The CIS

It should be noted that in 2010 CIS adopted Protocol for Gradual Formation of the Common Electricity Energy Market within the CIS. Parallel functioning of electricity energy of the members was ensured by 1998 CIS Treaty. This was the first step in the realization of a common electricity market. The Russian Federation was the driving force behind this initiative. However this process did not actualize for two reasons. First of all, parallel functioning of electricity energy of

---

689 ibid, Article 218.
690 ibid, Article 300.
691 ibid, Article 232, 239.
692 Annex XIV-A to the Association Agreements.

all CIS countries did not realize. Central Asian Countries still have disputes over the hydro-electricity resources. Secondly, after the formation of Eurasian Economic Union, Russia put its focus on common energy market within the EAEU, rather than the CIS. Thirdly, some of the countries in the region, mainly Armenia and Tajikistan still possess outdated systems for electricity energy transmission, making it difficult to ensure parallel functioning of electricity energy. All in all, though CIS has adopted a number of documents for energy, they have remained mainly on paper and have not been realized.

v. Key Findings

This sub-chapter examined the energy provisions of the RTAs in Eastern Europe, Central Asia and the Caucasus and their relationship with multilateral trade agreements.

The EAEU aim at a common market, while Association Agreements establish free trade zones. This is one of the important difference with regards to energy liberalization.

Based on the analysis, the following general traits of the region were observed. Firstly, inclusion of energy in the RTAs within the region is mostly politically motivated. Many of the countries in the region are dependent on energy import from Russia or in the case of Kazakhstan, on the transit of energy through Russia[693]. So, potential disrupt of the supply of the energy, as well as potential prevention of the transit of energy could be quite burdensome for these countries. Moreover, Russia has been using energy as a foreign diplomacy tool, showcased in many instances in Ukraine, Georgia or the Baltic states[694]. As such, the countries in the region have been trying provide some predictability of energy issues by inclusion of it in the RTAs.

Secondly, there is a general lack of trust for deeper energy integration within Eastern Europe, Central Asia and the Caucasus. Most of the CIS countries do not want the EAEU to turn into the disguised Soviet Union and of history repeating itself. The threat of the loss of sovereignty is therefore an important factor that

---

693 Nabi Ziyadullayev 'Qosudarstva Centralnoy Azii v Usloviax Qlobalizacii: Sovremennie Tendencii i Perspektivi' (Central Asian states in the globalization conditions: current tendencies and prospects) (2006) 6 (48) Centralnaya Aziya I Kafkaz, p. 152 <https://cyberleninka.ru/article/v/gosudarstva-tsentralnoy-azii-v-usloviyah-globalizatsii-sovremennye-tendentsii-i-perspektivy> accessed 23 December 2018.

694 Randall Newnham 'Oil, carrots and sticks: Russia's energy resources as foreign policy tool' (2011) 2(2) Journal of Eurasian Studies, p. 134.

make members cautious about trusting in energy integration within the EAEU and the CIS.

Thirdly, most energy markets of the CIS and the EAEU lack accountability and transparency and they are largely monopolized. These markets are focused on supply-side approach and are not open to competition. Even when there is not a monopoly, the companies operating in the energy sector come under tight control of the government. Not surprisingly, European Commission initiated an investigation against Russian energy company "Gazprom" because of its monopolization policy in a number of EU countries in 2012[695].

Fourthly, national energy policies of the CIS and the EAEU are fragmented and uncoordinated with each other. Members do not consult the CIS or EAEU on the development of new energy routes or energy policies. These matters are in the authority of the national authorities.

Fifthly, the current national energy policies of the CIS and the EAEU are largely dependent on fossil fuels and vulnerable to external shocks. Even in the case of the Kyrgyz Republic, which uses hydropower, the winter months bring severe shortages of energy. Renewables, such as solar and wind power cover only a small percentage in the overall energy mix[696]. Meanwhile, the policy of countries like the USA, Japan, the EU and other energy importing countries worldwide has shifted from energy imports to energy self-sufficiency – in other words to develop their own potential (shale gas, renewables etc.) and not depend on energy exporting countries, such as Russia. This necessitates change in energy policies of the region as well[697].

---

695 Yuliya Kukushkina, Elena Ostrovskaya 'Aktualnie Problemi i Perspektivi Sopryajeniya Processov Evraziyskoy i Zapadno Yevropeyskoy Ekonomiceskoy Inteqraciyii' (Actual problems and prospects of interconnection of processes of Eurasian and Western-European economic integration) (2013) 4 Vestnik mejdunarodnix orqanizaciy: obrazovanie, nauka, novaya ekonomika, p. 216 <https://cyberleninka.ru/article/v/aktualnye-problemy-i-perspektivy-sopryazheniya-protsessov-evraziyskoy-i-zapadnoevropeyskoy-ekonomicheskoy-integratsii> accessed 25 December 2018.

696 Tatyana Mirolyubova 'Perspektivi Ispolzovanie Vozobnovlyayemix Istochnikov Enerqii v Sisteme Racionalnoqo Prirodopolzovaniya v Reqione' (Prospects of use of renewable energy sources in the system of rational nature use in the region) (2010) 4 (7) Vestnik Permskoqo Universiteta, p. 80 <https://cyberleninka.ru/article/v/perspektivy-ispolzovaniya-vozobnovlyaemyh-istochnikov-energii-v-sisteme-ratsionalnogo-prirodopolzovaniya-v-regione> accessed 26 December 2018.

697 Irina Platonova 'Ustoycivoe Razvitie Mirovoy Ekonomiki i Konkurentosposobnost Rossii' (Sustainable development of world economy and competitivity of Russia) (2014) 9 Rossiyskiy vneshnoekonomiceskiy vestnik, p. 63 <https://cyberleninka.ru/

Lastly, the energy integration within the EAEU is artificially accelerated. While it took the EU several decades to gradually create pre-conditions for the establishment of the common energy market that exists now, the EAEU is trying to achieve this in a much more accelerated manner.

Trade in energy products and services have generally been outside of multilateral trade negotiations, therefore inclusion of these provisions is a novice feature of the recent RTAs. Slowly but steadily, RTAs have become a platform for liberalization and harmonization of energy policies across the different regions. It is true that energy liberalization progresses slowly, but despite this, RTAs provide provisions on energy sustainability, energy efficiency and use of renewable energy which encourage trade of energy products and services, therefore they are positively affecting multilateral trade. Moreover, having common energy market provides better access for countries to the energy markets of their RTA partners.

Since energy is a WTO-beyond issue, all the energy provisions of the RTAs create further standards than the WTO. The analysis did not find any progressive or innovative provisions within the RTAs, as most of them were covering the same issues. However, as multilateral trade does not cover energy and the importance of energy increases substantially, there is a merit in including energy in multilateralization of regionalism.

When it comes to energy, there is a resistance for liberalization and multilateralization from energy producing and exporting countries in the region. There are a number of reasons for this: (i) Energy is a high-income generating resource. Having a monopoly on energy sector and keeping the market closed for foreign players is therefore lucrative; (ii) The energy producing countries of the region are dependent on energy exports. In such countries energy is viewed as a strategic asset and not surprisingly these countries ensure tight control over the energy exports. (iii) Maintaining quantitative restrictions and limitations on energy production affect the price of energy resources in the world market. This is how OPEC is functioning. Major oil producing countries convene and discuss the energy production limits and quotas so that they could maintain favorable energy prices worldwide. Market liberalization is nearly impossible to achieve in such circumstances. (iv) Many energy rich countries provide subsidized energy to their local population. Cutting off the subsidization and providing equal prices to foreign and local consumers is a sensitive and almost a political issue

---

article/v/ustoychivoe-razvitie-mirovoy-ekonomiki-i-konkurentosposobnost-rossii> accessed 23 December 2018.

for such countries. Cutting off energy subsidization would affect the vulnerable strata of the population negatively, as well as cause consumer dissatisfaction.

All the above-mentioned reasons generate the resistance from the governments to indulge in multilateral negotiations for energy liberalization in the region. Energy is still viewed by energy producing countries as a sector of domestic priority and not surprisingly, many will oppose any negotiations for multilateralization of energy. A multilateral framework in such circumstances could only cover general principles for energy efficiency and energy saving, relationship of environment and energy. Any substantial multilateralization process would bring opposition from energy exporting and producing countries. Regionalization of energy provisions in the long run could lead to such multilateralization, but all in all, the current circumstances seem too immature to start multilateralization of energy yet.

4. Summary of the Chapter

This chapter looked into the multilateralization of WTO beyond issues, namely investment, competition and energy. The chapter concluded the following:

Among these 3 sectors, investment is the most viable sector for multilateralization. RTAs have provided common investment policy framework in the region and thus have united defragmented rules. Investment provisions of the RTAs can be used for further development of multilateral trade agreements, because they go further than WTO agreements, as well as bilateral investment treaties. Having one multilateral framework will harmonize the diverse national rules and regulations of investment and make the trade rules for investors easier and more accessible. However, issues central to investment liberalization, such as entry and stay of physical persons, visas, quotas, establishment of juridical persons can be quite sensitive for a number of countries which will resist this multilateralization process. So, the multilateralization process should focus instead on investment protection, dispute settlement procedures, definitions of investments.

RTAs have been successful in harmonizing scattered competition provisions. However, there is still a resistance towards the multilateralization of competition and lack of the adequate willingness from the countries. Competition is viewed as an internal affair by many and a number of states do not desire to concede their authority on this issue to any multilateral framework. The level of competition law and market conditions differ among countries. This necessitates a diverse approach to different countries. Furthermore, multilateralization of competition could negatively impact small and medium entrepreneurship in lesser developed countries which are not able to compete against transnational companies. A solution in this circumstances could be Trade Facilitation Agreement model, where members could the commitment level and date of entry into force of these commitments.

Energy is the least likely sector among the WTO beyond sectors that could be multilateralized. This is because there is a high resistance from energy producing and exporting countries. Even RTAs that include energy are mostly politically motivated and are not fully liberalizing this sector. Energy is still seen by many governments as a high income generating and government monopolized sector, so energy producing and exporting countries will resist any attempt to multilateralize this area. Any multilateralization therefore could only succeed in the long run, however in the short run multilateral frameworks could work around the main principles for energy efficiency, energy saving, relationship of environment and energy and other non-controversial areas within energy.

Chapter 5 Assessing Possibility of Multilateralization of the Regional Trade Agreements of Eastern Europe, Central Asia and the Caucasus

The current chapter of this book aims to elaborate how multilateralization of regionalism could be applied to Eastern Europe, Central Asia and the Caucasus region.

It is organized as following: Firstly, the criteria for assessing whether multilateralization of regionalism is possible in a certain area is introduced. Secondly, these criteria are applied to the RTAs of the region.

1. Criteria for the Multileralization of the Regionalism

i. OECD Criteria

In 2014, Organization for the Economic Cooperation and Development suggested a set of criteria to see if certain sector within the RTA could be easily multilateralized[698]. These criteria could be applied to both the areas where RTA measures went deeper than what is covered by the WTO (WTO plus), as well as to the sectors that are not covered by the WTO agreements (WTO beyond).

In general, the study concluded that whether a certain provision can be multilateralized depended on the following factors:

The widespread nature of the provisions: Based on the mentioned OECD study, when a certain trade measure is found in a majority of RTAs, it can be an indication of consensus among the countries accepting that measure. Understandably, the higher the consensus, the easier it is to multilateralize. On the contrary, when a measure is endorsed only by a handful of RTAs, it might be just an isolated case, as well as it might indicate that there are countries which do not find this measure attractive[699]. Hence, the less widespread measures

698 Iza Lejárraga 'Deep Provisions in Regional Trade Agreements: How Multilateral-friendly?: An Overview of OECD Findings' (2014) OECD Trade Policy Papers, No. 168 (OECD Publishing, Paris) , p. 12.

699 ibid.

may not be susceptible to multilateralization. It should be noted that the study itself does not elaborate the threshold of the widespread nature, but it suggests that participation of both developing and developed countries is necessary to consider that there is a critical consensus for a given measure[700].

Similarity of these provisions: This criterion has two different elements. Firstly, OECD study suggests that any given measure that is to be multilateralized should not contradict multilateral commitments of the countries[701]. That is to say these provisions should not contradict with the WTO provisions, as well as the provisions of the countries taken within other multilateral fora. For instance, if a RTA has an environmental provision which contradicts with Paris climate goals, there might be a resistance among countries for multilateralization of the given measure. Secondly, given measure not only should there be a widespread measure across the RTAs, but also it should be similar in its content, which would provide common ground for its multilateralization.

Discrimination towards non-parties: When a certain measure in the RTAs is less discriminatory towards non-parties, multilateralization can take place in a more flowing fashion. The reason for this lies with the notion that multilateralization of a measure may result in erosion of the preference[702]. This in turn leads the benefactors of the discrimination not to cooperate in multilateral fora. OECD study however suggests that this might not always be the case, as there are many instances during pre-WTO times that measures were multilateralized despite their highly discriminatory nature.

Implementation, transparency and enforceability: When a measure within the RTA is enforceable, parties take necessary steps in their domestic legislation to reflect it and if necessary implement reforms[703]. Thus, a highly enforceable, transparent and implementable measure is easier to multilateralize as parties would already have a mechanism to do so. On the contrary, when there is no enforceability mechanism and the provision is merely written in a best endeavor language show the hesitancy of the RTA parties to commit to it. Therefore, the likelihood that the measure will remain on paper and parties not take necessary steps for domestic implementation is high. Thus, they would also be unwilling to accept the provision in a multilateral forum. Therefore this criterion looks whether a certain provision is enforceable measure or

700 ibid.
701 ibid.
702 ibid.
703 ibid.

"best-endeavor" measure, whether WTO dispute settlement mechanism or another mechanism can be applied to it and how transparency provisions cover it.

Existence of political will to drive multilateralism and economic gains: Lastly, the study concluded that when there is a political will and economic gains, then multilateralization is easier to achieve. Even when all the criteria are met for multilateralization, but there is no political will, as well as there being no economic drive behind the multilateralization process, it will not happen. The mere example of the Brexit process demonstrates how politics can hinder trade liberalization in a tremendous way. So, political will is the driving force behind any multilateralization effort.

ii. Other Considerations

Apart from the criteria developed by the OECD, there are other considerations for multilateralising regionalism suggested in trade literature. For instance, Baldwin and Kawai compare the regionalism in North America, Europe and Asia and note that the multilateralization of regionalism is driven by different factors in different regions: a hegemon country (USA) in North America, by a group of strong leaders (Germany and France) in Europe and by a regional integration union (ASEAN) in the Asia[704]. So, existence of a strong integration union, a strong power or alliance willing and interested in multilateralization can create a favorable environment for multilateralization of regionalism.

Another factor is the economic gains pursued with multilateralization. It is argued that gains from multilateralization should outweigh any gain from bilateralism[705]. For instance, Asian Development Bank brings the case of Sri-Lanka – India free trade agreement and South East Free Trade Area where both of the countries participate, however since the bilateral FTA have better terms, trade is handled mostly through the bilateral FTA than the regional one[706]. The engagement level of the country in global production and supply chains also contribute to the economic gains. The more a country participates in the global supply and

---

704 Richard Baldwin, Masahiro Kawai 'Multilateralising Asian Regionalism' (2013) Asian Development Bank Institute Working Paper 431, p. 15 <https://www.adb.org/sites/default/files/publication/156286/adbi-wp431.pdf> accessed 08 May 2019.

705 'Multilateralizing Asian Regionalism: Approaches to Unraveling Asian Noodle Bowl' in Asian Economic Integration Monitor (2013, Asian Development Bank, Philippines), p. 57.

706 ibid.

production chains, the more it is interested in having more favorable trade facilitation arrangements and connectivity[707]. This in turn creates an amicable environment for multilateralization efforts for these issues.

All in all, having a driving force behind the multilateralization efforts, as well as having clear gains from the multilateralization, pave the way for multilateralization of regionalism.

2. Application of Criteria for Multilateralization of Regionalism to This Region

When it comes to the widespread nature of the provisions of the RTAs, it can be concluded that the widespread nature criterion is present in the region. First of all, although the region contains many more bilateral RTAs, the CIS, Association Agreements and the EAEU cover all the countries of the region. In particular, the CIS being the oldest RTA in the region, has covered until 2008 all the regional countries[708]. It has concluded several thousands of agreements between its members since its formation in various areas such as economic, cultural, social, political, military, legal, parliamentary cooperation and etc.[709]. All the EAEU members are also the CIS members, so these agreements are also valid in the EAEU. Secondly, not only do all the countries in the region participate in one or another RTA, but the level of development of the countries are also different. Based on World Bank classification, Ukraine, Georgia, Uzbekistan are lower middle income countries, while Russia, Armenia, Azerbaijan, Belarus, Moldova, Kazakhstan, Turkmenistan are upper middle income countries and Tajikistan is a low income country[710]. Participation of countries with different level of development in the same RTAs can be an indication that the areas within these RTAs enjoy general consensus for inclusion.

Regarding the scope of these provisions, it should be noted that the scope of these areas is different in each RTA, which was further explained in the previous

---

707 Evgeny Kanaev, Alexander Korolev 'Factory Asia and Asia-Pacific Regionalism: The Connectivity Factor Revisited' (2016) Higher School of Economics Research Paper WP BRP 27/IR/2016, p. 7.

708 Georgia left the CIS in 2008.

709 All the treaties of the CIS can be found at CIS's web-portal: <http://cis.minsk.by/reestr/ru/index.html#reestr/create> accessed 03 September 2018.

710 World Bank: The World by Income and Region <http://datatopics.worldbank.org/world-development-indicators/the-world-by-income-and-region.html> accessed 09 May 2019.

chapters. To summarize, the CIS has a more restricted scope for liberalization of trade in comparison with the EAEU and the Association Agreements. This is due to the fact that CIS treaties date earlier than the Association Agreements and the EAEU. Therefore the latter agreements are more liberal in their content and scope. Despite Association Agreements of the EU with Moldova, the Ukraine and Moldova are merely free trade agreements and the EAEU is an economic union, Association Agreements have captured most of the political, legal, environmental, economic and other disciplines, in one agreement. In other words, Association Agreements and the EAEU have quite similar scope of the elements reflected in these agreements despite them being different integration units.

With regards to similarity and homogeneity of the RTA provisions, the research compared rules of origin, trade facilitation and transparency, SPS and TBT, intellectual property, investment, competition and energy areas within the RTAs of the region. It concluded that SPS and TBT, intellectual property, trade facilitation and transparency, investment and competition were similar in their context. Especially, among these, investment was the most similar, because investment chapters were generally repeating existing bilateral investment treaties with some additions. The research also concluded that rules of origin and energy the following areas were the most dissimilar.

When it comes to the criterion of discrimination towards non-parties, the research concluded that SPS and TBT, rules of origin and energy areas discriminated towards non-parties. Among them, the most discriminatory area towards non-parties is the rules of origin, because rules of origin, from their nature, are designed to discriminate between RTA partners and non-parties and they are the instruments for the RTA partners to reap benefits of their RTA preferences. The research also concluded that areas such as investment, competition, intellectual property, trade facilitation and transparency were almost always automatically multilateralized. Of course, theoretically there is a possibility to keep these sectors closed to non-parties of the RTAs, but it requires more resources and administrative burdens from the countries implementing them.

The research also elaborated on the enforcement mechanism, as well as dispute settlement procedure to enforce the provisions of the RTAs. All the analyzed RTAs in the region have a mechanism of enforcement: EAEU Commission, CIS Secretariat, Association Councils. All the three enforcement mechanism were introduced in the previous chapters. Among them, the EAEU is more efficiently structured. It has only 5 institutional bodies (EAEU Supreme Economic Council, EAEU Intergovernmental Council, EAEU Commission, EAEU court and EAEU financial body which is yet to be established), whereas in the case of the CIS, there are 84 bodies of the CIS doing the same functions.

When it comes to enforcement and implementation, dispute settlement is central. Association Agreements' dispute settlement consists of consultation, mediation and arbitration[711]. Arbitration is applicable only to the trade related provisions of the Association Agreements. Where the parties do not comply with the ruling of the arbitration, the other party reserves its right to suspend or nullify its obligations under the agreement[712]. Dispute settlement for other provisions of the Association Agreements are referred to good faith consultations within Association Councils[713]. These include but are not limited to economic cooperation, environment, agriculture, financial cooperation, anti-fraud cooperation and etc.

Both the EAEU and the CIS have established special judicial bodies to oversee economic disputes. However, the dispute settlement procedure within the EAEU and the CIS is rather weak compared to the WTO Dispute Settlement Understanding. Besides, EAEU and CIS countries[714] normally do not take any trade related cases into the courts, but rather try to settle them politically. For instance, despite a number of trade escalations between the EAEU members, only a single case on non-compliance had been lodged at the EAEU court[715]. Moreover, this case involved Russia filing a complaint against Belarus, but no member filed any complaint against Russia[716]. Furthermore, although the decisions of the EAEU Court are mandatory, the treaty on the formation of the EAEU Court specifies that the decisions of the Court cannot cancel or change the norms of the EAEU, nor legislation of the members, and do not have the authority to create new norms[717]. The CIS Economic Court only determines the violations by the members and remedies for such violations, it is also not entitled to change any norms

711 EU – Georgia Association Agreement Chapter XIV 'Dispute settlement' (29 May 2014) <thttps://eeas.europa.eu/sites/eeas/files/association_agreement.pdf> accessed 23 August 2018.

712 ibid, Article 257.

713 ibid, Article 421.

714 Not all CIS countries have accepted Economic Court's jurisdiction. Azerbaijan, Armenia and Turkmenistan have not signed the statute of the court.

715 The reference point is the period from the start of the functioning of the EAEU Court until 1 August 2017.

716 *Russian Federation v Republic of Belarus*, Case No CE-1-1/1-16-BK (Russian Federation).

717 EAEU Treaty, Annex 2 (Statute of the Court of Eurasian Economic Union), art 101.

of the CIS[718]. As it can be seen, despite the fact that both CIS and the EAEU have mechanisms for solving economic issues, they are not reluctant to use them.

All in all, based on the analysis, it could be assumed that although there is an enforcement mechanism and provisions of the RTAs could be implemented to a certain degree. However, dispute settlement process is weak across the region which in practice could affect the enforceability of the provisions.

Regarding the political will to drive multilateralization, in the previous chapters, the research concluded that energy and competition areas witnessed more resistance towards liberalization. In both cases, these sectors were viewed as domestic and governments were not willing to enter into negotiations to further liberalize them. While there was a lesser degree of resistance towards rules of origin, trade facilitation and transparency, SPS and TBT, intellectual property and investment, the conditions were also different. For instance, there was no urgent need to further multilateralize trade facilitation and transparency. For intellectual property, there was a need for transitional periods and resources for any multilateralization process. It also was not beneficial to have the same level of TBT and SPS protection in all countries.

Investment and rules of origin were among the most pushed sectors for multilateralization by transnational companies. However, in rules of origin, the differences among the members are large, so the multilateral framework could only encompass general principles, documentary and administrative requirements. In investment, the differences are not so large, therefore political will to drive the multilateralization process is greater than the rules of origin area. Moreover, the region contains a lot of risks for investment[719], the investment image of the countries are not as favorable as the investment climate itself[720] and an investment crisis is being witnessed in Russia starting from 2014[721]. All these factors

718 The CIS Economic Court also gives interpretations of the CIS norms. See: Rules for the CIS Economic Court, Article 4–5 (6 July 1992) <http://sudsng.org/download_files/docs/dk17s021p_01.pdf> accessed 23 August 2018.

719 Alevtina Rusavskaya 'Investisiyii i Investisicionniy Potencial Reqiona' (Investments and investment potential of the region) (2012) 1(37) Ueks, p. 12 <https://cyberleninka.ru/article/v/investitsii-i-investitsionnyy-potentsial-regiona> accessed 21 December 2018.

720 Andrey Trofimenko 'Pryamie Inostrannie Investisiyii v Rossii: Problemi i Perspektivi' (Foreign Direct Investments in Russia: challenges and prospects) (2011) 3 (77) Izvestia IQEA, p. 119 <https://cyberleninka.ru/article/v/pryamye-inostrannye-investitsii-v-rossii-problemy-i-perspektivy> accessed 23 December 2018.

721 Yana Petrova 'Klyuchevie Problemi Privlecheniya Inostrannix Investisiy v Ekonomiku Rossiyii" (The key problems in attracting foreign investment to the economy of

can create an amicable atmosphere to liberalize investment, because all these factors combined stimulate the countries in the region to come up with policies to promote investment. Therefore, a policy of harmonizing rules and procedures for investment regulation can appear appealing for the countries in the current circumstances.

When it comes to the policy of expansion, the situation is different in Association Agreements, the CIS and the EAEU. In the case of the EAEU, there is a political will to widen the scope of the membership. The EAEU has been actively pursuing the enlargement. It currently holds negotiations on RTAs with a dozen of countries, yet only it was successful to sign a RTA only with Vietnam[722]. Though, these negotiations are more politically motivated than economically, they serve to the multilateralization process.

No political will to drive multilateralism are currently observed in the CIS. However, in the case of the Association Agreements, the EU has been trying to have free trade negotiations with a number of Eastern European, Caucasus and Central Asian countries, such as Armenia, Azerbaijan and Kazakhstan. However, the factor of Russia has been hindering this process, therefore currently limit of the membership to Association Agreements are Moldova, Georgia and the Ukraine. Political realities might change in future, but it seems that for now it does not seem feasible.

All in all, it seems that there is an expansion policy both in Association Agreements and the EAEU, however the expansion policy is politically motivated rather than economically. Therefore, so far it has not brought any feasible economic benefits. It also seems that investment might be the area where there is more political will towards multilateralization compared with other sectors analyzed in the research.

Russia) (2014) 102 (8) Nauchniy Jurnal KubQau, p. 2 <https://cyberleninka.ru/article/v/klyuchevye-problemy-privlecheniya-inostrannyh-investitsiy-v-ekonomiku-rossii> accessed 21 December 2018.

722 Marina Vladimirovna Lapenko 'Sozdanie zoni svobodnoy torqovli mejdu EAES i Respublikoy Vyetnam: itoqi pereqovornoqo prochessa' (Creation of free trade area between the EAEU and Republic of Vietnam: conclusions of the negotiation process) (2017)17 (2) Istoriya. Mejdunarodniye otnosheniye, p. 213 <https://cyberleninka.ru/article/v/sozdanie-zony-svobodnoy-torgovli-mezhdu-eaes-i-respublikoy-vietnam-itogi-peregovornogo-protsessa> accessed 21 December 2018.

3. Summary of the Chapter

This chapter analyzed a number of criteria which could lead to multilateralization of the provisions in the EAEU, the CIS and Association Agreements of the EU with Moldova, Georgia and the Ukraine. The results of the analysis is summarized in Chart 1.

The analysis showed that there was a certain degree of enforceability of the provisions of the RTAs despite their weak dispute settlement procedure. The EAEU's institutional structure is more advanced than the Association Agreements or the CIS. Moreover, the EAEU and the CIS have judicial bodies which can take cases of non-compliance, though the practice shows that the members prefer solving any disputes through the negotiations.

The chapter concluded that investment, trade facilitation and transparency, SPS and TBT and intellectually property answered to most of the criteria. However, for trade facilitation and transparency, there is not an urgent need for multilateralization as the WTO Trade Facilitation Agreement is recent. SPS and TBT is technically difficult to multilateralize, as every country's circumstances require different SPS and TBT system. For intellectual property multilateralization, more resources – such as financial assistance and transitional periods are necessary. In this background, multilateralization of investment emerged the area more susceptible to multilateralism in this particular region.

Chart 1. Multilateralization of RTA areas:

	Rules of origin	**Trade facilitation and**		**SPS and TBT**			**Energy**
Wide-spread nature of provisions	Wide-spread	Wide-spread	Wide-spread	Wide-spread	Wide-spread	Wide-spread	Wide-spread
Similarity of provisions	The EAEU/CIS RoO are different than Association Agreements RoO	Mostly similar	Mostly similar	Mostly similar	Mostly similar	Mostly similar	Very different
Discrimination towards non-parties	Discriminates	Automatically multilateralizes	Automatically multilateralizes	Discriminates	Automatically multilateralizes	Automatically multilateralizes	Discriminates
Implementation and enforceability	Enforceable, but weak dispute settlement	Enforceable, but weak dispute settlement	Enforceable, but weak dispute settlement	Enforceable, but weak dispute settlement	Enforceable, but weak dispute settlement	Enforceable, but weak dispute settlement	Enforceable, but weak dispute settlement
Existence of political will to drive multilateralization	Less resistance	Less resistance, but no urgent need for multilateralization	Less resistance, but more time needed to adjust the market	Less resistance, but technically difficult	Less resistance and high gains	Resistance to multilateralization	Resistance to multilateralization

Conclusion

Regionalism in the current decade has entered a new stage. With the limited advancement of the negotiations within the WTO, the quest of using regionalism as a tool to advancing multilateralism has re-emerged.

The goal of the research was to examine whether multilateralization of regionalism was possible in Eastern Europe, Central Asia and the Caucasus and if so, how to achieve it. For this aim, the research tested the following hypotheses in the Central Asia, Eastern Europe and the Caucasus region:

(i) RTAs are the most efficient tool for trade liberalization and multilateralization in this region.
(ii) Only innovative and progressive elements of these RTAs can be used in the multilateralization of regionalism and
(iii) RTA provisions with low cost and high gain can be used in multilateralization of regionalism.

The research introduced the discussion in five chapters. In the first chapter, the book provided information on legal basis of the RTAs in general, current processes in the WTO and introduced the concept of multilateralization of regionalism. In the second chapter the book elaborated on the geopolitical situation in Eastern Europe, Central Asia and the Caucasus and provided background information and specificities of the main RTAs in the region.

The third chapter focused on the traditional trade related sectors found in these RTAs, namely rules of origin, trade facilitation and transparency, intellectual property, SPS and TBT. In the next chapter the book provided comparative analysis of the trade related WTO beyond provisions of these RTAs, namely investment, competition and energy. The book provided information on each sector, the main issues confronted in the multilateralization of each sector, compared the substance of these sectors and provided key findings based on the comparative analysis.

The final chapter analyzed the criteria developed by the OECD in order to determine applicability of multilateralization of regionalism to any sector. The book applied these criteria to the RTAs of the region.

The Following Were Concluded Based on the Analysis of the Research Main Conclusions

Firstly, with the emergence of mega-regional trade deals, multilateralization of regionalism has taken a new course and has become easier to achieve. In this process, RTAs between hub and spoke countries create a natural environment for multilateralization. Furthermore, the expansion of the membership of the RTAs and the similarity of the provisions of RTAs make it easier to multilateralize. During the multilateralization process, a 'one size fits all' concept will not be effective. Requiring all the countries to commit to one set of rigid rules will be met with resistance from many countries. Instead, a multi-tier multilateralization or Trade Facilitation Agreement model – where a global framework could provide general principles, best practices and models – could be more efficient.

Secondly, in the context of Eastern Europe, the Caucasus and the Central Asia region, the RTAs that have more potential for multilateralization are the Eurasian Economic Union, Commonwealth of Independent States and Association Agreements of the EU with Moldova, Georgia and the Ukraine.

Thirdly, regarding the sectors that can be multilateralized, it was determined that rules of origin appeared to be one of the most urgent areas. For multilateralization of rules of origin to be effective, any multilateral framework could focus on documentary and administrative requirements and making rules of origin more flexible and less rigid.

The book showed that for trade facilitation and transparency, there was no urgent need for further development of the multilateral trade agreement. In the region analyzed, the theory and practice of the trade facilitation and transparency is not adequate and the main barrier in this multilateralization process are the willingness of the countries to make real, lasting and practical changes in the trade facilitation area.

With regards to intellectual property, this region has higher standards on issues such as geographical indications and enforcement provisions. Since both these areas are the topics where consensus has not been able to be forged within multilateral arena, with the increase and expansion of the RTAs, these provisions could be more widely accepted and included in the RTAs, which could lead to their eventual multilateralization. However, lesser developed countries face challenges in implementation of intellectual property, because instituting higher enforcement mechanisms also require resources, including financial and human resources, which lesser developed countries do not easily have access to. So, the multilateralization of intellectual property issues is possible, yet it would need transitional time and assistance for developing and least developed countries to adjust to this process.

Regarding SPS and TBT, the book suggested that multilateralization process should aim for achieving mutual recognition and equivalence system, where each country would recognize as equivalent the other country's SPS and TBT policy, even though it could be different. This will allow the countries to take into consideration their geographical and cultural characteristics when designing proper SPS and TBT policy, yet still be able to export to other countries in the region without hurdles.

The book also pointed out that investment was the area with potential for multilateralization. RTAs have provided common investment policy framework in the region and thus have united defragmented rules. Regarding competition, there is still a resistance towards the multilateralization and lack of the adequate willingness from the countries. Competition is still viewed as internal affair by many and a number of states do not desire to concede their authority on this issue to any multilateral framework. Furthermore, the level of competition law and market conditions differ among countries. This necessitates a diverse approach to different countries. A solution in this circumstances could be Trade Facilitation Agreement model, where members could the commitment level and date of entry into force of these commitments.

The research found energy as the least likely sector among the WTO beyond sectors that could be multilateralized. This is because there is a high resistance form energy producing and exporting countries. Even RTAs that include energy are mostly politically motivated and are not fully liberalizing this sector. Energy is still seen by many governments as a high income generating and government monopolized sector, so energy producing and exporting countries will resist any attempt to multilateralize this area. Any multilateralization therefore could only succeed in the long run, however in the short run multilateral frameworks could work around the main principles for energy efficiency, energy saving, relationship of environment and energy and other non-controversial areas within energy.

This research also analyzed criteria developed by the OECD to assess multilateralization of regionalism – Widespread nature and similarity, discrimination towards non-parties, implementation and enforceability and political will to drive multilatearlization. It concluded that investment was the area which complied with most of the criteria, as well as the political and economic environment (institutionalization, willingness to expand, resistance to multilateralize, discrimination towards non-parties) within the region was good enough to drive the multilateralization process for investment.

Coming back to the hypotheses of the research, let us assess them:

i. RTAs are the most efficient tool for trade liberalization and multilateralization in this region.
The research provided arguments to support this. The RTAs had liberal provisions in all areas covered by the research and there was an empirical data presented throughout the research showing the advancement of trade in the region. Moreover, not all the countries in the region are the WTO members, therefore not all of them abide by the WTO commitments. Thus, RTAs appear to be the most efficient tool for trade liberalization, as well as consequent multilateralization process in the region.

ii. Innovative and progressive elements of these RTAs can be used in the multilateralization of regionalism.
The research proved that this hypothesis was invalid. It established that even though some areas lacked any innovative and progressive elements, yet they still had potential for multilateralization. For instance, in the SPS and TBT, the RTAs mostly reiterated the concepts introduced by the WTO, however they further developed some concepts such as regionalization, labeling and marking requirements that could be potentially used in the multilateralization process. So, the research concluded that multilateralization process can be driven not only on innovativeness and progression, but rather on how these provisions affect the multilateral trade. In fact, the similarity of provisions in the RTAs makes it easier to proceed to multilateralism.

iii. RTA provisions with low cost and high gain can be used in multilateralization of regionalism.
The research proved that this hypothesis is valid. A provision that benefits most of the stakeholders, but also confronts less resistance from the government, is easier to multilateralize. For instance, competition and energy are two sectors with high gain for trade, however their multilateralization would face more resistance by the governments and local business, therefore, the conditions are not yet ripe for the multilateralization of these areas.

The research concluded that in Eastern Europe, Central Asia and the Caucasus region currently, investment was the area with strongest potential multilateralization process. In this background, a Trade Facilitation Model – where countries could notify their implementation timelines, resources and commitment levels could be more efficient. Moreover, any multilateral agreement could cover the main principles and best practices, while the details of implementation could be left to national authorities.

For the analysis of the research, multilateralization of regionalism was not seen as a global framework covering all the countries. Rather, it was seen as a plurilateral agreement – a framework joining together a significant amount of countries in a certain region, thus unifying and harmonizing defragmented rules across the region. In this regard, this research focused only on the RTAs in Eastern Europe, Central Asia and the Caucasus. The research did not elaborate on a more global framework, as a thorough analysis of the RTAs in the different regions is necessary, if multilateralization process to cover more countries.

The current trade realities demand new approaches from the WTO. The rising role of mega-regional arrangements is irreversible. In this background, the WTO should take a leading role in advancing multilateralization of regionalism or it will lose its central role as a key rule-setting forum.

References

1. Abbott F., 'Intellectual Property Provisions of Bilateral and Regional Free Agreements in Light of US Federal Law' (2006) 12 UNCTAD – ICTSD Project on IPRs and Sustainable Development Issue Paper
2. Acharya R. et al., "Landscape" in *Preferential Trade Agreement Policies for Development: A Handbook* (2011, World Bank, Washington)
3. Acharya R., *Regional Trade Agreements and the Multilateral Trading System* (2016, Cambridge University Press, Cambridge)
4. Adolf H., 'Trade Related Aspects of Intellectual Property Law and Developing Countries' (2001) 39-1 Developing Economies
5. Apostolov M., 'Mexanizmi uprosheniya procedure torqovli v reqionalnoy torqovoy inteqracii' (Mechanisms of facilitation of trade procedures in regional trade integration), Eurasian Commission publication <http://www.eurasiancommission.org/ru/act/integr_i_makroec/dep_makroec_pol/seminar/Documents/article%20on%20MA%20presentation%20v3%20clean.pdf> accessed 19 December 2017
6. Arestov A., 'Osobennosti I Protivorechiya Ekonomiceskoy Inteqraciyii Stran SNQ' (Specificities and challenges of economic integration of the CIS) (2009) 2 Finansi: Teoriya I Praktika <https://cyberleninka.ru/article/v/osobennosti-i-protivorechiya-ekonomicheskoy-integratsii-stran-sng> accessed 25 December 2018
7. Atik S., 'Regional Economic Integrations in Post-Soviet Eurasia: An Analysis of Causes of Inefficiency' (2014) 109 Procedia-Social and Behavioral Sciences
8. Aydin U., 'International Competition Network: Cooperation and Convergence in Competition Laws' (2010) 11(3) Rekabet
9. Baier S., Bergstrand J., Feng M., 'Economic Integration Agreements and the Margins of International Trade' (2014) 93 Journal of International Economics
10. Baldwin R., 'The World Trade Organization and the Future of Multilateralism' (2016) 30 (1) The Journal of Economic Perspectives
11. Baldwin R., Evenett S., Low R., 'Beyond Tariffs: Multilateralising Deeper RTA Commitments' (2007) <https://www.wto.org/english/tratop_e/region_e/con_sep07_e/baldwin_evenett_low_e.pdf> accessed 26 March 2018
12. Baldwin R. 'Multilateralising 21st Century Regionalism' (2014) OECD Global Forum on Trade Reconciling Regionalism and Multilateralism in

Post-Bali World, <https://repository.graduateinstitute.ch/record/286980/files/Baldwin_OECD_2013.pdf> accessed 23 July 2018

13. *WTO, Multilateralising Regionalism: Challenges for the Global Trading System* edited by Balwin R. and Low P. (Cambridge University Press, Cambridge, 2009)
14. Baldwin R., Kawai M., 'Multilateralising Asian Regionalism' (2013) Asian Development Bank Institute Working Paper 431 <https://www.adb.org/sites/default/files/publication/156286/adbi-wp431.pdf> accessed 08 May 2019
15. Baldwin R., Thornton P., "Multilateralising Regionalism" (2008) CEPR Policy Report <https://cepr.org/active/publications/books_reports/viewreport.php?cvno=P185> accessed 25 July 2018
16. Baldwin R., 'Multilateralising Regionalism: Spaghetti Bowls as Building Blocks on the Path to Global Free Trade' (2006) NBER Working Paper 12545, p. 3 <https://www.nber.org/papers/w12545.pdf> accessed 7 April 2019
17. Baldwin R. 'The Causes of Regionalism' (1997) 20 (7) World Economy <https://onlinelibrary.wiley.com/doi/abs/10.1111/1467-9701.00107> accessed 21 December 2018
18. Baldwin R., 'Trade and Industrialization After Globalisations' 2nd Unbundling: How Building and Joining Supply Chain are Different and Why it Matters' (2011) NBER Working Paper 17716 <https://www.nber.org/papers/w17716.pdf> accessed 07 April 2019
19. Balmaceda M., 'Belarus: Oil, Gas, Transit Pipelines and Russian Foreign Energy Policy' (2006) Institute for the Analysis of Global Security, Global Market Briefings
20. Barcelo III J.J., 'Harmonizing Preferential Rules of Origin in the WTO System' (2006) Cornell Law Faculty Publications <https://www.peacepalacelibrary.nl/ebooks/files/CLFP_Barcelo_Harmonizing_Preferential.pdf> accessed 11 March 2017
21. Bhagwati J, *Termites in the Trading System: How Preferential Agreements Undermine Free Trade* (2008, Oxford University Press, Oxford)
22. Biryukova O., 'Qlobalnie Tsepokci Stoimosti I Voprosi Torqovoy Politiki' (Global value chains and trade policy issues) (2016) 6 Economy and business, p. 6 <https://cyberleninka.ru/article/v/globalnye-tsepochki-stoimosti-i-voprosy-torgovoy-politiki> accessed 22 December 2018
23. Blackhurst R., Otten A., 'Trade and Foreign Direct Investment' (1996) WTO <https://www.wto.org/english/news_e/pres96_e/pr057_e.htm> accessed 18 January 2018

24. Bond I., 'Contested Space: Eastern Europe between Russia and the EU' (2017) Center for European Reform publication <https://www.cer.eu/sites/default/files/pb_eastern_part_IB_9march17.pdf> accessed 12 April 2019
25. Brenton P., Manchin M., 'Making EU Trade Agreements Work: The Role of Rules of Origin' (2003) 26 (5) World Economy
26. Brenton P., Imagawa H., 'Rules of Origin, Trade and Customs' (2005) The Customs Modernization Handbook, World Bank <https://siteresources.worldbank.org/INTEXPCOMNET/Resources/Customs_Modernization_Handbook.pdf> accessed 6 February 2017
27. Brown C.P. The Mega-Regional Trade Arrangements and the Future of the WTO' (2016) Council on Foreign Relations Discussion Paper <https://onlinelibrary.wiley.com/doi/full/10.1111/1758-5899.12391> accessed 15 August 2018
28. Brusick P., Alvarez A.M., Cernat L., 'Competition Provisions in Regional Trade Agreements: How to Assure Development Gains' (2005) UNCTAD Publication <http://unctad.org/en/docs/ditcclp20051_en.pdf> accessed 21 May 2018
29. Cadot O., Melo J., 'Why OECD Countries Should Reform Rules of Origin' (2008) 23 The World Bank Research Observer 1
30. Cachet T., 'The World Trade Organization Trade Facilitation Agreement: Legal Consequences and Impact on Union Customs Code' (2017) 12 (2) Global Trade and Customs Journal
31. Chase K., 'Multilateralism Compromised: The Mysterious Origins of GATT Article XXIV' (2006) 5(1) World Trade Review
32. Choi W.-M., 'Defragmenting Fragmented Rules of Origin of Regional Trade Agreements: A Building Block to Global Free Trade' (2010) 13 Journal of International Economic Law
33. Cottier T., Malumfashi G., Matteotti-Berkutova S., Nartova O., de Sepibus J., Bigdeli S.Z., 'Energy in WTO Law and Policy' (2010) <https://www.wto.org/english/res_e/publications_e/wtr10_7may10_e.pdf> accessed 15 September 2017
34. Curtis J.M., 'Intellectual Property Rights and International Trade' 2012 CIGI Papers No 3 <https://www.cigionline.org/sites/default/files/no.3.pdf> accessed 13 March 2018
35. Dent C., *New Free Trade Agreements in the Asia-Pacific* (Palgrave Macmillan, New York, 2006)
36. Dryakin A., 'Enerqeticeskaya Diplomatiya Rossii v Aziatsko-Tixookeanskom Reqione: Osnovnie Aspekti i Napravleniya' (Energy diplomacy of Russia in Asian-Paific region: main aspects and directions) (2014) 4

(32) Izvestie Vuzov: Povoljskiy reqion. Qumanitarnie nauki, p. 106 <https://cyberleninka.ru/article/v/energeticheskaya-diplomatiya-rossii-v-aziatsko-tihookeanskom-regione-osnovnye-aspekty-i-napravleniya> accessed 35 December 2018

37. Duval Y., Neufeld N., Utoktham C., 'Do Trade Facilitation Provisions in Regional Trade Agreements Matter? Impact on Trade Costs and Multilateral Spillovers' (2016) Asia-Pacific Research and Training Network Series Working Paper No164
38. Ebbs T., Trebilcock M., *Research Handbook on WTO and Technical Barriers to Trade* (2013, Edward Edgar, UK)
39. Efremova K., 'Ot reqionalisma k transreqionalizmu: Teoreticeskoe osmislenie novoy realnosti' (From regionalism to trans-regionalism: Theoretical thinking of new reality) (2017) 58 (2) Sravnitelnaya politika
40. Eliason A., 'The Trade Facilitation Agreement: A New Hope for the World Trade Organization' (2015) 14(4) World Trade Review
41. Estevadeordal A., Suominen K., 'Rules of Origin: A World Map and Trade Effects' (2004) 7th Annual Conference on Global Economic Analysis: Trade, Poverty and Environment
42. Faradjirad A., Xezerzadeh A., 'Vneshnaya politika Rossii v Yuzhnem Kafkaze pri Vladimire Putina' (Russia' foreign policy in South Caucasus in Vladimir Putin's time) (2010) 13 Centralnaya Aziya I Kafkaz 4 <https://cyberleninka.ru/article/v/vneshnyaya-politika-rossii-na-kavkaze-pri-vladimire-putine> accessed 31 October 2018
43. Flanagan S., 'The Turkey-Russia-Iran Nexus: Eurasian Power Dynamics' (2012) 36 (1) The Washington Quarterly 1
44. Fulponi L., Shearer M., Almeida J., 'Regional Trade Agreements – Treatment of Agriculture' (2011) OECD Food, Agriculture and Fisheries Papers, No. 44, OECD Publishing
45. Gasiorek M., Augier P., Lai-Tong C., 'Multilateralising Regionalism: Relaxing Rules of Origin or Can Those PECS Be Flexed? (2007) 03 CARIS Working Papers, Centre for the Analysis of Regional Integration at Sussex, University of Sussex <https://ideas.repec.org/p/ari/wpaper/03.html> accessed 30 July 2018
46. Geraets D., Carroll C., Williems A.R., 'Reconciling Rules of Origin and Global Value Chains: The Case for Reform' (2015) 18 (2) Journal of International Economic Law
47. Hafez Z., Weak Discipline: GATT Article XXIV and the Emerging WTO Jurisprudence on RTAs' (2003) 79 (4) North Dakota Law Review

48. Harris J., 'Building Inclusive Rules of Origin in the XXI Century' (2017) International Center for Trade and Sustainable Development and Inter-American Development Bank Publication <http://e15initiative.org/wp-content/uploads/2015/09/RTA-Exchange-Rules-of-Origin-Jeremy-Harris-Final.pdf> accessed 30 July 2018
49. Harrison M., 'The Soviet Economy: 1917–1991. Its Life and After-life'(2017) 1137 Warwick Economic Research Papers
50. Hassan E., Yaqub O., Diepeveen S., *Intellectual Property and Developing Countries. A Review of the Literature* (2010, Rand, California)
51. Hilpold P., 'Regional Integration According to Article XXIV – Between Law and Politics' (2003) 17 (87) Max Planck Yearbook of United Nations Law
52. Hoekman B., Mavroidis P., 'Economic Development, Competition Policy and the World Trade Organization' (2002) World Bank Policy Research Working Paper 2917 <https://openknowledge.worldbank.org/bitstream/handle/10986/19221/multi0page.pdf?sequence=1&isAllowed=y> accessed 3 May 2019
53. Hoekman B, 'Multilateral Cooperation in a World of Preferential Trade Agreements' (2015) 21 (2) The Brown Journal of World Affairs
54. Hoekman B., 'The WTO Trade Facilitation Agreement: Milestone, Mirage or Mistake?' (2014) Prepared for a Columbia University/John Hopkins University conference on the world trade system, Washington DC, October 1–2, 2014
55. Ho C., 'A Collision Course between TRIPS Flexibilities and Investor-State Proceedings' (2016) 6 (3)k UC Irvine Law Review
56. Ippolit D., 'Mnoqostoronnost I Regionalism v Ramkax VTO I Sovremennoy Mejdunarodnoy Torqovle' (Multilateralislm and regionalism in the framework of the WTO and contemporary international trade) (2016) 10 Mejdunarodnaya ekonomika
57. Isachenko T., 'Soqlasheniye po uprosheniyu procedur torqovli otkrivaet novie vozmojnosti' (Agreement on Trade Facilitation opens new opportunities) (2014) 7 (1) Mosti
58. Jarova A.K., *Zashita intellektualnoy sobstvennosti* (Protection of intellectual property) (2017, Yurayt, Moscow)
59. Jewell C., 'The Artist's Resale Right: A Fair Deal for Visual Artists' (2017) WIPO Magazine <http://www.wipo.int/wipo_magazine/en/2017/03/article_0001.html> accessed 30 August 2017
60. Jones V.C., Martin M.F., 'International Trade: Rules of Origin' (2011) 4 (3) Journal of Current Issues in Globalization

61. Kanaev E., Korolev A., 'Factory Asia and Asia-Pacific Regionalism: The Connectivity Factor Revisited' (2016) Higher School of Economics Research Paper WP BRP 27/IR/2016
62. Kang J.W., Ramizo D., 'Impact of Sanitary and Phitosanitary Measures and Technical Barriers on International Trade' (2017) Asian Development Bank Paper 82352 <https://mpra.ub.uni-muenchen.de/82352/1/MPRA_paper_82352.pdf> accessed 28 April 2019
63. Karliuk M., 'The Eurasian Economic Union: An EU-like Legal Order in the Post-Soviet Space? (2015) National Research University Higher School of Economics research papers <https://wp.hse.ru/data/2015/09/23/1075393178/53LAW2015.pdf> accessed 22 July 2017
64. Katsoulis S., 'Multilateralising Regionalism and the Case of the EU' in "The EU at a Crossroads" edited by Despina Anagnostopoulou, Ioannis Papadopoulos and Lina Papadopoulou (2016, Cambridge Scholars Publishing, Newcastle)
65. Ketcheson J., 'Investment Arbitration: Learning from Experience' in '*Shifting Paradigms in International Investment Law: More Balanced, Less Isolated, Increasingly Diversified*' edited by S. Hindelang and M. Krajewski (2016, Oxford University Press, UK)
66. Kim J.B., Kim J., 'The Role of Rules of Origin to Provide Discipline to the GATT Article XXIV Exception' (2011) 14 (3) Journal of International Economic Law
67. Koraboev I., 'Ot Reqionalnoy Inteqracii Centralnoy Azii k Evraziyskomu Interacionnomu Prostranstvu? Menyayushaya Dinamika Postsovetskoqo Reqionalizma' (From regional integration of Central Asia to Eurasian Integration Space? Changing dynamics of post-Soviet regionalism) (2010) 3 (8) Evraziyskoe Ekonomiceskaya Inteqraciya <https://cyberleninka.ru/article/v/ot-regionalnoy-integratsii-tsentralnoy-azii-k-evraziyskomu-integratsionnomu-prostranstvu-menyayuschayasya-dinamika-postsovetskogo> accessed 26 December 2018
68. Kosov Y.V., Toropiqin A.V., Marishev A.A., 'Uprosheniye prosedur mirovoy torqovli: problema i puti resheniya' (Simplification of global trade procedures: problems and solution ways) (2014) Управленческое консультирование 8
69. Kozlova S., 'Vstuplenie Rossii v VTO: Opit stran SNQ' (Russia's accession to the WTO: Experience of CIS countries' (2011) 5 Biznes v Zakone <https://cyberleninka.ru/article/v/vstuplenie-rossii-v-vto-opyt-stran-sng> accessed 31 October 2018

70. Kvashnina I., 'Inostrannie investisiyii v Rossii: vozmojnosti I oqraniche-nii' (Foreign investments in Russia: possibilities and limitations) (2014) 12 Rossiyskiy vneshnoekonomicheskiy vestnikm <https://cyberleninka.ru/article/v/inostrannye-investitsii-v-rossiyu-vozmozhnosti-i-ogranicheniya> accessed 21 December 2018
71. Kukushkina Y., 'Znacenie Requlirovanie Torqovli v Ramkax VTO dlya Enerqidialoqa Rossii s Evropeyskim Soyuzom' (Important of trade regulation in the framework of WTO for energy dialogue of Russia with European Union) (2014) 4 Finansi: Teoriya I Praktika <https://cyberleninka.ru/article/v/znachenie-regulirovaniya-torgovli-v-ramkah-vto-dlya-energodialoga-rossii-s-evropeyskim-soyuzom> accessed 25 December 2018
72. Kukushkina Y., Ostrovskaya E., 'Aktualnie Problemi i Perspektivi Sopryaje-niya Processov Evraziyskoy i Zapadno Yevropeyskoy Ekonomiceskoy Inteq-raciyii' (Actual problems and prospects of interconnection of processes of Eurasian and Western-European economic integration) (2013) 4 Vest-nik mejdunarodnix orqanizaciy: obrazovanie, nauka, novaya ekonomika <https://cyberleninka.ru/article/v/aktualnye-problemy-i-perspektivy-sopryazheniya-protsessov-evraziyskoy-i-zapadnoevropeyskoy-ekonomicheskoy-integratsii> accessed 25 December 2018
73. Kuruk P., 'Negotiating Competition Policy in Multilateral Trade Agreements: European Union Overtures to West Africa and the WTO' (2015) 36 (3) University of Pennsylvania Journal of International Law 3
74. Kushnirenko A., Spartak A., 'Dvadcatiletniy Yubiley SNQ: Itoqi I Perspektivi Razvitiya' (Twentieth anniversary of the CIS: Outcomes and prospects) (2011) 10 Rossiyskiy vneshnoekonomimceskiy vestnik <https://cyberleninka.ru/article/v/dvadtsatiletniy-yubiley-sng-itogi-i-perspektivy-razvitiya> accessed 25 December 2018
75. Kuzmin N., Centralnaya Aziya Posle Operatsiy v Afqanistane' (Central Asia after the operations in Afghanistan) (2003) 1 "Centralnaya Aziya i Kafkaz" Jurnal Socialno Politiceskix Issledovaniy <http://www.fergananews.com/articles/1406> accessed 31 October 2018
76. Kuznetsova Q.V., *Mejdunarodnaya torqovlya tovarami i usluqami* (International trade of goods and services) (2017, Yurayt, Moscow)
77. Langille J., 'Neither Constitution nor Contract: Understanding the WTO by Examining the Legal Limits on Contracting out through Regional Trade Agreements Note' (2011) 86 (5) New York University Law Review
78. Lapenko M., 'Sozdanie zoni svobodnoy torqovli mejdu EAES i Respublikoy Vyetnam: itoqi pereqovornoqo prochessa' (Creation of free trade area between the EAEU and Republic of Vietnam: conclusions of the negotiation

process) (2017) 17 (2) Istoriya. Mejdunarodniye otnosheniye <https://cyberleninka.ru/article/v/sozdanie-zony-svobodnoy-torgovli-mezhdu-eaes-i-respublikoy-vietnam-itogi-peregovornogo-protsessa> accessed 21 December 2018

79. Laumulin M., 'Diskussiya Po Problemam Evraziyskoy Inteqracii' (Discussion on the problems of Eurasian integration) (2014) 17 Centralnaya Aziya I Kavkaz 3
80. Laumulin M., 'Strateqiceskie Interesi Rossii v Qosudarstvax Centralnoy Azii na Sovremennom Etape' (Strategic interests of Russia in Central Asian countries in current stage) (2009) 3 (63) Centralnaya Aziya I Kafkaz <https://cyberleninka.ru/article/v/strategicheskie-interesy-rossii-v-gosudarstvah-tsentralnoy-azii-na-sovremennom-etape> accessed 26 December 2018
81. Leal-Arcas R., Grasso C., Rios J.A., *Energy Security, Trade and the EU: Regional and International Perspectives* (2016, Edward Elgar Publishing Limited, Cheltenham)
82. Leal-Arcas R., Grasso C., Rios J.A., 'Multilateral, Regional and Bilateral Energy Governance' (2014) Queen Mary University of London Legal Studies Research Paper N 188/2014
83. Leichtova M., *Misunderstanding Russia: Russian Foreign Policy and the West* (2016, Routledge, Abingdon)
84. Lejárraga I. 'Multilateralising Regionalism: Strengthening Transparency Disciplines in Trade' (2012), 152 OECD Trade Policy Papers (OECD Publishing, Paris)
85. Lejárraga I., 'Deep Provisions in Regional Trade Agreements: How Multilateral-friendly?: An Overview of OECD Findings' (2014) OECD Trade Policy Papers 168 (OECD Publishing, Paris)
86. Lesher M., Mirodout S., 'Analysis of the Economic Impact of Investment Provisions in Regional Trade Agreements' (2005) 36 OECD Trade Policy Paper <http://www.oecd-ilibrary.org/docserver/download/322248021805.pdf?expires=1516769068&id=id&accname=guest&checksum=0909AD65E913DF06FBDEC949206B80EE> accessed 24 January 2018
87. Linott D., Reyxlin F., 'Enerqetika i Bezopasnost: Qlobalnie Vizovi' (Energy and security: Global challenges) (2005) 3 (39) Centralnaya Aziya I Kafkaz <https://cyberleninka.ru/article/v/energetika-i-bezopasnost-globalnye-vyzovy> accessed 26 December 2018
88. Lombaerde P., Garay L.J., 'Preferential Rules of Origin and the Multilateral Trading System: Pro-development Policy Options' (2007) UNU-CRIS Working Paper W2007-14

89. Malceva V., Chupina D., 'Reqionalnie i Meqareqionalnie Torqovie Soqlasheniye: Torqovlya Selskoxozyaystvennoy Produkciey v Transtixookeanskim Partnerstve' (Regional and mega-regional trade agreements: Trade in agricultural products in Transpacific Partnership) (2017) Vestnik mejdunarodnix orqanizaciy: obrazovanie, nauka, 1 novaya ekonomika <https://cyberleninka.ru/article/v/regionalnye-i-megaregionalnye-torgovye-soglasheniya-torgovlya-selskohozyaystvennoy-produktsiey-v-transtihookeanskom-partnerstve> accessed 22 December 2018
90. Mann H., 'Investment Liberalization: Some Key Elements and Issues in Today's Negotiating Context' (2007) in Issues in International Investment Law: Background Papers for the Developing Country Investment Negotiator's Forum <https://www.iisd.org/pdf/2007/inv_liberalization.pdf> accessed 26 April 2018
91. Marhold A., *Fossil Fuel Subsidy Reform in the WTO: Options for Constraining Dual Pricing in the Multilateral Trading System* (2017, International Center for Trade and Sustainable Development, Geneva) <https://www.researchgate.net/publication/321722933_Fossil_Fuel_Subsidy_Reform_in_the_WTO_Options_for_Constraining_Dual_Pricing_in_the_Multilateral_Trading_System> accessed 26 December 2018
92. Marhold A., 'The World Trade Organization and Energy: Fuel for Debate' (2013) 2 (8) ESIL Reflections
93. Marocchi T., 'EU-Russia Relations: Towards an Increasingly Geopolitical Paradigm' (2017) Henrich Boll Stiftung publications <https://eu.boell.org/sites/default/files/uploads/2017/07/eu-russia-relations_towards-an-increasingly-geopolitical-paradigm.pdf> accessed 12 April 2019
94. Mavroidis P., 'Always Look at the Bright Side of Non-delivery: WTO and Preferential Trade Agreements, Yesterday and Today' (2011) 10(3) World Trade Review
95. McDougall R., 'Evaluating the Implementation Obligations of the Trade Facilitation Agreement in the Context of Existing Multilateral Trade Rules' (2017) International Center for Trade and Sustainable Development publication <https://www.ictsd.org/sites/default/files/research/evaluating_the_implemenation_of_the_tfa.pdf> accessed 21 April 2019
96. Medalla E., Balboa J., 'ASEAN Rules of Origin: Lessons and Recommendations for Best Practice' (2009) ERIA Discussion Paper series ERIA-DP-2009-17 <http://www.eria.org/ERIA-DP-2009-17.pdf> accessed 19 April 2019
97. Meliado F., 'Private Standards, Trade and Sustainable Development: Policy Options for Collective Action' (2017, ICTSD, Geneva)

98. Mirolyubova T., 'Perspektivi Ispolzovanie Vozobnovlyayemix Istochnikov Enerqii v Sisteme Racionalnoqo Prirodopolzovaniya v Reqione' (Prospects of use of renewable energy sources in the system of rational nature use in the region) (2010) 4 (7) Vestnik Permskoqo Universiteta <https://cyberleninka.ru/article/v/perspektivy-ispolzovaniya-vozobnovlyaemyh-istochnikov-energii-v-sisteme-ratsionalnogo-prirodopolzovaniya-v-regione> accessed 26 December 2018
99. Mixaylenko E., *Stariy i noviy reqionalizm: Teoreticeskiy diskurs* (Old and new regionalism: Theoretical discussion) (2014, Izdatelstvo Uralskoqo universiteta, Ekaterinburg)
100. Mixaylenko E., 'Slojnosti Postroenie Rosiyskoqo Reqionalizma na Post-Sovetskom Prostranstve' (Challenges of establishment of Russian regionalism in post-Soviet space) (2015) 400 Vestnik Tomskoqo Qosudarstennoqo Universiteta, p. 83 <https://cyberleninka.ru/article/v/slozhnosti-postroeniya-rossiyskogo-regionalizma-na-postsovetskom-prostranstve> accessed 26 December 2018
101. Moga T., Alexeev D., 'Post-Soviet States Between Russia and the EU: Reviving Geopolitical Competition? A Dual Perspective' (2013) 13 (1) Connections
102. Movchan V., Shportyuk V., 'EU – Ukraine DCFTA: The Model for Eastern Partnership Regional Trade Cooperation' (2012) 445 CASE network Studies and Analyses
103. Mostafa G., Mahmood M., 'Eurasian Economic Union: Evolution, Challenges and Possible Future Directions' (2018) 9 (2) Journal of Eurasian Studies
104. Neufeld N., 'Trade Facilitation Provisions in Regional Trade Agreements: Traits and Trends' (2014) 5 (1) Journal of International Commerce, Economics & Policy
105. Neufeld N., 'Trade Facilitation under the Regional Trade Agreement Umbrella: Origins and Evolution', in *Regional Trade Agreements and the Multilateral Trading System*, edited by Rohini Archaya (2016, Cambridge University Press, Cambridge)
106. Newnham R., 'Oil, Carrots and Sticks: Russia's Energy Resources as Foreign Policy Tool' (2011) 2(2) Journal of Eurasian Studies
107. Obolenskiy V., 'Pereqovori o Sozdanii Torqovix Superblokov I Interesi Rossii' (Negotiation on formation of trade super-blocks and interests of Russia) (2013) 11 Rossiyskiy Vneshnoekonomiceskiy Vestnik <https://cyberleninka.ru/article/v/peregovory-o-sozdanii-torgovyh-superblokov-i-interesy-rossii> accessed 22 December 2018

108. OECD (2015), 'Regional Trade Agreements and Agriculture', OECD Food, Agriculture and Fisheries Papers, No. 79, OECD Publishing.
109. Omelicheva M., 'Russia's Foreign Policy Toward Iran: A Criticial Geopolitics Perspective' (2012) 14 (3) Journal of Balkan and Near Eastern Studies
110. Orbie J. et al., '*Europe's Global Role: External Policies of the European Union*' (2008, Routledge, Abingdon)
111. Ortiz R.M., 'Mega-regionals: What is going on?' In "*Mega-Regional Trade Agreements: Game Changers or Costly Distractions for World Trading System?*" (2014) World Economic Forum publication <http://www3.weforum.org/docs/GAC/2014/WEF_GAC_TradeFDI_MegaRegionalTradeAgreements_Report_2014.pdf> accessed 8 April 2019
112. Panagariya A., 'Challenges to the Multilateral Trading System and Possible Responses' (2013) 7 Economics
113. Petrova Y., 'Klyuchevie Problemi Privlecheniya Inostrannix Investisiy v Ekonomiku Rossiyii" (The key problems in attracting foreign investment to the economy of Russia) (2014) 102 (8) Nauchniy Jurnal KubQau <https://cyberleninka.ru/article/v/klyuchevye-problemy-privlecheniya-inostrannyh-investitsiy-v-ekonomiku-rossii> accessed 21 December 2018
114. Petrovsky V., 'Growth, Governance and Human Development: Post-Soviet Transition in North and Central Asia' (2002) Asia Pacific Center for Security Studies <https://apcss.org/Publications/Edited%20Volumes/GrowthGovernance_files/Pub_Growth%20Governance/Pub_GrowthGovernancech12.pdf> accessed October 23, 2018
115. Pezard S., Radin A., Szayna T., Larrabee S., *European Relations with Russia: Threat Perceptions, Responses and Strategies in the Wake of the Ukrainian Crisis* (2017, Rand Corporation, California)
116. Piermartini R.M., Budetta M., "A Mapping of Regional Rules on Technical Barriers to Trade." (2009) In A. Estevadeordal, K. Suominen, and R. Tech, eds., *Regional Rules in the Global Trading System* (Cambridge: Cambridge University Press)
117. Platonova I., 'Ustoycivoe Razvitie Mirovoy Ekonomiki i Konkurentosposobnost Rossii' (Sustainable development of world economy and competitivity of Russia) (2014) 9 Rossiyskiy vneshnoekonomiceskiy vestnik <https://cyberleninka.ru/article/v/ustoychivoe-razvitie-mirovoy-ekonomiki-i-konkurentosposobnost-rossii> accessed 23 December 2018
118. Pokrovskaya V.V., *Tamojennoe delo* (Customs work) (2017, Moscow, Yurayt)
119. Poluektov A., 'Transatlanticeskoe Torqovoe I Investicionnoe Partnerstvo Mejdu ES I SShA: Proobraz Obnovlennoy VTO?' (Transatlantic Trade

and Investment Partnership Between EU and USA: model of renewed WTO?) (2016) 2 (6) Torqovoaya Politika <https://cyberleninka.ru/article/v/transatlanticheskoe-torgovoe-i-investitsionnoe-partnerstvo-mezhdu-es-i-ssha-proobraz-obnovlennoy-vto> accessed 26 December 2018

120. Pominova I., 'Risks and Benefits for the Russian Federation to Participate in the Energy Charter: Comprehensive Analysis' (2014) Energy Charter Secretariat Knowledge Center <https://energycharter.org/fileadmin/DocumentsMedia/Occasional/Russia_and_the_ECT_en.pdf> accessed 09 September 2017
121. Portanskiy A., 'Ot Bretton-Vudsa do Buenos Ayresa' (From Bretton-Woods to Buenos-Aires) (2017) 3 (11) Torqovaya politika <https://cyberleninka.ru/article/v/ot-bretton-vudsa-do-buenos-ayresa> accessed 22 December 2018
122. Portanskiy A., 'Mirovaya Tendenciya Reqionalizma I Inteqrasiya v SNQ' (The global tendency of regionalism and integration in the CIS) (2011) 11 Rossiyskoy vneshnoekonomicheskoy vestnik
123. Portanskiy A., 'O Perspektivax Meqaregionalnix Torqovix Soqlasheniy' (About the perspectives of mega-regional trade agreements) (2017) 3 Mir novel ekonomiki
124. Portanskiy A., 'Posle Nairobi VTO Vinujdena Menyatsya' (After Nairobi, WTO must change) (2016) 3 Rosiyskiy vnesneoekonomicheskiy vestnik
125. Reichman J., 'Universal Minimum Standards of Intellectual Property Protection under the TRIPS Component of the WTO Agreement' (1995) 29 International Lawyer
126. Rusavskaya A., 'Investisiyii i Investisicionniy Potencial Reqiona' (Investments and investment potential of the region) (2012) 1(37) Ueks <https://cyberleninka.ru/article/v/investitsii-i-investitsionnyy-potentsial-regiona> accessed 21 December 2018
127. Ruyqa I., Ruskix O., 'Sovremennie tendenchii rinka pryamix inostrannix investisiy' (The modern tendencies of the direct investment market) (2015) 3 Konsept <https://cyberleninka.ru/article/v/sovremennye-tendentsii-rynka-pryamyh-inostrannyh-investitsiy>accessed 21 December 2018
128. Qlazyev S.Y., Chuskin V.I., Tkachuk S.P., *Yevropeyskiy soyuz i Yevraziyskoe ekonomicheskoe soobshestvo: sxodstvo i razlicie processov inteqrachionnoqo stroitelstvo,* (European Union and Eurasian Economic Community: similarities and differences of the process of integration building) (2013, Vikor Media, Moscow)
129. Schill S., 'The Multilateralization of International Investment Law: Emergence of a Multilateral System of Investment Protection on Bilateral

Grounds' (2010) 2 (1) Trade, Law and Development <http://www.tradelawdevelopment.com/index.php/tld/article/viewFile/2%281%29%20TL%26D%2059%20%282010%29/41> accessed 21 December 2018

130. Serqunin A., Tixonov V. '"Vostochnoe Partnerstvo" I Rossiyskie Interesi na Kafkaze' ("Eastern Partnership" and Russia's interests in the Caucasus) (2010) 4 Izvestiya Vuzov: Severo Kafkazskiy region. Seriya: Obshestvennie nauki <https://cyberleninka.ru/article/v/vostochnoe-partnerstvo-i-rossiyskie-interesy-na-kavkaze> accessed 31 October 2018
131. Shkutko O., 'Mnoqostoronneye Requlirovanie Torqovix Otnosheniy: Potensial i Vozmojnosti Transformachiyi' (Multilateral regulation of trade relations: potential and opportunities for transformation) (2018) 37 (1) Sbornik nauchnix trudov uchenix I aspirantov
132. Shleifer A., Tresiman D., 'A Normal Country: Russia After Communism' (2005) 19 (1) Journal of Economic Perspectives
133. Shipovich L., 'Vliyania Inostrannix Investisiy na Finansoviy Krizis v Rossii' (Impact of foreign investment in financial crisis in Russia) (2013) 32 (323) Vestnik Chelyabinskoqo Qosudarstvennoqo Universiteta <https://cyberleninka.ru/article/v/vliyanie-inostrannyh-investitsiy-na-finansovyy-krizis-v-rossii> accessed 21 December 2018
134. Shumilov V.M., *Pravo Vsemirnoy Torqovoy Orqanizachii* (World Trade Organization Law) (2017,Yurayt, Moscow)
135. Spartak A., 'Metamorfozi Processa Reqionalizacii: Ot Reqionalnix Torqovix Soqlasheniy k Meqareqionalnim Proektam' (Metamorphosis of regionalization process: From regional trade agreements to mega-regional projects) (2017) 10 (4) Konturu qlobalnix transformaciy: politika, ekonomika, pravo <https://cyberleninka.ru/article/v/metamorfozy-protsessa-regionalizatsii-ot-regionalnyh-torgovyh-soglasheniy-k-mezhregionalnym-proektam> accessed 23 December 2018
136. Starix S., 'Osobennosti osushestvleniya tamojennoqo dela v ramkax Evraziyskoqo ekonomicheskoqo soyuza' (Characteristing of customs formalities in the framework of the Eurasian Economic Union) (2016) 1 Mejdunarodniy jurnal qumanitarnix I yestestvennix nauk <https://cyberleninka.ru/article/n/osobennosti-osuschestvleniya-tamozhennogo-dela-v-ramkah-evraziyskogo-ekonomicheskogo-soyuza> accessed 29 November 2018
137. Starodubcev I., 'Rossiysko-Tureckoe Sotrudnicestvo: Sovremennoe Sostayanie I Perspektivi' (Russian-Turkish cooperation: current situation and prospects) (2012) 1 Vestnik MQIMO <https://cyberleninka.ru/article/v/rossiysko-turetskoe-sotrudnichestvo-sovremennoe-sostoyanie-i-perspektivy> accessed 25 December 2018

138. Stoler A., 'TBT and SPS Measures in Practice" chapter in "Preferential Trade Agreement Policies for Development: A Handbook" (2011) World Bank Resources <http://siteresources.worldbank.org/INTRANETTRADE/Resources/C11.pdf> accessed 16 November 2017
139. Storojcuk V., 'Opredelenie strain proisxojdeniya tovarov na usloviyax soqlasheniy o svobodnoy torqovle, zaklyuchennix Ukrainoy so stranami SNQ' (Determination of rules of origin of goods on the conditions of the agreements of free trade, concluded by Ukraine with the countries of CIS) (2014) Viunik 45 <http://www.visnuk.com.ua/ru/pubs/id/7829> last accessed 15 December 2017
140. Tabarovskaya M., Sherov-Iqnatyev V., 'VTO Posle Nayrobi: Vizovi So Storoni Meqareqionalnix Soqlasheniy I Koalichionnaya Aktivnost Rossiyi' (WTO after Nayrobi: Challenges from the mega-regional agreements and coalition activity of Russia) (2017) 1 (9) Torqovaya politika
141. Tarr D., 'The Eurasian Economic Union Among Russia, Belarus, Kazakhstan, Armenia and Kyrgyz Republic: Can It Succeed Where Its Predecessor Failed?'(29 September 2015) World Bank Publications <http://as.vanderbilt.edu/gped/documents/DavidTarrEurasianCustomsUnion--prospectsSept282015.pdf> accessed 1 April 2018
142. Trofimenko A., 'Pryamie Inostrannie Investisiyii v Rossii: Problemi i Perspektivi' (Foreign Direct Investments in Russia: challenges and prospects) (2011) 3 (77) Izvestia IQEA <https://cyberleninka.ru/article/v/pryamye-inostrannye-investitsii-v-rossii-problemy-i-perspektivy> accessed 23 December 2018
143. Tsume E., 'Soqlasheniye ob uproshenii prosedur torqovli: vozmojnosti i uqrozi dlya chastnoqo sektora s tochki zreniiya razvivayushixsya stran' (Trade Facilitation Agreement: opportunities and threats for the private sector from the point of view of the developing states) (2014) Tamojenniy nauchniy journal 2
144. van der Loo G., 'The EU's Association Agreements and DCFTAs with Ukraine, Moldova and Georgia: A Comparative Study' (2017) <http://www.3dcftas.eu/system/tdf/Comparitve%20GVDL%2024.6.17_final_0.pdf?file=1&type=node&id=360&force=> accessed 27 August 2018
145. Van Grasstek C., *The History and Future of World Trade Organization* (2013, World Trade Organization Publications, Geneva)
146. van Rauch G., *History of Soviet Russia* (Praeger Publishers, New York, 1972)
147. Vinokurov E., 'Obshiy Elektroenerqeticeskiy Rinok SNQ kak Instrument Ekonomiceskoqo Razvitiya i Reqionalnooy Inteqracii' (Common electricity energy market of CIS as a tool of economic development and regional

integration) (2008) 1 (1) Evraziyskoe Ekonomiceskoe Inteqrasiya <https://cyberleninka.ru/article/v/obschiy-elektroenergeticheskiy-rynok-sng-kak-instrument-ekonomicheskogo-razvitiya-i-regionalnoy-integratsii> accessed 26 December 2018

148. Vivas-Eugui D., 'Regional and Bilateral Agreements and a TRIPS-Plus World: The Free Trade Area of Americas' (2002) 1 Quaker United Nations Office, TRIPS Issues Papers <http://homepages.3-c.coop/tansey/pdfs/ftaa-a4.pdf> accessed 27 August 2017
149. Volinchuk A., 'Rossiya v Evrazii: Balans Qeoekonomiceskix i Qeopoliticeskix Instrumentov Inteqracii' (Russia in Eurasia: Balance of geo-economic and geo-political instruments of integration) (2018) 1(99) Rossiya I ATR <https://cyberleninka.ru/article/v/rossiya-v-evrazii-balans-geoekonomicheskih-i-geopoliticheskih-instrumentov-integratsii> accessed 26 December 2018
150. Willis B., 'The Arguments For and Against TRIPS Agreement' (2013) <http://www.e-ir.info/2013/12/23/the-arguments-for-and-against-the-trips-agreement/> accessed 17 August 2017
151. Wilson J.S., Mann C.L., & Otsuki T., 'Assessing the Benefits of Trade Facilitation: A Global Perspective' (2005), 28/6 World Economy <www.researchgate.net/profile/Tsunehiro_Otsuki/publication/4997218_Assessing_The_Benefits_Of_Trade_Facilitation_A_Global_Perspective/links/02e7e52308a1ac8ef8000000.pdf> accessed 8 April 2017
152. Wolcock S., 'EU Policy Towards Free Trade Agreements' (2007) ECIPE Working Paper No 03/2007
153. Xalifazade M., 'Amerikanskaya Politika 'Perezaqruzki' Otnosheniy s Rossiyey i Yujniy Kafkaz' (American policy of reloading relations with Russia and South Caucasus) (2014) 17 (3) Centralnaya Aziya I Kavkaz
154. Yeliseyev A., 'EAES I Perspektivniiye Zoni Svobodnoy Torqovli (EAEU and Prospective Free Trade Areas)' Belarus Institute for Strategic Studies (2015) 6 Evraziyskoye obozrenie
155. Yesdauletova A., 'Kazakhstan's Energy Policy: Its Evolution and Tendencies' (2009) 6 (4) Journal of US-China Public Administration
156. Yu P.K., 'The Objectives and Principles of the TRIPS Agreement' (2009) 46 (979) Houston Law Review
157. Yuldasheva G., 'Iran v Centralnoy Aziatskoy politike Rossii' (Iran in the Central Asian politics of Russia) (2014) 17 (3) Centralnaya Aziya I Kavkaz
158. Zaqashvili V., 'VTO I Meqaregionalnie Torqovie Soqlashenie' (WTO and mega-regional trade agreements) (2017) 5 Rosiyskiy vneshnoekonomiceskoy vestnik

159. Zhiltsov S., 'Truboprovodi v Centralnoy Azii I v Kaspiyskom reqione: noviy etap borbi' (Pipelines in the Central Asia and the Caucasus region: new stage of fight) (2014) 17 (3) Centralnaya Aziya I Kavkaz
160. Ziyadullayev N., 'Qosudarstva Centralnoy Azii v Usloviax Qlobalizacii: Sovremennie Tendencii i Perspektivi' (Central Asian states in the globalization conditions: current tendencies and prospects) (2006) 6 (48) Centralnaya Aziya I Kafkaz <https://cyberleninka.ru/article/v/gosudarstva-tsentralnoy-azii-v-usloviyah-globalizatsii-sovremennye-tendentsii-i-perspektivy> accessed 23 December 2018
161. Zubiashvili T., 'Aspects of Post-Soviet Economy Against the Backdrop of Association Agreement with European Union' (2017) 6 (1) Ecoforum

List of Laws and Regulations

1. Agreement on Rules of Origin (15 April, 1994), Marrakesh Agreement Establishing the World Trade Organization, Annex 1A, <http://docsonline.wto.org>
2. Amendments to the Annex to the Convention on Facilitation of International Maritime Traffic (7 July 2005) <www.imo.org>
3. Berne Convention for the Protection of Literary and Artistic Works (September 9, 1886) <http://www.wipo.int/treaties/en/text.jsp?file_id=283698>
4. CIS Investor Rights Convention (28 March 1997) <http://investmentpolicyhub.unctad.org/Download/TreatyFile/3127>
5. CIS Treaty on the Cooperation in the Field of Copyright and Related Rights (6 May 1995) <http://www.wipo.int/wipolex/en/other_treaties/details.jsp?group_id=21&treaty_id=377>
6. CIS Treaty on Mutual Recognition of the Results of Accreditation Work on Conformity Assessment Procedures (May 21, 2003)
7. CIS Treaty on the Prevention of Use of False Trademarks and Geographical Indications (4 June 1999) <http://www.wipo.int/wipolex/en/details.jsp?id=12428>
8. CIS Intergovernmental Treaty on the Implementation of a Coordinated Competition Policy, 24 December 1993, Ashgabat
9. CIS Agreement for Implementation of the Harmonized Antimonopoly Policy dated 25 January 2000. Annex 1. Regulations on the Prevention of Monopolistic Activity and Unfair Competition dated 25 January 2000. Annex 2. Regulations on the Interstate Council for Antimonopoly Policy dated 25 January 2000 <http://cis.minsk.by/reestr/ru/index.html#reestr/view/text?doc=1000>

10. CIS Free Trade Agreement (18 October 2011) <http://cis.minsk.by/reestr/ru/printPreview/text?id=3183>
11. Customs Code of the Customs Union (27 November 2009) <https://docs.eaeunion.org>
12. Decision N7, dated 31 May 2016 of the Eurasian Economic Council on the concept of the formation of common gas market of the EAEU
13. Decision N8, dated 31 May 2016 of the Supreme Eurasian Economic Council on the adoption of the Concept of common EAEU oil and petroleum products market.
14. Decision N12, dated 8 May 2015 of the Supreme Eurasian Economic Council on the adoption of the Concept of common EAEU electricity market.
15. EAEU – Vietnam Free Trade Agreement (29 May 2015) <https://docs.eaeunion.org>
16. EAEU Customs Code (26 December 2016) <docs.eaeunion.org>
17. EU – Moldova Association Agreement, EU-Georgia Association Agreement, EU-Ukraine Association Agreement (29 May 2014) <trade.ec.europa.eu/doclib>
18. EU – South Korea FTA (15 October 2009) <eur-lex.europa.eu>
19. Enabling Clause: WTO Decision on Differential and More Favorable Treatment Reciprocity and Fuller Participation of Developing Countries (28 November 1979) <http://docsonline.wto.org>
20. GATS: General Agreement on Trade in Services (15 April, 1994), Marrakesh Agreement Establishing the World Trade Organization, Annex 1B, <http://docsonline.wto.org> accessed 20 August 2016
21. GATT: General Agreement on Tariffs and Trade (30 October1947) <http://docsonline.wto.org>
22. International Convention on the Simplification on the Simplification and Harmonization of Customs Procedures (Kyoto Convention), Specific Annex K, E1/F2 (1974) <www.wcoomd.org>
23. International Maritime Organization Guidelines for the Use of Electronic Certificates (20 April 2016) <www.imo.org>
24. North-American Free Trade Agreement (17 December 1992) <www.sice.oas.org/trade/nafta/naftatce.asp>
25. OECD Policy Brief 'Trade Facilitation: The Benefits of Simpler, more Transparent Border Procedures' (OECD Observer, 2003) <www.oecd.org/trade/facilitation/8920454.pdf>
26. OECD 'Hard Core Cartels' (2000) <http://www.oecd.org/competition/cartels/2752129.pdf>

27. OECD 'Recommendation Concerning Effective Action Against Hard Core Cartels' (25 March 1998) (98)35/FINAL <http://www.oecd.org/daf/competition/2350130.pdf> accessed 9 May 2018
28. OECD 'Benchmark definition of foreign direct investment' (2008) <https://www.oecd.org/daf/inv/investmentstatisticsandanalysis/40193734.pdf>
29. Protocol on the protection and defense of the rights for the objects of intellectual property, Annex 26 to the Treaty on the Establishment of the Eurasian Economic Union (29 May 2014) <docs.eaeunion.org>
30. Protocol on the protection and defense of the rights for the objects of intellectual property, Annex 26 to the Treaty on the Establishment of the Eurasian Economic Union (29 May 2014) <docs.eaeunion.org>
31. The EAEU Treaty on the information-communication technologies and informational interaction within the framework of the EAEU, Annex 3 to the EAEU Treaty, <docs.eaeunion.org>
32. Treaty on harmonized system of confirmation of the origin of goods, exported from customs territory of the Eurasian Economic Union (22 mart 2016) <https://docs.eaeunion.org>
33. Treaty on harmonized system of confirmation of the origin of goods, exported from customs territory of the Eurasian Economic Union (22 mart 2016) <https://docs.eaeunion.org>
34. Treaty on Rules of Origin of Goods from Developing and Least Developed Countries (12 December 2008) <https://docs.eaeunion.org>
35. Treaty on the Establishment of the Free Trade Area in Commonwealth of Independent States (15 April 1994)
36. Treaty on the Rules of Origin of the Goods in Commonwealth of Independent States (20 November 2009) <docs.eaeunion.org>
37. Treaty on Unified Rules of Origin of Goods (25 January 2008) <https://docs.eaeunion.org>
38. Transparency Mechanism for Regional Trade Agreements (14 December 2006) WT/L/671, 18 December 2016 <http://docsonline.wto.org>
39. United Nations Center for Trade Facilitation and Electronic Business (UN/CEFACT) Recommendation and Guidelines on establishing a Single Window (Recommendations 33) (July 2005) and United Nations Center for Trade Facilitation and Electronic Business Recommendation on Establishing a Legal Framework for International Trade Single Window (Recommendation 35) (December 2010) <www.unece.org>
40. UNCTAD 'Consumers, Multilateral Competition Policy and the WTO: Technical Report' (2003) <https://www.wto.org/english/tratop_e/dda_e/symp03_ci_tech_report_e.pdf>

41. UNCTAD. Investment Provisions in Economic Integration Agreements (2006). <http://unctad.org/en/docs/iteiit200510_en.pdf>
42. UNCTAD 'World Investment Report 2007' (2007) <http://unctad.org/en/Docs/wir2007p4_en.pdf>
43. U.N. Conference on Trade and Development (UNCTAD), The United Nations Set of Principles and Rules on Competition, U.N. Doc.TD/RBP/CONF/10/Rev.2 (2000), <http://unctad.org/en/docs/tdrbpconf10r2.en.pdf.> a
44. Understanding on the Interpretation of the Article XXIV of the GATT (15 April 1994) <http://docsonline.wto.org>
45. World Customs Organization, Rules of Origin Handbook
46. WTO Doha Ministerial Declaration (adopted 14 November 2011) WT/MIN(01)/DEC/1 <https://www.wto.org/english/thewto_e/minist_e/min01_e/mindecl_e.htm>
47. WTO Nairobi Ministerial Declaration (adopted 19 December 2015) WT/MIN(15)/DEC <https://www.wto.org/english/thewto_e/minist_e/mc10_e/mindecision_e.htm>
48. WTO, *European Communities – Conditions for the Granting of Tariff Preferences to Developing Countries – Appellate Body Report* (7 April 2004) WT/DS246/AB/R
49. WTO, General Council Decision 'WTO Committee on Regional Trade Agreements' (6 February 1996) WT/L/127, 7 February 1996 < https://www.wto.org/english/tratop_e/region_e/127.pdf>
50. WTO, Negotiating Group on Rules 'Compendium of Issues related to Regional Trade Agreements' (1 August 2002) TN/RL/W/8/Rev.1
51. WTO Agreement on Sanitary and Phytosanitary Measures, Art 2 (April 15, 1994) Marrakesh Agreement Establishing the World Trade Organization, Annex 1A <docs.wto.org>
52. WTO Agreement on Trade-Related Aspects of Intellectual Property Rights, Art 9.1 (April 15, 1994) Marrakesh Agreement Establishing the World Trade Organization, Annex 1C <docs.wto.org>
53. WTO Ministerial Decision on Preferential Rules of Origin for Least-Developed Countries (7 December 2013) <http://docsonline.wto.org>
54. WTO Ministerial Decision on Preferential Rules of Origin for Least Developed Countries (19 December 2015) <http://docsonline.wto.org>
55. WTO Survey "Rules of Origin Regime in Regional Trade Agreements" WT/REG/W/45, 5 April 2002
56. WTO Trade Facilitation Agreement (7 December 2013), Bali Ministerial Decision <http://docsonline.wto.org>

57. WTO Singapore Ministerial Decision, WTO/MIN(96)/DEC, 18 December 1996
58. WTO Services Sectoral Classification List MTN.GNS/W/120, 10 July 1991
59. WTO Council for Trade Special Session, USA proposal on energy services S/CSS/W/24, 18 December 2000

Court Cases

1. Case C-393/92 *Gemeente Almelo and Others v.Energiebedrijf IJsselmij NV*, European Court of Justice, 27 April 1994
2. *Russian Federation v Republic of Belarus*, Case No CE-1-1/1-16-BK (Russian Federation) EAEU Court

Erlanger Schriften zum Öffentlichen Recht

Herausgegebenvon Max-Emanuel Geis, Heinrich de Wall, Markus Krajewski, Bernhard W. Wegener, Andreas Funke und Jan-Reinard Sieckmann

Band 1 Ingo Mehner: Privatisierung bayerischer Kreiskrankenhäuser. 2012.

Band 2 Claudius Fischer: Disziplinarrecht und Richteramt. 2012.

Band 3 Jan Schubert: Die Handelskooperation zwischen der Europäischen Union und den AKP-Staaten und deren Vereinbarkeit mit dem GATT. 2012.

Band 4 Michael Link: Open Access im Wissenschaftsbereich. 2013.

Band 5 Adolf Rebler: Die Genehmigung der Durchführung von Großraum- und Schwertransporten. 2014.

Band 6 Heidrun M.-L. Meier: Das Kunsthochschullehrernebentätigkeitsrecht. Der Hochschullehrer im Spannungsverhältnis zwischen Dienstrecht und grundrechtlicher Freiheit. 2015.

Band 7 Michaela Tauschek: Das Abstandsgebot in Richtlinie 2012/18/EU („Seveso-III-Richtlinie") und seine Auswirkungen auf die Erteilung von Baugenehmigungen. Deutsche Behörden zwischen Baurecht, Umweltrecht und Europarecht. 2016.

Band 8 Tina Linti: Rechtsrahmen und Regulierung Privater Militär- und Sicherheitsunternehmen unter besonderer Berücksichtigung ihrer Einsatzmöglichkeiten in UN-Friedensmissionen. 2018.

Band 9 Jörg Bundle: Verfassungsrechtliche Probleme Großer Koalitionen. 2019.

Band 10 Jahn-Rüdiger Albert: Gefahrenprognose im Ausweisungsrecht nach strafrechtlicher Verurteilung. 2020.

Band 11 Seljan Verdiyeva: Regional Trade Agreements in Eastern Europe, Central Asia and the Caucasus: Is Multilateralization of Regionalism possible?. 2020.

www.peterlang.com

FSC
www.fsc.org
MIX
Papier | Fördert
gute Waldnutzung
FSC® C083411

Kolibri 360 GmbH
Ferdinand-Jühlke-Straße 7
99095 Erfurt, Deutschland
produktsicherheit@kolibri360.de

Druck:
CPI Druckdienstleistungen GmbH
im Auftrag der
Kolibri 360 GmbH
Ferdinand-Jühlke-Str. 7
99095 Erfurt